UNLOCK

Second Edition

4

Listening, Speaking & Critical Thinking

STUDENT'S BOOK WITH DIGITAL PACK

Lewis Lansford and Robyn Brinks Lockwood
with Chris Sowton, Jessica Williams
and Christina Cavage

CAMBRIDGE
UNIVERSITY PRESS

CAMBRIDGE
UNIVERSITY PRESS & ASSESSMENT

Shaftesbury Road, Cambridge CB2 8EA, United Kingdom

One Liberty Plaza, 20th Floor, New York, NY 10006, USA

477 Williamstown Road, Port Melbourne, VIC 3207, Australia

314–321, 3rd Floor, Plot 3, Splendor Forum, Jasola District Centre, New Delhi – 110025, India

103 Penang Road, #05–06/07, Visioncrest Commercial, Singapore 238467

Cambridge University Press & Assessment is a department of the University of Cambridge.

We share the University's mission to contribute to society through the pursuit of education, learning and research at the highest international levels of excellence.

www.cambridge.org
Information on this title: www.cambridge.org/9781009031486

First published 2014
Second edition 2019
Second Edition update published 2021

20 19 18 17 16 15 14 13 12 11 10 9 8

Printed in the Netherlands by Wilco BV

A catalogue record for this publication is available from the British Library

ISBN   978-1-009-03148-6   Listening, Speaking and Critical Thinking Student's Book with Digital Pack 4
ISBN   978-1-009-03136-3   Listening, Speaking and Critical Thinking Student's eBook with Digital Pack 4

CONTENTS

MAP OF THE BOOK

UNIT	VIDEO	LISTENING	VOCABULARY	
1 GLOBALIZATION Listening 1: A radio programme about the global food industry (Environment) Listening 2: A presentation on the global film industry (Business)	NBA making a play for China	**Key listening skill:** Activating prior knowledge **Additional skills:** Understanding key vocabulary Using your knowledge Listening for main ideas Listening for detail Listening for opinion Understanding cause and effect Taking notes on main ideas and detail Synthesizing **Pronunciation for listening:** Consonant clusters	Globalization vocabulary	
2 EDUCATION Listening 1: A meeting between a student and a careers adviser (Education) Listening 2: A conversation between students about paths towards a medical profession (Education)	Langton School science programme	**Key listening skills:** Listening for advice and suggestions Making inferences **Additional skills:** Using your knowledge Understanding key vocabulary Listening for main ideas Listening for opinion Taking notes on main ideas and detail Synthesizing **Pronunciation for listening:** Certain and uncertain intonation	Academic adjectives to describe professions (e.g. *manual, medical, technical*)	
3 MEDICINE Listening 1: A college seminar about pandemics (Medicine) Listening 2: A debate about flu vaccinations (Medicine)	New 'health tablet' gives instant test results	**Key listening skills:** Identifying contrasting opinions Strengthening points in an argument **Additional skills:** Understanding key vocabulary Using your knowledge Listening for attitude Listening for detail Taking notes on main ideas Synthesizing **Pronunciation for listening:** Intonation in tag questions	Health science vocabulary	
4 THE ENVIRONMENT Listening 1: A lecture about habitat destruction (Environment) Listening 2: A talk about the decline of desert habitats (Environment)	Cloning endangered species	**Key listening skills:** Distinguishing main ideas from details Taking notes on main ideas and details **Additional skills:** Understanding key vocabulary Using your knowledge Listening for main ideas Listening for detail Summarizing Listening for opinion Listening for text organization Synthesizing **Pronunciation for listening:** Pauses in prepared speech	Verbs to describe environmental change	

GRAMMAR	CRITICAL THINKING	SPEAKING
Modals of present and past probability	Analyzing and using data in pie charts Using data to support an argument	***Preparation for speaking:*** Presenting data Describing a pie chart Drawing conclusions from data ***Speaking task:*** Give a presentation using data from a pie chart.
The future continuous Stating preferences with *would*	Prioritizing criteria Using priorities to evaluate options	***Preparation for speaking:*** Giving an opinion and making suggestions Agreeing and disagreeing respectfully Compromising and finalizing a decision ***Pronunciation for speaking:*** Certain and uncertain intonation ***Speaking task:*** Decide as a group which candidate should receive a scholarship.
Conditionals: • The third conditional • Review of the second conditional – unreal situations	Analyzing background and motivation	***Preparation for speaking:*** Creating persuasive arguments ***Speaking task:*** Role-play a debate
Multi-word prepositions The past perfect	Organizing information in a presentation	***Preparation for speaking:*** Giving background information and explaining a problem Using signposting language in a presentation ***Speaking task:*** Give a problem and solution presentation.

UNIT	VIDEO	LISTENING	VOCABULARY	
5 ARCHITECTURE Listening 1: A conversation between two property developers (Urban planning) Listening 2: A housing development meeting (Urban planning)	The skyscraper	**Key listening skills:** Understanding figurative language Understanding strong and tentative suggestions *Additional skills:* Understanding key vocabulary Using your knowledge Listening for main ideas Listening for detail Listening for attitude Taking notes on main ideas Synthesizing *Pronunciation for listening:* Emphasis in contrasting opinions	Academic vocabulary for architecture and transformation	
6 ENERGY Listening 1: A radio programme about the island of El Hierro, Spain (Culture; Environment) Listening 2: A chaired meeting about saving energy in an office (Environment)	Jeju Island goes carbon-free	**Key listening skills:** Understanding digressions Understanding persuasive techniques *Additional skills:* Understanding key vocabulary Using your knowledge Listening for main ideas Listening for detail Listening for text organization Taking notes on detail Synthesizing *Pronunciation for listening:* Intonation related to emotion	Academic vocabulary for networks and systems	
7 ART AND DESIGN Listening 1: A radio report about graffiti (Art and design; Culture) Listening 2: An informal debate about public art (Art and design)	Contemporary African art sale	**Key listening skills:** Inferring opinions Distinguishing fact from opinion *Additional skills:* Understanding key vocabulary Predicting content using visuals Using your knowledge Listening for main ideas Listening for detail Listening for opinion Making inferences Taking notes on opinion Synthesizing *Pronunciation for listening:* Stress in word families	Academic vocabulary related to art (e.g. *appreciate, interpret, analyze*)	
8 AGEING Listening 1: A finance podcast (Economics) Listening 2: Two student presentations on ageing in different countries (Social anthropology)	Never too old to code	**Key listening skill:** Understanding specific observations and generalizations *Additional skills:* Using your knowledge Understanding key vocabulary Listening for main ideas Listening for detail Taking notes on main ideas and detail Synthesizing *Pronunciation for listening:* Elision and intrusion	Academic verbs for support and assistance	

GRAMMAR	CRITICAL THINKING	SPEAKING
Future forms: • *Will* and *be going to* for predictions and expectations	Comparing and evaluating solutions	***Preparation for speaking:*** Identifying problems and suggesting solutions: • Presenting a problem • Making polite suggestions • Responding to suggested solutions ***Pronunciation for speaking:*** Emphasizing a word or idea to signal a problem ***Speaking task:*** Discuss a housing problem and possible solutions.
Connecting ideas The passive voice	Analyzing and evaluating problems and solutions	***Preparation for speaking:*** Keeping a discussion moving: • Asking for input in a discussion, summarizing and keeping a discussion moving • Dealing with interruptions and digressions ***Pronunciation for speaking:*** Using a neutral tone of voice ***Speaking task:*** Participate in a discussion about an energy problem and possible solutions.
Relative clauses	Using debate statements and responses Preparing for a debate: • Evaluating reasons • Analyzing evidence	***Preparation for speaking:*** Language for debates: • Expressing contrasting opinions • Restating somebody's point • Using language for hedging ***Pronunciation for speaking:*** Stress in hedging language ***Speaking task:*** Participate in an informal debate about whether public money should be spent on public art.
Verbs with infinitives or gerunds	Analyzing and using data from a line graph	***Preparation for speaking:*** Referencing data in a presentation: • Explaining details and trends in a graph • Explaining causes and effects ***Pronunciation for speaking:*** Contrastive stress in numbers and comparisons ***Speaking task:*** Give a presentation using graphical data

YOUR GUIDE TO UNLOCK

Unlock your academic potential

Unlock Second Edition is a six-level, academic-light English course created to build the skills and language students need for their studies (CEFR Pre-A1 to C1). It develops students' ability to think critically in an academic context right from the start of their language learning. Every level has 100% new inspiring video on a range of academic topics.

Confidence in teaching.
Joy in learning.

Better Learning WITH UNLOCK SECOND EDITION

Better Learning is our simple approach where insights we've gained from research have helped shape content that drives results. We've listened to teachers all around the world and made changes so that *Unlock* Second Edition better supports students along the way to academic success.

CRITICAL THINKING

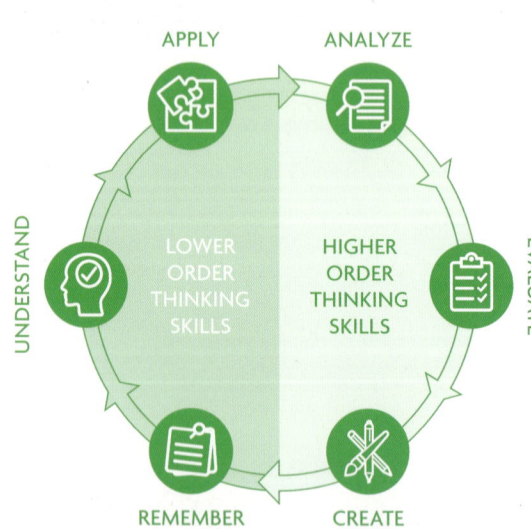

APPLY
ANALYZE
UNDERSTAND
EVALUATE
LOWER ORDER THINKING SKILLS
HIGHER ORDER THINKING SKILLS
REMEMBER
CREATE

Critical thinking in *Unlock* Second Edition …

- is **informed** by a range of academic research from Bloom in the 1950s, to Krathwohl and Anderson in the 2000s, to more recent considerations relating to 21st Century Skills
- has a **refined** syllabus with a better mix of higher- and lower-order critical thinking skills
- is **measurable**, with objectives and self-evaluation so students can track their critical thinking progress
- is **transparent** so teachers and students know when and why they're developing critical thinking skills
- is **supported** with professional development material for teachers so teachers can teach with confidence

… so that students have the best possible chance of academic success.

INSIGHT

Most classroom time is currently spent on developing lower-order critical thinking skills. Students need to be able to use higher-order critical thinking skills too.

CONTENT

Unlock Second Edition includes the right mix of lower- and higher-order thinking skills development in every unit, with clear learning objectives.

RESULTS

Students are better prepared for their academic studies and have the confidence to apply the critical thinking skills they have developed.

DIGITAL CLASSROOM MATERIAL

The *Unlock* Second Edition Digital Classroom Material …

- offers extra, **motivating** practice in speaking, critical thinking and language
- provides a **convenient** bank of language and skills reference informed by our exclusive Corpus research 👁
- is easily **accessible** and **navigable** from students' mobile phones
- is fully **integrated** into every unit
- provides Unlock-**specific** activities to extend the lesson whenever you see this symbol 📱

… so that students can easily get the right, extra practice they need, when they need it.

INSIGHT

The digital classroom material is most effective when it's an integral, well-timed part of a lesson.

CONTENT

Every unit of *Unlock* Second Edition is enhanced with bespoke digital classroom material to extend the skills and language students are learning in the book. The symbol 📱 shows when to use the material.

RESULTS

Students are motivated by having relevant extension material on their mobile phones to maximize their language learning. Teachers are reassured that the material adds real language-learning value to their lessons.

RESEARCH

We have gained deeper insights to inform *Unlock* Second Edition by …

- carrying out **extensive market research** with teachers and students to fully understand their needs throughout the course's development
- consulting **academic research** into critical thinking
- refining our vocabulary syllabus using our **exclusive Corpus research** 👁

… so that you can be assured of the quality of *Unlock* Second Edition.

INSIGHT

- Consultation with global Advisory Panel
- Comprehensive reviews of material
- Face-to-face interviews and Skype™ calls
- Classroom observations

CONTENT

- Improved critical thinking
- 100% new video and video lessons
- Clearer contexts for language presentation and practice
- Text-by-text glossaries
- Digital workbook with more robust content
- Comprehensive teacher support

RESULTS

"Thank you for all the effort you've put into developing Unlock Second Edition. As far as I can see, I think the new edition is more academic and more appealing to young adults."

Burçin Gönülsen,
Işık Üniversity, Turkey

Unlock your knowledge

Encourages discussion around the themes of the unit with inspiration from interesting questions and striking images.

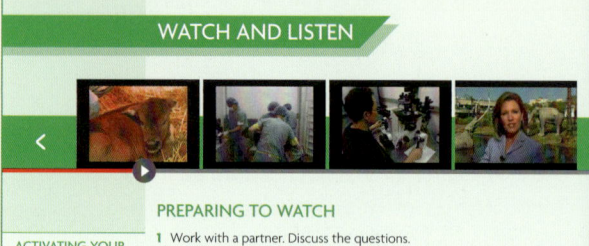

UNL○CK YOUR KNOWLEDGE

Work with a partner. Discuss the questions.

1 What is deforestation?
2 What are its causes and effects?
3 Other than deforestation, what things do people do that affect the environment?
4 How can people use natural resources without harming the environment?

Watch and listen

Features an engaging and motivating video which generates interest in the topic and develops listening skills.

WATCH AND LISTEN

ACTIVATING YOUR KNOWLEDGE

PREPARING TO WATCH

1 Work with a partner. Discuss the questions.

1 Can you think of any animals that have disappeared or are endangered?
2 What role do humans play in making an animal extinct or endangered?
3 What can people do to prevent more animals from becoming extinct?

LISTENING

Listening 1

Provides information about the topic and practises pre-listening, while-listening and post-listening skills. This section may also include a focus on pronunciation which will further enhance listening comprehension.

LISTENING

LISTENING 1

UNDERSTANDING KEY VOCABULARY

PREPARING TO LISTEN

1 You are going to listen to a lecture about habitat destruction. Before you listen, read the words and definitions. Then complete the sentences with the correct form of the words in bold.

adapt (v) to adjust to different conditions
coastal (adj) on or related to land by the sea or ocean
conservation (n) the act of being careful not to waste water, energy, etc.
exploit (v) to use something in a way that helps you (or unfairly for an advantage)

Language development

Practises the vocabulary and grammar from Listening 1 and pre-teaches the vocabulary and grammar for Listening 2.

⊙ LANGUAGE DEVELOPMENT

MULTI-WORD PREPOSITIONS

GRAMMAR

Multi-word prepositions are two- or three-word phrases that function like one-word prepositions (*of, on, by*). Multi-word prepositions include:

• two-word phrases (*apart from, according to*)
• three-word phrases (*by means of, as well as*)

Like one-word prepositions, multi-word prepositions are followed by nouns, noun phrases and gerunds. They show the relationship between two things. For example, *in front of* shows location.

Listening 2

Presents a second listening text on the topic, often in a different format, and serves as a model for the speaking task.

LISTENING 2

PREPARING TO LISTEN

1 Work with a partner. Discuss the questions.

1 What is a desert?
2 Are there any desert areas in your country? If so, where are they?
3 What kinds of plants, animals or products do you find in the desert?

2 You are going to listen to a talk about desert habitats. Before you listen, read the sentences and write the words in bold next to the definitions.

1 Antarctica usually has a **harsh** winter with extremely cold temperatures.

USING KNOW

UNDERSTA KEY VOCAB

SPEAKING

Critical thinking

Develops the lower- and higher-order thinking skills required for the speaking task.

Preparation for speaking

Presents and practises functional language, pronunciation and speaking strategies for the speaking task.

Speaking task

Uses the skills and language learned throughout the unit to support students in producing a presentational or interactional speaking task. This is the unit's main learning objective.

Objectives review

Allows learners to evaluate how well they have mastered the skills covered in the unit.

Wordlist

Lists the key vocabulary from the unit. The most frequent words used at this level in an academic context are highlighted. ⊙

SPEAKING

CRITICAL THINKING

At the end of this unit, you are going to do the speaking task below.

> Give a presentation about a change in the environment and discuss possible solutions.

Organizing information in a presentation

PREPARATION FOR SPEAKING

GIVING BACKGROUND INFORMATION AND EXPLAINING A PROBLEM

Background information is often necessary to put a problem in context. In other words, you need to say *why* it is a problem. One way of structuring this background information is to give main ideas, examples of those ideas and details to clarify the examples:

Let's begin by looking at some background information from the United Nations Environment Programme. The United Nations reports in *Global Deserts Outlook* that ...

Humans have learned to exploit the resources of the desert for survival and profit by adapting their behaviour, culture and technology to its harsh environment. To give you an example, tribes such as the Tuareg...

SPEAKING TASK

> Give a presentation about a change in the environment and discuss possible solutions.

PREPARE

1 Look back at the outline for the research you did in Critical thinking. Add any new information you would like to include.

2 Prepare a short introduction. Make notes based on your research from Critical thinking. Think about what kind of background information to include in your introduction in order for the audience to understand the problems in your presentation. Use language from Preparation for speaking to help you.

3 Look back at your proposed solutions in your outline. What kind of information could you include in your conclusion? Use signposting language from Preparation for speaking to help you.

4 Refer to the Task checklist below as you prepare your presentation.

OBJECTIVES REVIEW

1 Check your learning objectives for this unit. Write *3, 2* or *1* for each objective.

3 = very well   2 = well   1 = not so well

I can ...

watch and understand a video about cloning endangered species.   _____

distinguish main ideas from details.   _____

take notes on main ideas and details.   _____

organize information in a presentation.   _____

use multi-word prepositions.   _____

---

2 Use the *Unlock* Digital Workbook for more practice with this unit's learning objectives.

⊙ UNLOCK ONLINE

WORDLIST

consumer (n) ⊙	labour (n) ⊙	profit (n) ⊙
discount (n) ⊙	multinational (adj)	prosperity (n) ⊙
domestic (adj) ⊙	outsourcing (n)	purchase (v) ⊙
goods (n) ⊙	overseas (adv) ⊙	supply chain (n)
greenhouse (n)	produce (n) ⊙	transport (n) ⊙
import (v) ⊙	produce (v) ⊙	
investigate (v) ⊙	production costs (n)	

⊙ = high-frequency words in the Cambridge Academic Corpus

Unlock offers 56 hours per Student's Book, which is extendable to 90 hours with the Digital Pack, and other additional activities in the Teacher's Manual and Development Pack.

Unlock is a paired-skills course with two separate Student's Books per level. For levels 1–5 (CEFR A1 – C1), these are **Reading, Writing and Critical Thinking** and **Listening, Speaking and Critical Thinking**. They share the same unit topics so you have access to a wide range of material at each level. Each Student's Book provides access to the Digital Pack.

Unlock Basic has been developed for pre-A1 learners. **Unlock Basic Skills** integrates reading, writing, listening, speaking and critical thinking in one book to provide students with an effective and manageable learning experience. **Unlock Basic Literacy** develops and builds confidence in literacy. The *Basic* books also share the same unit topics and so can be used together or separately, and **Unlock Basic Literacy** can be used for self-study.

Student components

Resource	Description	Access

Student's Books	• Levels 1–5 come with the Digital Pack (Digital Workbook, Digital Classroom Material, downloadable audio and video)
	  – Levels 1–4 (8 units)
	  – Level 5 (10 units)
	• *Unlock Basic Skills* comes with downloadable audio and video (11 units)
	• *Unlock Basic Literacy* comes with downloadable audio (11 units)
		• The Digital Pack (Digital Workbook, Digital Classroom Material, downloadable audio and video) is accessed on our **learning platform** via the unique code inside the front cover of the Student's Book
		• The audio and video are downloadable from the Student's Resources section on the **learning platform**

Digital Workbook	• Levels 1–5 only • Extension activities to further practise the language and skills learned • All-new vocabulary activities in the Digital Workbook practise the target vocabulary in new contexts	• The Digital Workbook is on our **learning platform** and is accessed via the unique code inside the front cover of the Student's Book
Digital Classroom Material	• Levels 1–5 only • Extra practice in speaking, critical thinking and language	• Please go to **cambridgeone.org** to access the digital classroom material. • Students use the same login details as for the **learning platform**, and then they are logged in for a year
Video	• Levels 1–5 and *Unlock Basic Skills* only • All the video from the course	• The video is downloadable from the Student's Resources section on the **learning platform**
Audio	• All the audio from the course	• The audio is downloadable from the Student's Resources section on the **learning platform**

Teacher components

Resource	Description	Access
Teacher's Manual and Development Pack	• One manual covers Levels 1–5 • It contains flexible lesson plans, lesson objectives, additional activities and common learner errors as well as professional development for teachers, *Developing critical thinking skills in your students* • It comes with downloadable audio and video, vocabulary worksheets and peer-to-peer teacher training worksheets	• The audio, video and worksheets are downloadable from the Teacher Resources section on the **learning platform**
Presentation Plus	• Software for interactive whiteboards so you can present the pages of the Student's Books and easily play audio and video, and check answers	• Presentation Plus is available from the Teacher Resources section on our **learning platform**

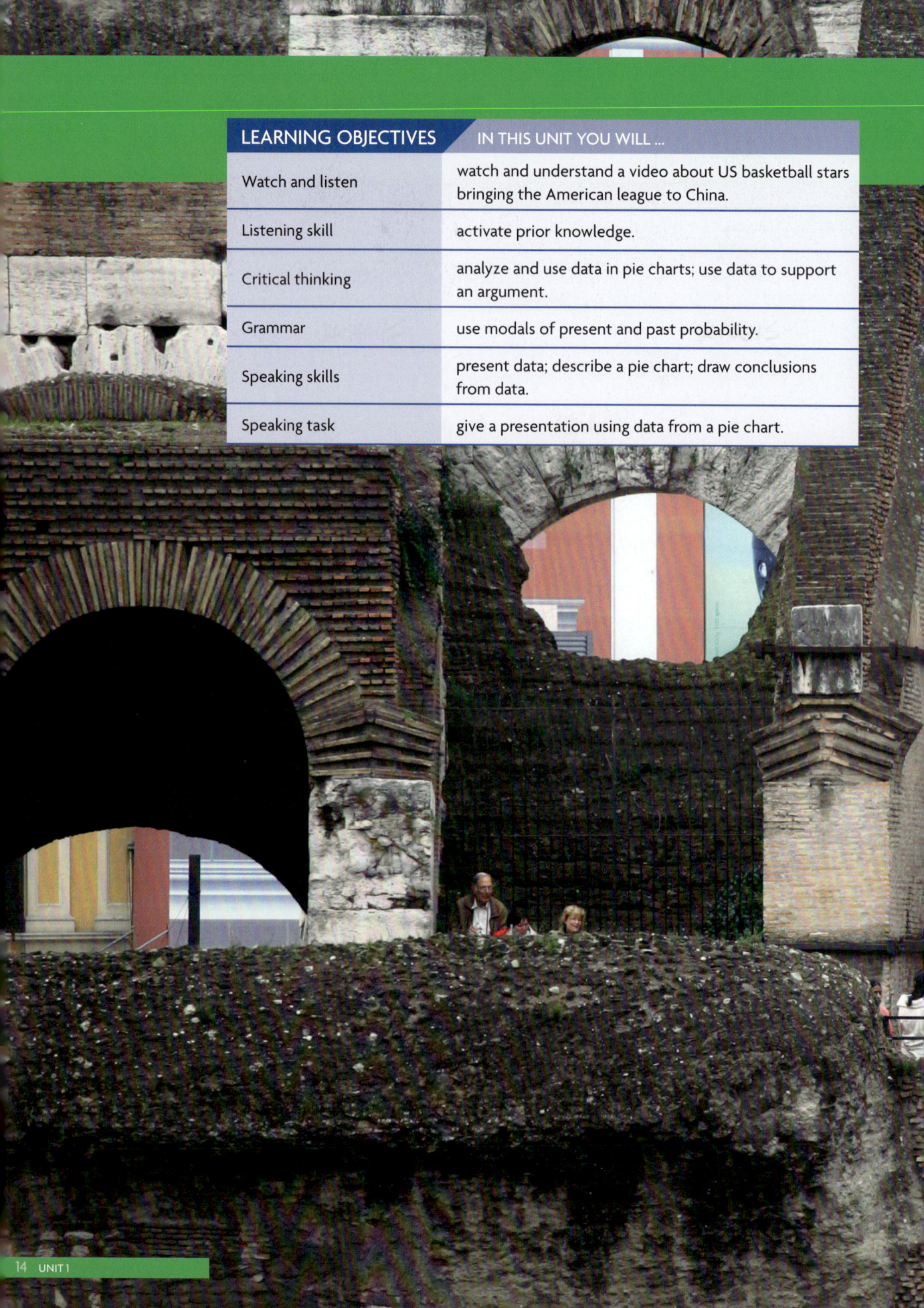

LEARNING OBJECTIVES	IN THIS UNIT YOU WILL ...
Watch and listen	watch and understand a video about US basketball stars bringing the American league to China.
Listening skill	activate prior knowledge.
Critical thinking	analyze and use data in pie charts; use data to support an argument.
Grammar	use modals of present and past probability.
Speaking skills	present data; describe a pie chart; draw conclusions from data.
Speaking task	give a presentation using data from a pie chart.

GLOBALIZATION

UNL🔓CK YOUR KNOWLEDGE

Work with a partner. Discuss the questions below.

1 Do you read any international magazines or watch foreign television programmes or films? Give examples of your favourites.

2 Do you like fashion or music from other countries? Why / Why not?

3 What international restaurants are there in your city or country? What do they serve?

4 Do you buy any foods from other countries at the supermarket? If so, what foods do you buy?

PLUS

PREPARING TO WATCH

1 Work with a partner and answer the questions.

1 Do you enjoy watching international sporting events on television, that is, sports that are popular in many different countries? Which ones? Why do you like these sports?

2 How often do you watch *live* sporting events? How much does it cost to watch them?

3 Do you support a team? Do you have any clothes or anything else with the name or picture of the team?

2 Look at the pictures from the video. Discuss the questions with a partner.

1 In which country is the game being played? Do you think basketball is popular there? Why / Why not?

2 What are the players doing when they are not playing basketball?

3 Why do you think they are doing these things?

GLOSSARY

NBA (abbr) National Basketball Association; the men's professional basketball league in the United States and Canada

charm offensive (n phr) a strong effort to make people like you

NBA-sponsored facilities (n phr) buildings and equipment that are paid for by the NBA

merchandising and broadcast deals (n phr) agreements to put games on television and sell things associated with the teams, such as T-shirts and hats

go from strength to strength (phr) to become more and more successful

have their way (phr) to get what they want

WHILE WATCHING

3 ▶ Watch the video. Write *T* (true) or *F* (false) next to the statements below. Correct the false statements.

_____ 1 The NBA players were in China to celebrate the opening of a new sports facility.

_____ 2 The NBA players were in China to make basketball more popular.

_____ 3 The NBA teams came to China to play a game during the main basketball season.

_____ 4 The NBA player, Jeremy Lin, is from China.

_____ 5 The Chinese market is of increasing importance to the NBA.

4 ▶ Read the main ideas. Watch the video again and add supporting details for each main idea.

1 The NBA players went to China on a charm offensive.

_____

2 The Chinese market is very valuable to the NBA.

_____

3 The players enjoyed themselves in China.

_____

5 Work with a partner. Discuss the questions and give reasons for your answers.

1 Do you think the visits to China and other parts of the world by the NBA will continue? Why / Why not?

2 What kind of impact do you think the visit had on the children who met the players, and the fans who watched the games?

3 Do you think the NBA will have teams outside North America in the future? Why / Why not? If so, what countries might come first?

4 What do you think the players learned during their visit to China?

DISCUSSION

6 Work with a partner and answer the questions.

1 Would you like to attend an NBA game? Why / Why not?

2 Do you think the international popularity of American basketball will continue to grow? Why / Why not?

3 What other sports are popular outside the country where they began? Why do you think they became global?

4 Are there any sports that originated in your country or region that have become popular in other places? Which one(s)? Why do you think its popularity has spread?

LISTENING

LISTENING 1

PREPARING TO LISTEN

UNDERSTANDING KEY VOCABULARY

1 Read the sentences and write the words in bold next to the definitions.

1 I **purchase** apples from the local farm shop to help the environment.
2 As an educated **consumer** I often read the labels on my shopping.
3 Some farmers **produce** fruit and vegetables to sell locally.
4 The UK **imports** its bananas from other countries and then sells them in local markets.
5 Scientists **investigate** the reasons climate change is getting worse.
6 According to the label on the pasta sauce, it is made **overseas**.
7 In cold climates, many types of fruit can be grown in **greenhouses**.

a _____ (v) to buy something
b _____ (adv) in, from, or to other countries
c _____ (n) someone who buys or uses goods or services
d _____ (v) to bring products in from another country to sell or use
e _____ (n) a building used to grow plants that need constant warmth and protection
f _____ (v) to create something or bring it into existence
g _____ (v) to carefully examine something, especially to discover the truth about it

SKILLS

Activating prior knowledge

Thinking about what you already know about the topic before you listen can help you connect it to your own personal experiences or past studies. It can also help you predict what information you might hear or think about what you might like to know about the topic. You can activate your prior knowledge by asking questions about the topic, looking at photos related to the topic, thinking about the title of the lecture or talk, or talking with a classmate about the topic.

You can ask questions such as:

• What do I already know about this topic?
• What experiences have I had that relate to this topic?
• What have I read or heard about this topic before?
• What do I think about this topic?

Activating prior knowledge will make it easier to understand key information when you listen the first time. It can also help you evaluate the information, based on what you already know.

2 You are going to listen to a radio programme called *The 48,000-km fruit salad*. Before you listen, work with a partner. Think about the programme name and look at the photo below. Choose the topics that you think will be included. Give reasons why.

1 Supermarkets	5 Specialist food shops
2 Environmental pollution	6 UK businesses in other countries
3 Job creation	7 Shipping food by aeroplane
4 International companies	8 Ways to make healthy food

WHILE LISTENING

3 🔊 1.1 Listen to the interview between a customer and a reporter and check your answers to Exercise 2.

4 🔊 1.1 Listen again and complete the student's notes. Then compare notes with a partner.

Name of programme: The world close up
Main topic: (1) _____ GLOBALIZATION _____
Customer interviewed: (2) _____ David Green _____
Customer is buying more (3) _____ fruits _____ and (4) _____ vegetables _____ in order to eat more
(5) _HEALTHILY_.

Item	Tomatoes	(6) _BANANAS_	Grapes	Blueberries	(7) _KIWIS_
Country	Morocco	Colombia	(8) _South Africa_	Argentina	New Zealand
Kilometres	3,500	(9) _8,500_	(10) _9,600_	(11) _11,100_	18,800

The lettuce is (12) _____ local _____, but the farm it came from could have (13) _____ transported _____.
Fruit and vegetables from hot countries must be grown in greenhouses, and this
(14) _____ increase products CO₂ _____

Total kilometres travelled (15) _48000_
Problems with food travelling: long food (16) _____ and a huge carbon _FOOTPRINT_
(17) _____ emission _____
| LONG FOOD SUPPLY CHAIN | supply chain |

5 Read the statements. Write T (true) or F (false). Then correct the false statements.

_T_ 1 Most of the food David is buying is imported.

_____

_F_ 2 David usually tries to eat foods that are grown locally.

_____

_F_ 3 The global food industry limits the types of fruit people eat.

_____

_F_ 4 You can be sure that locally grown food has not travelled.

_____

_F_ 5 Locally grown food is always environmentally friendly.

_____

POST-LISTENING

6 🔊 1.2 Listen to the extracts from the radio programme. Choose the statement (a–c) which best matches the reporter's opinion.

1 a Cheap food can have hidden negative effects.
  b Cheap food costs less for consumers.
  c Cheap food is better for the environment.

2 a Shipping fruit by air is a good thing.
   b Shipping fruit by air is not environmentally friendly.
   c Shipping fruit by air is cheap and easy.
3 a Shipping fruit around the world might contribute to global warming.
   b The price of fruit at the supermarket is too high because of air travel.
   c If we don't eat enough locally grown fruit, we won't be healthy.

PRONUNCIATION FOR LISTENING

Consonant clusters

A consonant cluster is a group of consonants without a vowel between them, for example /gr/ or /spl/.

Mixtures of consonant sounds can cause problems with note-taking. If you mishear the speaker, you might write the wrong word. Consonant clusters can be heard at the start of words (_grow_, _fly_, _cross_) or at the end of words (_cost_, _past_, _find_).

7   1.3 Listen to the consonant clusters in these sentences. Write the word the speaker says.

1 These agricultural products are already going _ABROAD_ .
2 We _GROW_ many kinds of tea on this plantation.
3 The police regularly _FIND_ illegal imports.
4 The company _PRODUCES_ more crops overseas last year.
5 The bananas are _TIMED_ so that they ripen together.
6 _FIND_ the crops causes air pollution.
7 The products _PASS_ through customs easily.
8 I want to know why these routes _COST_ more.

[handwritten notes in margin: to RIPE / MATURE → Amadurecer / RIPE – Madura / TIMED / AMADUREçAM]

8   1.4 Listen and complete the student's notes. Then read the notes and check that the words make sense in the context.

There hasn't been much (1) _support_ from the government over the issue of imported agricultural crops. There are (2) _three_ issues with this. (3) _firstly_ , nearly a (4) _1/6th_ of all imported fruit cannot grow in our (5) _climate_ . Secondly, the (6) _stage_ should help our own farmers rather than foreign growers. Finally, we should not fall into the (7) _trap_ of not (8) _growing_ enough food. What (9) _would_ happen if it didn't (10) _rain_ and we were left with a food shortage?

[handwritten: ✱ Fall into the TRAP – cair na armadilha]

DISCUSSION

9 Work with a partner. Discuss the questions.

1 What kind of fresh foods are available in your country? Are they produced locally or overseas?
2 Are these fresh foods available all year or only at specific times? Why?
3 Do you check the origin of food when you buy it by reading the label? Where does it come from?
4 Do you think most people in your city or country buy food that has travelled long distances? Why / Why not?

⊙ LANGUAGE DEVELOPMENT

MODALS OF PRESENT AND PAST PROBABILITY

You can use modals to show how sure or unsure you are of something in the present or past. In the present, use a modal + infinitive. In the past, use a modal + *have* + past participle.

It **might be** a British company. (present)
It **might have been** a British company. (past)

Use *must* when you are certain that something is true because there is strong evidence, or when you think there is only one logical conclusion.

These avocados **must be** from Mexico. The label says 'avocados from Mexico'. (present)
These avocados **must have come** from Mexico. I saw the shipping box come in yesterday from Mexico. (past)

Use *can't* or *couldn't* when you are absolutely certain that something is not true.

Abdul **can't be** from Oman. He has an Egyptian passport. (present)
His flight **can't have arrived** in Dubai yet. It's only nine o'clock. (past)
This jumper **can't be** from Japan. The tag says 'made in Scotland'. (present)
She **couldn't have bought** her car in the UK. She was living in Turkey at the time. (past)

When you think something is possible, but you are not sure, use *may (not), might (not)* or *could*.

The company **could be** British, but I'm not really sure. (present)
The supermarket **might have imported** the bananas from Colombia. (past)
Eun Sook **may not have worked** in the UK before. (past)

Only use contractions (short forms) with *could* and *can*.

most certain ↑ *must* (something is true)
couldn't, can't (something is not true)

least certain ↓ *may (not), might (not), could*

GRAMMAR

1 Circle the correct modal and verb form. Use the information in brackets to help you.

→ (Possibility)

1 Alana *couldn't have bought / may have bought* tickets to Ecuador last week. She asked me about ticket prices. (guessing)

2 Ahmed *must be / could be* from Oman. I saw his passport earlier. (the only logical conclusion)

3 I *might have lost / must have lost* my passport on the way home from work. It was in my pocket when I left work, and then it wasn't there when I got home. (the only logical conclusion)

4 Jan's new company *might send / must send* her to Dubai next week. They do a lot of international business, and she thinks a large meeting is happening in the next ten days. (guessing)

5 My new smartphone *can't be / must be* from Tahiti. There isn't a big smartphone industry there. (impossible)

6 Luis *may have lived / must have lived* in South Korea for a while. He speaks fluent Korean, and I saw a Korean company on his CV. (the only logical conclusion)

PLUS

2 Look again at Exercise 1. How would the meaning of each sentence change if the other modal and verb form was used?

3 Complete the statements with modals of present and past probability. Use the given verbs and the clues in brackets to help you. Sometimes more than one answer is possible.

1 These fruit and vegetables __must be__ (be) grown locally – I bought them at the farm shop. (present – logical conclusion)

2 Your phone __could have been__ (be) made overseas and exported to be sold in other countries. (past – logical conclusion) ← May have been / Must have been

3 Your lunch __might contain__ (contain) only food products that were produced in this country. (present – guess) may / could

4 Fifty years ago, goods that were produced locally __May have been / Could have been__ (be) cheaper than goods that were produced overseas. (past – guess)

5 This film __Couldn't have been__ (be) based on an older British film. The writer said it was American! (past – impossible)

4 Discuss these questions with a partner. Use the structures *could be / may be / must be* or *could have / may have / must have* in your answers.

1 Where do you think the clothes you are wearing today were made?

2 Think about the kind of car you would like to buy. Where do you think it was made? What other countries buy that car?

3 Do you have friends from other countries? Where are they from? What other countries have they visited or lived in?

GLOBALIZATION VOCABULARY

5 Complete the text with the correct words and phrases from the box. Use the Glossary on page 190 to help you.

> goods   imported   multinational   outsourcing   produce
> prosperity   purchase   supply chain   transport

Globalization is positive. Thanks to advances in (1)_____, a wide range of (2)_____ can now be shared around the world. For example, fresh food can be (3)_____ from different countries via lorry, plane and ship. Although this makes the (4)_____ longer, with more people involved before the (5)_____ reaches the customer, there's an amazing variety of fruit and vegetables to choose from. Even if your country doesn't grow kiwis, you can (6)_____ them in supermarkets all year round! Companies are now (7)_____; Coca-Cola is an American company, but it has offices in Argentina, Japan and Spain. Globalization can bring a lot of (8)_____ to countries. The trend in (9)_____ — when a company gets services from an outside supplier — has been very beneficial for some countries. For example, India is a leader in supplying IT customer services for companies all over the world. Globalization is definitely making the world smaller!

LISTENING 2

PREPARING TO LISTEN

UNDERSTANDING KEY VOCABULARY

1 Choose the best definition (a–b) for the bold word or phrase (1–7).

1 Over the years, Starbucks has become a **multinational** company, now operating in over 75 countries.
   a active in one country
   b active in several countries

2 You have to pay taxes on any **goods** you buy when visiting another country.
   a items for sale
   b services

3 Companies try to save on **production costs**, so that they can make money when the product is sold later.
   a the money spent to make something
   b the money spent to sell something

4 The film director was excited when he learned his film earned a **profit** after just one week in cinemas.
   a good review
   b financial gain

5 The film director promised to use only **domestic** products when filming outside the country.
   a related to other countries
   b related to a person's own country

6 **Labour** costs can be expensive because they include wages, benefits and taxes.
   a work
   b materials

7 If you buy three cinema tickets rather than just one, you get a **discount**.
   a a reduction in price
   b an increase in price

2 You are going to listen to a presentation on the film industry. Before you listen, discuss the questions in pairs.

USING YOUR KNOWLEDGE

1 What is your favourite film? Where do you think it was made? Where do you think most films are made?

2 Why might a film director choose a different location in which to make their film?

handwritten: ☆ Ghallywood for Gana

WHILE LISTENING

3 🔊 1.5 Listen to the presentation about the film industry and take notes. List the countries where the United States makes films and the reasons why.

Countries	Reasons
1 CANADA *torgnto* *Hollywood north*	discount on labour *ots most bulet* tax credits 60% *(Columbia + 18%)*
2 Mexico	*FREE from some TAPES* *BRINGS JOBS and MONEY to people*
3 MIDDLE EAST UNITED EMIRATES	tax – *incentives* great locations
4 USA	*Agricultural town – hollywood* *Big budget films* *>50 outside* *>25% outside USA*

4 🔊 1.5 Listen to the presentation again. Number the statements in the order they are discussed. Then listen again and check your answers.

a Hollywood itself has become more multinational. __1__
b Films made in Mexico are considered exports. __3__
c Canada is sometimes called 'Hollywood North'. __2__
d Another popular area for filming is the Middle East. __4__

5 🔊 1.5 Listen to the presentation again and complete the pie chart with the words and phrases from the box.

> Overseas   Overseas and Domestic   Domestic

WHERE AMERICAN FILMS ARE MADE

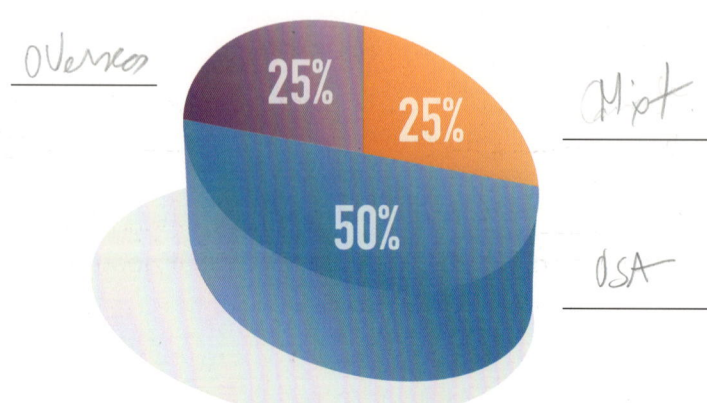

Overseas — 25%
Mixt. — 25%
USA — 50%

POST-LISTENING

6 Read the sentences from the presentation. Underline the cause of the action in each sentence.

1 In order to get this tax credit, one of the two highest-paid actors in the film must be Canadian.

2 Since films made in Mexico are considered exports, they are free from some taxes, making Mexico an appealing location for film-makers.

3 Jordan helps producers avoid taxes, such as the VAT, or Value Added Tax, that is added to goods and services that are bought. Therefore, more and more films are being made there.

7 Look at the sentences in Exercise 6 again. Circle the language that links the cause and effect in each sentence.

8 Complete the sentences with your own ideas. Then compare with a partner.

1 Due to the film industry becoming more multinational,

_____ .

2 Many film producers are making films overseas. As a result,

_____ .

3 Films are not always made in Hollywood. Consequently,

_____ .

4 Producing films overseas earns profits for both countries, which therefore

_____ .

DISCUSSION

9 Work with a partner. Describe a film that you enjoy watching. Then discuss the questions.

1 Where is the film set?

2 Do you think the film was made there or somewhere else? Why do you think so?

10 Work with a partner. Use ideas from Listening 1 and Listening 2 to discuss the following questions.

1 Do you know if any Hollywood films are made in your country? What benefits do you think your country can offer a film director?

2 Do you think films being made around the world is a good thing? Why / Why not?

3 When a film is made in multiple international locations, what cost considerations do companies need to make? Think about the supermarket in Listening 1, for example.

SPEAKING

CRITICAL THINKING

At the end of this unit, you are going to do the speaking task below.

> Give a presentation on how we can ensure that workers in developing countries are paid fairly for the goods and services we import.

How long 3 min →

SKILLS

Using data to support an argument

To make strong, convincing arguments, it is important to use reliable data. If you do not, then your argument may just be seen as an opinion rather than one based on facts. Data is sometimes shown in pie charts, which are a useful tool for presenting data in an easy-to-understand format. Pie charts are used to show percentages. The sections of a pie chart represent portions of 100%, or the entire circle.

UNDERSTAND

1 Look at the pie chart. Answer the questions.

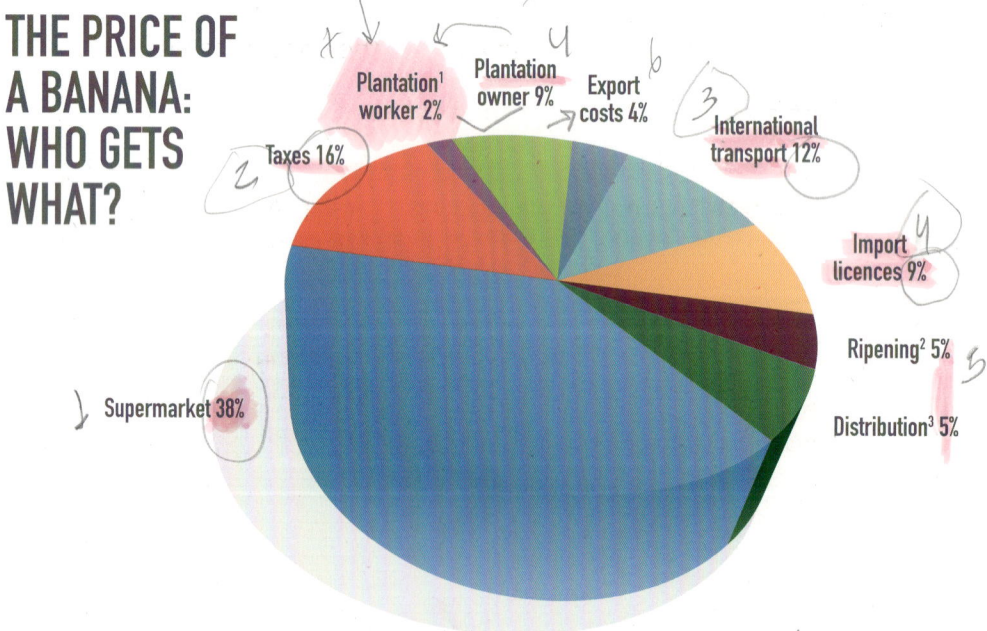

THE PRICE OF A BANANA: WHO GETS WHAT?

Plantation[1] worker 2%
Plantation owner 9%
Export costs 4%
International transport 12%
Taxes 16%
Import licences 9%
Ripening[2] 5%
Distribution[3] 5%
Supermarket 38%

[1] **plantation** (n) a large farm on which a particular crop is grown
[2] **ripening** (n) (of fruit or vegetables) becoming mature and ready to eat
[3] **distribution** (n) the act of spreading or supplying something

1 What does each section of the chart represent? How many different activities are presented?

_____

2 Which information in the pie chart do you find most surprising? Tell a partner why.

_____

3 If the government reduced taxes on bananas to 10%, what would happen to the other percentages in the chart? What about if supermarkets demanded a higher share of income?

_____

ANALYZING AND USING DATA IN A PIE CHART

2 Does the data in the pie chart support or oppose the following statements? Write *S* (support) or *O* (oppose).

ANALYZE

1 The cost of transporting bananas from the plantation to the supermarket accounts for the largest share of the price. __O__

2 Import licences contribute nearly the same amount to the price of bananas as international transport costs. __O__

3 The ripening process accounts for a much bigger share of the price of bananas than the growing process. __O__ *Fertilizing , planting*

4 Taxes contribute the smallest amount to the price of bananas. __O__

3 Work with a partner and answer the questions.

worth the cost
High RISK.

1 Why is so much of the price of bananas made up of supermarket costs? Does the figure seem reasonable to you? *NO*

2 Why is the cost of growing bananas such a small component of the overall cost? *?*

3 Why do plantation owners receive much more than the workers? Do you think this is fair? → *Exploitation / inequality*

4 What effect would doubling the amount of money plantation workers receive have on the overall price of bananas? If this happened, do you think there would be any other effects?

none

small effect on general price

- Plantation owner ↓
tips ↓
- Supermarket ↓

4 In this unit's speaking task, you are going to give a presentation agreeing or disagreeing with one of the statements below. Look at the statements. With a partner, say if you agree or disagree with them. Write notes explaining why / why not.

1 Food producers and exporters should be responsible for helping workers in developing countries get a fair deal.

_9% _ _ 4% _

_2% _

2 Governments in importing countries should take the lead in sharing their income from the food trade with workers in developing countries.

Tags 16% _Input licenses 9%_
int. transport 12%

3 Consumers should put pressure on supermarkets and distributors to do more for workers in developing countries.

faire answers _36%_

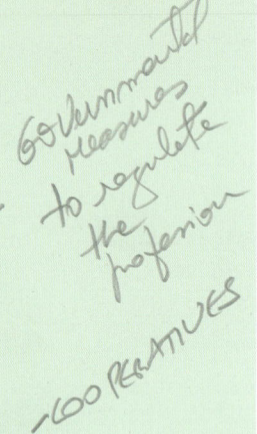

Governments measures
- to regulate the profession

- COOPERATIVES

FAIR TRADE MOVEMENT

_↓_

initiative

5 Choose one of the statements in Exercise 4. Answer the questions about your statement.

1 What data in the pie chart on page 28 can you use to support your argument?

Percentages from Tapas, internet, transport and
Input loans

2 What data in the chart contradicts your view? What can you do to minimize this problem?

Percentage from Supermarkets huge

3 Do you need any other information to support your argument? Where could you find this?

How to ↓ the info from Supermarkets

PRESENTING DATA

> **SKILLS**
>
> Charts present data in a way that makes it easy to understand. When giving a presentation, you can use charts to explain information that supports your point of view. You can make good use of the information by drawing general and specific conclusions from it, using figures such as fractions or percentages to describe it and listing points and conclusions using sequential language (*firstly*, *next*, etc.).

1 Complete the introduction to the presentation. Use the words and phrases from the box.

> a lot of discussion   consider   I'd like to talk about
> many people believe   others have pointed out
> look at   they say   would like to show

(1) *I'd like to talk about* where your money goes when you buy a cup of coffee. There has been (2) *a lot of discussion* in the media recently about fair prices for the people in countries who grow crops like coffee. (3) *Many people believe* that it's not right that a cup of coffee can cost £3 or more, of which the farmers only get a few pennies. However, (4) *others have pointed out* that the coffee beans are only one part of the cost of supplying a cup of coffee. (5) *They say* that the other ingredients, such as milk and sugar, are also a big part of the cost of a cup of coffee. However, I (6) *would like to show* that in a typical coffee shop, the ingredients are only a small part of the overall cost. Let's (7) *look at* some data. If you (8) *consider* the information in this chart ...

2 🔊 1.6 Listen and check your answers to Exercise 1.

PLUS

DESCRIBING A PIE CHART

3 Look at the pie chart for the price of a cup of coffee in the UK. Complete the sentences with the phrases from the box.

> accounts for   a total of   each make up   more than a quarter of
> the largest part   three parts are related to   they make up

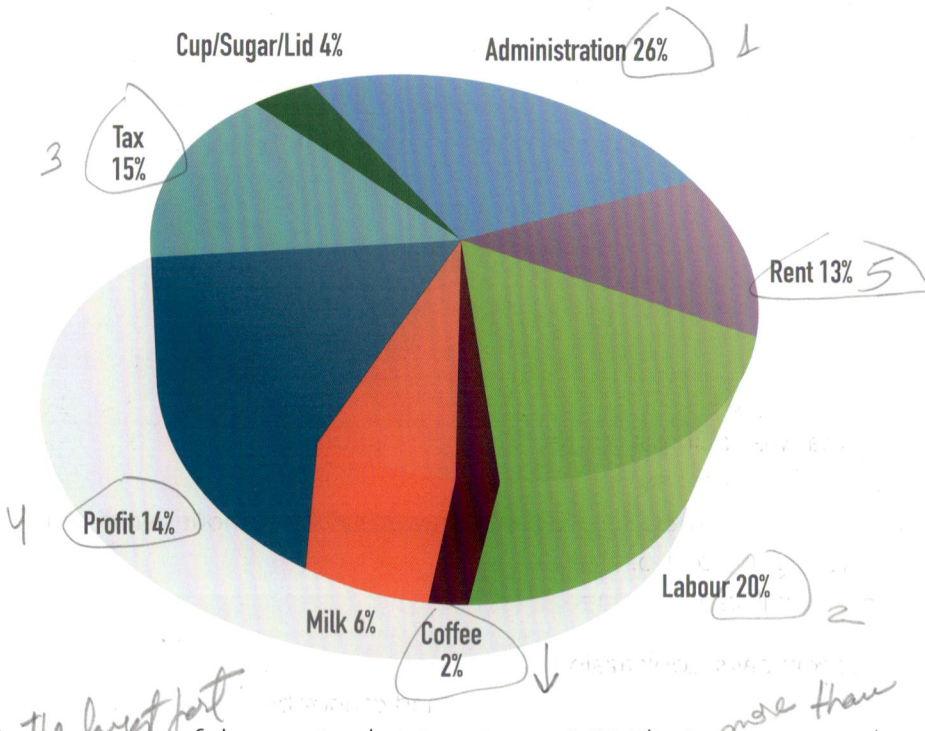

THE PRICE OF A CUP OF COFFEE IN THE UK

Cup/Sugar/Lid 4%   Administration 26%   1

Tax 15%   3

Rent 13%   5

Profit 14%   4

Milk 6%   Coffee 2%   Labour 20%   2

1 _the largest part_ of the cost is administration, at 26%. That's _more than a quarter of_ the cost per cup.

2 Labour _accounts for_ 20% of the cost.

3 Tax, profit and rent _each make up_ about 14% of the cost, or _a total of_ 42% of the price of a cup of coffee.

4 _3 parts are related to_ the product you take away – milk at 6%; the cup, sugar and lid at 4%; and the coffee itself at 2%. Together, _they make up_ 12% of the price you pay.

```
  15
  14
  13
  ----
  42
```

DRAWING CONCLUSIONS FROM DATA

4 🔊 1.7 Listen to the next part of the presentation. Number the expressions in the order you hear them.

a as you can see ... _3_
b This pie chart shows ... _1_
c which you'll notice accounts for ... _5_
d Finally, I'd like to draw your attention to ... _7_
e Next ... _6_
f Firstly ... _2_
g Secondly ... _4_

5 Match the sentence halves.

1 You can see that in a typical cup of coffee, _e_
2 This data shows that the raw ingredients only _a_
3 This means that it may be possible _d_
4 Looking at the chart, we can conclude _c_
5 In summary, the data shows that the two biggest _b_

a account for 12% of the price you pay.
b parts of the cost of a cup of coffee are administration and labour.
c that we could pay coffee farmers a lot more for coffee beans, and coffee drinkers wouldn't notice the difference.
d to increase the price we pay for raw materials without significantly raising the cost of a cup of coffee.
e the milk can cost three times as much as the coffee itself.

6 Work in pairs. Look again at the pie chart in Exercise 3. Which data surprises you? Which data is 'fixed' and cannot be changed, and which is flexible?

Tap, Admin. (?) | Flexible → Pro Fit TAX LABOUR everything

SPEAKING TASK

▶ Give a presentation on how we can ensure that workers in developing countries are paid fairly for the goods and services we import.

PREPARE

1 Look back at the presentation statement you chose in Exercise 4 and your notes in Exercise 5 in Critical thinking. Add any additional information that may help you.

2 Using the information in the pie chart in Critical thinking, organize your points in the order you want to speak about them. Remember to put the most important points first and to support your points with data. Use language from the Preparation for speaking section in your points.

3 Write notes and a conclusion to help organize your presentation.

4 Refer to the Task checklist below as you prepare your presentation.

TASK CHECKLIST	✔
Set the context in the introduction.	
Describe the pie chart.	
Support your view with data.	
Draw a conclusion supported by the pie chart.	

PRESENT

5 Work with a partner. Take turns giving your presentation. Remember to use language from the Preparation for speaking section to organize your talk and to present data. When your partner has finished, ask them questions about their presentation. Say whether you agree or disagree with them and why.

OBJECTIVES REVIEW

1 Check your learning objectives for this unit. Write *3*, *2* or *1* for each objective.

3 = very well   2 = well   1 = not so well

I can ...

watch and understand a video about US basketball stars bringing the American league to China.   _____

activate prior knowledge.   _____

analyze and use data in pie charts.   _____

use data to support an argument.   _____

use modals of present and past probability.   _____

present data.   _____

describe a pie chart.   _____

draw conclusions from data.   _____

give a presentation using data from a pie chart.   _____

2 Use the *Unlock* Digital Workbook for more practice with this unit's learning objectives.

WORDLIST		
consumer (n) ⊙	labour (n) ⊙	profit (n) ⊙
discount (n) ⊙	multinational (adj)	prosperity (n) ⊙
domestic (adj) ⊙	outsourcing (n)	purchase (v) ⊙
goods (n) ⊙	overseas (adv) ⊙	supply chain (n)
greenhouse (n)	produce (n) ⊙	transport (n) ⊙
import (v) ⊙	produce (v) ⊙	
investigate (v) ⊙	production costs (n)	

⊙ = high-frequency words in the Cambridge Academic Corpus

LEARNING OBJECTIVES	IN THIS UNIT YOU WILL ...
Watch and listen	watch and understand a video about a school where students work on real science.
Listening skills	listen for advice and suggestions; make inferences.
Critical thinking	prioritize criteria; use priorities to evaluate options.
Grammar	use the future continuous; state preferences with *would*.
Speaking skills	give an opinion and make suggestions; agree and disagree respectfully; compromise and finalize a decision.
Speaking task	decide as a group which candidate should receive a scholarship.

UNLOCK YOUR KNOWLEDGE

Work with a partner. Discuss the questions.

1 Which careers require a lot of study? Which do not?

2 What subjects do you have to study to become …
   • a teacher?
   • a doctor?
   • a lawyer?
   • a businessperson?

3 Would you like to work in a medical profession?
   Why / Why not?

PLUS

TECHNOLOGY ——— COSMOLOGY ASTRONOMY

PREPARING TO WATCH

1 Work with a partner and answer the questions.

1 What science subjects do most high school students in your country study? *PHYSICS, CHEMICALS BIOLOGY*

2 What kinds of things do they do in science classes? Describe a typical lesson.

3 Do students need to pass a science exam to finish school or go to university? Is it more important to pass the exam or get some experience with real science?

4 What do you like about science courses? What do you dislike?

2 Look at the pictures from the video. Discuss the questions with a partner.

1 What area of science do you think the video will discuss?

2 What do you think the device in the second picture might be? What do you think is its purpose?

3 What is the device in the third picture? Is it something you usually find in schools?

4 Students like those in the fourth picture designed the device in the second picture. Does this seem unusual to you? Why / Why not?

GLOSSARY

research facility (n) a place where scientists work to make discoveries

radiation (n) a form of energy that comes from a nuclear reaction and can be dangerous in large amounts

corruption of data (phr) damage to or loss of information

ground-breaking (adj) based on completely new ideas

absolutely phenomenal (adj phr) completely amazing

WHILE WATCHING

3 ▶ Watch the video. Write *T* (true) or *F* (false) next to the statements below. Correct the false statements.

_____ 1 The students at the Simon Langton School conduct experiments similar to those of professional scientists.

_____ 2 The Simon Langton School science curriculum closely follows the government's recommendations.

_____ 3 The students' work is designed to help them to pass their exams.

_____ 4 Langton students are conducting advanced research in physics and health science.

_____ 5 This kind of science curriculum is quite unusual.

4 ▶ Watch again. Match these ideas to the speakers in the video.

1 Tom Stevenson, former student at the Simon Langton School
2 Becky Parker, Head of Physics at the Simon Langton School
3 Christopher Cundy, student at the Simon Langton School
4 Tom Ziessen, Engaging Science Manager at the Wellcome Trust

a I believe that experience, and not exams, is a better way to learn science.
b The curriculum at Langton is the only one of its kind.
c The work I did at school can help protect astronauts.
d It's an amazing opportunity for us to work on these real world problems.

5 Work with a partner. Discuss the questions and give reasons for your answers.

1 Why doesn't the school follow the government science curriculum?
2 How do you think a school knows if its curriculum is successful?
3 What can explain the success of students at Simon Langton School?
4 Do you think its success could be copied at other schools? Why / Why not?

DISCUSSION

6 Work with a partner and answer the questions.

1 Is the science curriculum in your country similar to the Simon Langton School curriculum? Describe similarities and differences.
2 If you could choose, would you like to study a curriculum like Langton's? Why / Why not?
3 Do you think schools do a good job of preparing high school students for university? For work? Explain your answer.
4 What role should practical experience play in education?

LISTENING

PREPARING TO LISTEN

USING YOUR KNOWLEDGE

1 Tick (✔) the statements that are true for you. Then discuss them with a partner.

1 I have visited a careers adviser. ☑
2 I know what career path I want to pursue. ☑
3 I know a lot about the field I want to study or work in. ☑
4 I know what I need to do for my future career. ☑
5 I have taken steps to prepare for my career. ☑

UNDERSTANDING KEY VOCABULARY

2 Read the definitions. Complete the sentences with the correct form of the words in bold.

---

academic (adj) related to subjects that require thinking and studying
acquire (v) to get or receive something, or to learn something
adviser (n) someone whose job is to give advice about a subject
internship (n) a period of time during which someone works for a company or organization in order to get experience of a particular type of work
mechanical (adj) related to machines
specialist (n) someone with a lot of skill or experience in a subject
understanding (n) knowledge about a subject
vocational (adj) providing skills and education that prepare you for a specific trade or profession

---

1 John did his _internship_ at an advertising firm last summer. He learned a lot about how he could use his marketing degree after graduating.
2 To become a doctor, students need to study _academic_ subjects such as Biology and Chemistry.
3 Kayo had to design _mechanical_ parts for an aeroplane engine for her Engineering project.
4 Taking English classes and practising with others every day will help you _acquire_ the language much faster than studying on your own.
5 I have a greater _understanding_ of government since I took a course in Political Science.
6 Li visited her university careers _adviser_ to help her choose her course of study.

7 People who study to become engineers often have good _Vocation_ training because they take specific courses focused on different aspects of Engineering.

8 After she became a doctor, Carolina took additional courses to become a sports medicine _specialist_.

3 Work with a partner. Describe your study or career interests. Use the words from Exercise 2.

WHILE LISTENING

4 🔊 2.1 Listen to the meeting between a student and a careers adviser. Then answer the questions.

LISTENING FOR MAIN IDEAS

1 What is Laura trying to make a decision about?
   what to do after graduate, considering go to a college but she don't know what exactly to do.

2 What field is she interested in working in?
   ENGINEERING

3 What do Laura and the careers adviser decide she should do?
   Find more about Engineering courses. Talking with some engineers about their work

5 Circle the correct answers.

1 Laura is considering studying *Engineering* / *Maths*.

2 Laura is interested in space flight, so her adviser suggests *Electrical* / *Mechanical* Engineering.

3 Laura feels a degree in Engineering would be very *academic* / *vocational*.

4 Laura prefers *academic study* / *manual work*.

5 Laura would rather *talk to someone* / *read information on websites*.

6 Laura says she would enjoy *the academic side of Engineering* / *designing and making things*.

Listening for advice and suggestions

In situations like a careers advice meeting, advice and suggestions are key points to listen out for. These are common phrases used to give strong advice and suggestions:

Strong Advice

You should (consider) ... / You ought to (consider) ... / I recommend ...

Suggestions

You might ... / You could ... / Have you thought about ... ? / Wouldn't you like/rather ... ? / I think ...

TAKING NOTES ON DETAIL

6 🔊 **2.1** Listen to the meeting again. Look at the notes that Laura took during the meeting with her careers adviser. Complete the notes with details that Laura missed.

1 Choose a career that will use _Maths_ and _Physics_ skills.
2 Consider _Mechanical_ Engineering.
3 Also consider Aerospace _n_ .
4 Find out more about Engineering _degrees_ .
5 Visit some _Universities_ and colleges and discuss Engineering _courses_ .
6 Attend the _Career_ fair.
7 Talk to _graduates_ at the fair about their _Jobs_ .
8 Contact a _Computer_ Engineering firm and arrange a _visit_ .

PRONUNCIATION FOR LISTENING

Certain and uncertain intonation

You can sometimes understand speakers' level of certainty by listening to their intonation. Intonation is the rise and fall of pitch in a person's voice. Rising intonation, with a questioning intonation, often indicates uncertainty. Falling intonation often indicates certainty.

🔊 **2.2** Listen to these examples from Listening 1.

The world will always need engineers! ↘ (certain)

Maybe you should consider Mechanical Engineering, then. ↗ (uncertain)

I'd like to study something technical, that's for sure. ↘ (certain)

Maybe I could do an internship at an Engineering firm. ↗ (uncertain)

7 🔊 2.3 Listen to the statements and questions. Does the speaker sound certain or uncertain? Write *C* (certain) or *U* (uncertain).

1 __U__ *consider, and you?*
2 __C__ *really want to be doctor*
3 __C__ *should consider*
4 __C__ *I'm considering studying*
   ~C Make quite definitely.
5 __C__ *I'll always be interested in*
6 __U__ *I think I can do that*
   I wouldn't mind need
7 __C__ *I wouldn't mind need*
8 __U__ *I might enjoy?*

8 Compare your answers with a partner. Do you agree? Why / Why not?

POST-LISTENING

9 Read the statements that Laura and the careers adviser made. Do the words and phrases in bold show they are certain or uncertain about what they are saying? Write the bold words or phrases in the correct column in the table.

1 It would **definitely** be a way to use your Maths and Physics skills.
2 I'd like to study something technical, that's **for sure**.
3 I **wonder** if I should try something more vocational.
4 Maybe you should **consider** Mechanical Engineering, then.
5 Okay, but I'm **not sure** if that would be for me.

certain	uncertain

10 Now change each sentence in Exercise 9 to make the opposite meaning.

1 It might be a way to use your Maths and Physics skills.
2 _____
3 _____
4 _____
5 _____

DISCUSSION

11 Work with a partner. Discuss the questions.

1 What advice do you think Laura should follow? Why do you think this is the best advice?
2 What advice also applies to the field of study or career that interests you?
3 What piece of advice would you add?

THE FUTURE CONTINUOUS

GRAMMAR

The future continuous is used to talk about an action that will be in progress at a specific time in the future.

We **will be taking** a holiday next summer.

Everyone **is going to be** taking time off next summer.

To form the future continuous, use *will* or *be going to* with *be* and the *–ing* form of the verb.

We **will be studying** for our final exams in the second week of December.

We **are going to be studying** for our final exams in the second week of December.

Will you **be studying** for your final exams in the second week of December?

Are you **going to be working** at Head Office next week?

In the negative, *will not be* can be contracted to *won't be*.

I definitely **won't be studying** Nursing.

You can add an adverb after *will* or *be going to* to show degrees of certainty. Common adverbs are *certainly, definitely, likely* and *probably*. In the affirmative, put the adverbs after *will* or *be*.

I **will definitely be studying** for my final exams in the second week of December.

Laura **is certainly going to be attending** the careers fair.

In the negative, put the adverbs before *won't*.

I **probably won't be having** much fun until after final exams are finished.

Sometimes the future continuous and *will* + infinitive have a very similar meaning, especially when the future event will happen at an indefinite time.

He **will choose** his career path later this year.

He **will be choosing** his career path later this year.

 PLUS

1 Complete the sentences with the future continuous form of the verb in brackets. Use *will* or *be going to* as noted.

1 I believe more women _____ Engineering in the coming years. (will / study)

2 In the future, almost everyone _____ mobile phones. Soon landlines will become a thing of the past! (be going to / use)

3 _____ you _____ the careers fair next week? (will / visit)

4 Zahra is studying Engineering. She _____ three more Engineering courses next term to prepare for her internship. (will / take)

5 You won't see me next week. I _____ some different college open days. (will / attend)

6 The careers adviser _____ you on Thursday to discuss a time to meet. (will / call)

7 _____ Martin _____ a university this year? (be going to / choose).

8 John is starting an internship at a local firm. He _____ from Monday to Friday (be going to / work).

2 Insert the adverb in the correct place in the sentences.

1 I won't be studying on Friday night. (certainly)

2 I will be studying next week because I have an exam. (definitely)

3 I won't be attending the match on Thursday afternoon because I haven't finished my research project yet. (probably)

4 I will be asking for help before Tuesday. I just don't understand this Maths assignment. (likely)

3 Work with a partner. Take turns asking and answering these questions. Give answers using the future continuous.

1 What are your plans after exams?

2 Where will you go on your next holiday from studying or work?

3 What do you see yourself doing in five years' time? In ten years' time?

STATING PREFERENCES WITH *WOULD*

GRAMMAR

Use *would rather* to express or ask questions about preferences.

I'd rather take a vocational course.

Would you **rather** start work right after graduation?

In the negative, use *would rather not* + verb.

I would rather not study far from home.

Use *would* (or *'d*) with verbs of preference, such as *like* and *prefer*.

I'd like to start working as soon as possible.

I'd prefer it if you studied a bit longer.

Would you **prefer** a short course to an academic degree?

Use *would rather* with the base form of a verb. Do not use *to*.

I would rather study Engineering.

Use *would like* and *would prefer* with an infinitive.

I would like/prefer to study Engineering.

You can use *would prefer* and *prefer* with a noun or an infinitive. You can also use a gerund (the *-ing* form of a verb) with *prefer*, but not *would prefer*.

Laura **would prefer an internship** at an Engineering company.

Laura **prefers to work / working** at an Engineering company.

Use *or* in questions about preference to offer a choice between two things. Use the base form of the verb after *or*.

Would you **like to study at a university or do a vocational course?**

4 Complete the sentences with the correct form of the verb.

1 Let's talk about your courses for next term. Would you rather *take / to take* Art History or Music Appreciation?

2 You need to consider where you want to work. Would you prefer *work / to work* at a big company or a small one?

3 She prefers *participate / participating* in team projects.

4 Would you like *stay / to stay* at home and study?

5 He prefers *work / working* with his hands.

6 Many parents would rather *see / to see* their children go to college than start work immediately after secondary school.

5 Rewrite each sentence using *would rather* or a verb of preference.

1 Do you prefer to work for a lot of money or for career satisfaction?

_____

2 I want to study a diploma course.

_____

3 Do they want to apply to a university in Riyadh?

_____

4 He wants to consider studying Medicine.

_____

5 Does she want to take a theoretical course?

_____

6 I don't want to start working right away.

_____

LISTENING 2

PREPARING TO LISTEN

1 Read the definitions. Complete the sentences with the words in bold.

> **complex** (adj) involving a lot of different but related parts
> **manual** (adj) involving the use of the hands
> **medical** (adj) relating to the treatment of disease and injury
> **physical** (adj) relating to the body
> **practical** (adj) relating to experience, real situations or actions rather than to ideas or imagination
> **professional** (adj) relating to a job that needs special education or training
> **secure** (adj) dependable; not likely to change
> **technical** (adj) relating to the knowledge, machines or methods used in science and industry

1 My adviser encouraged me to get a job in the ——————— profession, such as being a doctor or nurse.
2 My manager relies on me to have the ——————— knowledge to solve problems, while she is better at dealing with people.
3 My brother exercises every day; he jogs, lifts weights and swims. He is in good ——————— shape.
4 Some jobs, like assembling cars, require ——————— labour.
5 My parents want me to go to university so that I can have a ——————— job.
6 The robot was made from a ——————— combination of materials.
7 I want a ——————— job, so that I have a regular salary.
8 My decision to work instead of study was ——————— because I needed the money to pay my rent.

2 You are going to listen to a conversation between Adam, a student who is interested in a career in medicine, and a medical student. Before you listen, read Adam's notes and discuss the questions in pairs.

USING YOUR KNOWLEDGE

Medical Jobs

Emergency Medical Technician (EMT)
Works independently on an ambulance. Helps people in emergency situations, assessing a patient's condition and performing emergency medical procedures before they get to hospital. Must be self-confident. Requires excellent driving skills.

Accident and Emergency (A&E) Nurse
Works in the Accident and Emergency, or A&E, department of a hospital, dealing with patients as they arrive. Must have a high-level understanding of the human body and medicines and be able to assess patients quickly and correctly.

Which job do you think ...
- requires closer work with hospital staff?
- requires making decisions on your own?
- requires you to be sure of yourself and your abilities?
- requires more training?
- provides more excitement and adventure?
- requires more academic study?

Give reasons for your answers.

WHILE LISTENING

TAKING NOTES ON MAIN IDEAS

3 2.4 Listen to the conversation between Adam and the medical student. Write notes about the pros and cons for each job. Then compare your notes with a partner.

emergency medical technician (EMT)	A&E (Accident and Emergency) nurse

LISTENING FOR MAIN IDEAS

4 2.4 Listen to the conversation again. What is Adam's job preference? Summarize the reasons for his preference.

____

____

LISTENING FOR OPINION

5 Tick (✔) the speaker who expressed each opinion about the job. Then listen again and check your answers.

	medical student	Adam
1 That's a tough job. Exciting, but tough.	✔	
2 It seems like a great way to really help people.		
3 You have to be very independent and confident.		
4 It would involve a lot more complex study.		
5 It would be great to actually work after so much study.		
6 It may not be the ideal course for you.		
7 I imagine the pay would be better.		
8 That's a great idea.		

6 Work in pairs and discuss these questions. Do the speakers provide any support for or evidence of their opinions? If not, what evidence do you think they could give? Do you agree with them?

POST-LISTENING

SKILLS

Making inferences

When listening, you can *make inferences* (draw conclusions) from clues rather than get information directly from someone's words. These clues can include tone (the pitch, or the way a person's voice goes up or down when speaking), facial expressions and the emotion in someone's voice.

Consider these sentences: 'You're late' and 'You're here'. What clues would tell you if the speaker was angry, concerned, surprised or relieved?

7 Work with a partner. Discuss the questions below. Think about tone and emotion.

1 What does the medical student really think Adam should do? How do you know?
2 What are the most important factors in a job for Adam? How do you know?

MAKING INFERENCES

DISCUSSION

8 Work with a partner. Use your notes from Listening 1 and 2 to discuss the following questions.

1 Would you prefer to do a practical, vocational diploma, or a more academic university degree? Why?
2 How will you (or did you) make the decision about your education?
3 What kind of career do you think you would like to have? Who can help you reach this goal?

SYNTHESIZING

SPEAKING

CRITICAL THINKING

At the end of this unit, you are going to do the speaking task below.

> Decide as a group which candidate should receive the Mah Scholarship.

Prioritizing criteria

Making a choice from a number of options can be difficult. Sometimes understanding what is most and least important to you in a particular situation can help you make a better decision about what to do.

 **EVALUATE**

1 Look at the list of job criteria. Rank them from 1 to 10 in order of importance to you. (1 = most important, 10 = least important)

to make a lot of money _____
to feel challenged every day _____
to be friends with my colleagues _____
to work for a well-known company _____
to travel for work _____
to speak more than one language _____
to have job security _____
to have an easy commute _____
to manage other people _____
to be creative _____

2 Work with a partner. Compare your top three (1–3) and your bottom three (8–10) answers. Do you agree? Give reasons for the way you have prioritized the options.

Using priorities to evaluate options

Groups of people (project teams, managers or groups of students) often need to decide how to use money or other resources. This involves discussing priorities, ranking criteria and evaluating different options. You can give more 'weight' (or significance) to the criteria which you think are more important. This can be especially useful when it is difficult or not obvious how to make a decision.

3 Work with a partner. Read the text about the Mah Scholarship. Imagine you are committee members selecting applicants. Which criteria do you feel are the most important for receiving the Mah Scholarship? Rank them from 1 to 5 (1 = most important, 5 = least important). Discuss your reasons.

SCHOLARSHIPS

THE MAH SCHOLARSHIP
Information
Application forms
Application process
FAQs

JOBS

CONTACT US

The Mah Scholarship

The Mah Scholarship was started by Hong Kong billionaire Mah-Tak Hung, the successful businessperson behind the Mah Foundation. The Mah Scholarship pays the fees and expenses each year for one student, of any nationality, who wants to study in Hong Kong.

A committee of current students and academics evaluates the applications, interviews candidates and decides who will receive the scholarship.

Requirements:

- Applicants must be accepted to a course of study at a Hong Kong university.
- Applicants should show that their work after finishing the course will contribute to society.
- Applicants must apply in writing to the Mah Foundation.
- If chosen, applicants must participate in an interview by phone or video.

The final selection is made based on a student's grades and test scores, the quality of the written application and the student's financial need.

1 must be studying a course that contributes to society _____
2 must include a good written application _____
3 must have a good interview _____
4 must have good grades and test scores _____
5 must be in financial need _____

4 Compare your answers with another pair. Did you rank the criteria in the same way? Why / Why not? Change your ranking if the other pair convinces you that their ideas are better.

5 Work in a small group. Discuss the questions and note your ideas. You will use this information for the speaking task at the end of this unit.

> The Mah Foundation committee has chosen five finalists for the scholarship. The table below summarizes its assessment of each applicant.

1 Which proposed course of study in the table will make the greatest contribution to society? Which will make the smallest contribution? Why?

_____

_____

2 Rank each proposed course of study in the table from 1 to 10, according to level of contribution to society. (1 = the smallest contribution, 10 = the greatest contribution)

name	interview score	written application score	test average	financial need	proposed course of study
	Note: All scores are out of 10 possible points.				
Lee Jin-Sil	9	7	4	6	_____ Hotel Management
Adam Al Zamil	6	9	7	3	_____ Doctor
Yasmin Saleh	4	7	6	8	_____ Chinese
Tomomi Nonaka	6	5	9	4	_____ Mechanical Engineering
Thomas Nguyen	7	4	9	6	_____ Law

GIVING AN OPINION AND MAKING SUGGESTIONS

1 Match the sentence halves to make suggestions and give opinions. Which sentences make suggestions? Which give opinions?

1 I think the most important _____
2 I think _____
3 Why don't we _____
4 What if we say that _____
5 Have you considered _____
6 I feel it's important _____

a rank the proposed courses of study according to their contribution to society?
b to really focus on the applicants' potential contribution to society.
c looking at the applicants' family situation?
d the least important thing is the students' written application.
e factor is probably financial need.
f academic score is the most important factor?

PLUS

2 2.5 Listen and check your answers.

AGREEING AND DISAGREEING RESPECTFULLY

SKILLS

In a discussion where speakers have different opinions, it is important to use formal language to disagree respectfully with what someone has said. You can do this in several ways.

- Using modal verbs before making a point:
  Yes, I can see that. It **may** not be the ideal course for you.

- Apologizing before disagreeing with someone's point:
  Sorry, but I have to disagree. I think being a doctor is a very practical job!

- Saying you recognize someone's point and then adding a *but* ... clause:
  Yes, **but** it seems like a great way to really help people when they need it.

3 Read someone's responses to another speaker. Is the person agreeing or disagreeing? Write *A* (agree) or *D* (disagree). Which responses are formal and which are informal?

1 I can see what you're saying, but … _____
2 I couldn't agree more. _____
3 I think that's right. _____
4 I'm not sure I share that point of view. _____
5 No way. _____
6 Yes, but have you considered other factors? _____
7 I'm with you on that point. _____

4 Work in pairs. Take turns reading your statements below and responding. Use language from Exercise 3 and your own ideas.

Student A

1 Chinese will be the most important world language in the future.
2 Engineering is one of the best subjects you can study in college.
3 Lawyers are some of the most important people in society.

Student B

4 Everyone should be able to study at college for free.
5 It is more important to be able to speak English than to write it.
6 It is more important to do good work individually than to be able to work well as a group.

COMPROMISING AND FINALIZING A DECISION

5 Complete the sentences with the words from the box.

> agreement   decision   point   right   that   understandable

1 I see. That's _____ .
2 OK, I see your _____ .
3 You might be _____ about that.
4 I think we can all agree with _____ .
5 Yes. We've made a _____ .
6 I think we've come to an _____ .

6 🔊 2.6 Listen and check your answers.

PRONUNCIATION FOR SPEAKING

CERTAIN AND UNCERTAIN INTONATION

7 🔊 2.6 Listen again. Do the sentences from Exercise 5 use certain or uncertain intonation? Write *C* (certain) or *U* (uncertain).

1 _____
2 _____
3 _____
4 _____
5 _____
6 _____

8 Work in pairs. Take turns saying the sentences in Exercise 5 with either certain or uncertain intonation. Can your partner tell whether you're being certain or uncertain?

SPEAKING TASK

> Decide as a group which candidate should receive the Mah Scholarship.

PREPARE

1 Look back at the criteria, the table and your answers to Exercise 5 in Critical thinking. Add any new ideas or information to your notes.

2 Refer to the Task checklist below as you prepare for your discussion.

TASK CHECKLIST	✔
Give your opinion on criteria and priorities.	
Compromise with your group.	
Come to an agreement with your group.	
Respectfully disagree and make suggestions.	

DISCUSS

3 Get back into the group you worked with in Critical thinking. Rank the candidates from the table in Critical thinking, Exercise 5. Use the language in Preparation for speaking to help you.

4 Based on your discussion from Exercise 3 and your work in Critical thinking, decide who should receive the scholarship.

5 Choose one person from your group to present your choice for the scholarship to the class. Have him or her give reasons for the choice. Did everyone pick the same candidate? Who were the second- and third-place candidates?

OBJECTIVES REVIEW

1 Check your learning objectives for this unit. Write *3, 2* or *1* for each objective.

3 = very well   2 = well   1 = not so well

I can ...

watch and understand a video about a school where students work on real science. _____

listen for advice and suggestions. _____

make inferences. _____

prioritize criteria. _____

use priorities to evaluate options. _____

use the future continuous. _____

state preferences with *would*. _____

give an opinion and make suggestions. _____

agree and disagree respectfully. _____

compromise and finalize a decision. _____

decide as a group which candidate should receive a scholarship. _____

2 Use the *Unlock* Digital Workbook for more practice with this unit's learning objectives.

UNL☮CK
ONLINE

WORDLIST		
academic (adj) ⊙	mechanical (adj) ⊙	specialist (n) ⊙
acquire (v) ⊙	medical (adj) ⊙	technical (adj) ⊙
adviser (n)	physical (adj) ⊙	understanding (n) ⊙
complex (adj) ⊙	practical (adj) ⊙	vocational (adj)
internship (n)	professional (adj) ⊙	
manual (adj) ⊙	secure (adj) ⊙	

⊙ = high-frequency words in the Cambridge Academic Corpus

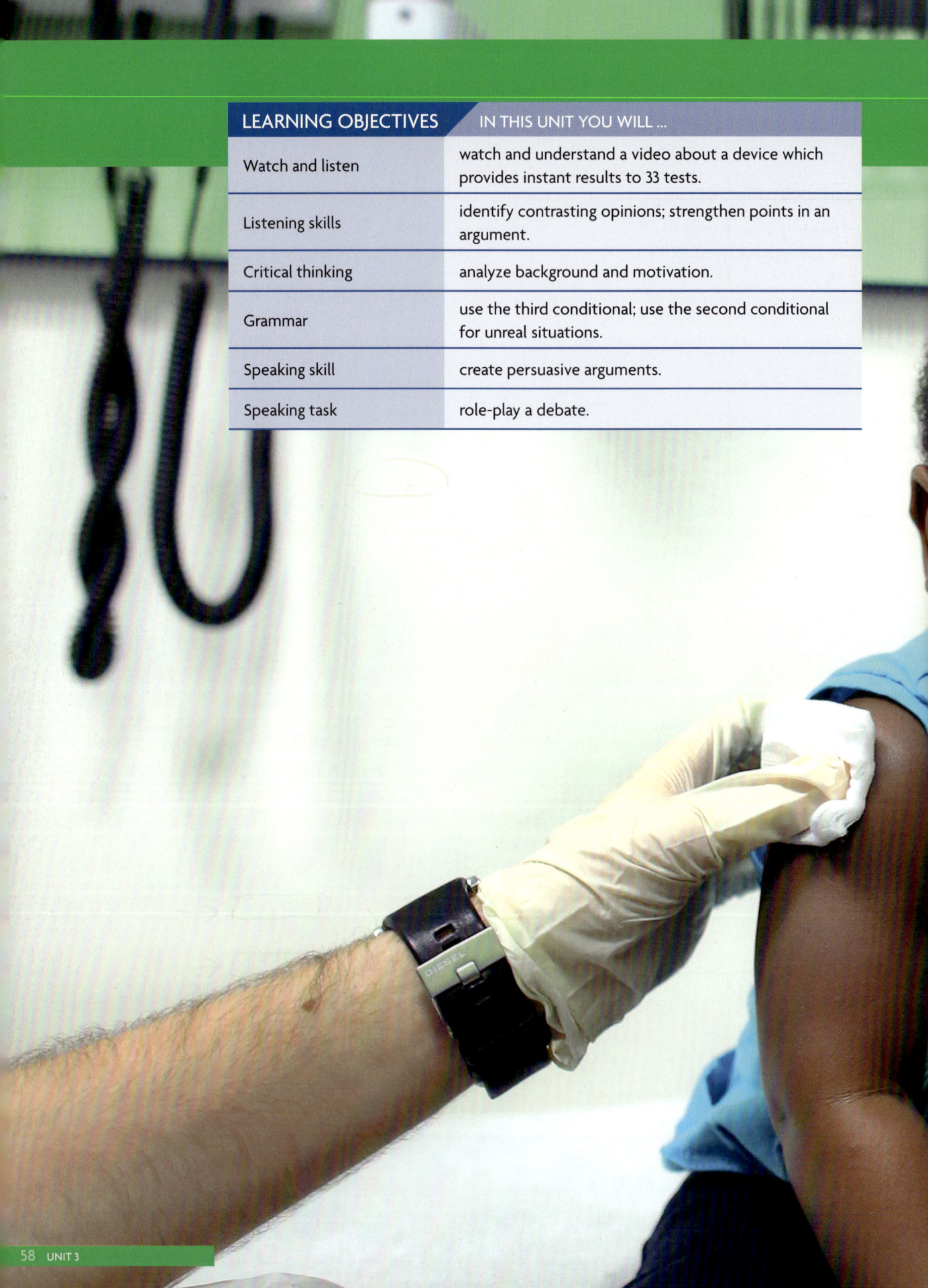

LEARNING OBJECTIVES	IN THIS UNIT YOU WILL ...
Watch and listen	watch and understand a video about a device which provides instant results to 33 tests.
Listening skills	identify contrasting opinions; strengthen points in an argument.
Critical thinking	analyze background and motivation.
Grammar	use the third conditional; use the second conditional for unreal situations.
Speaking skill	create persuasive arguments.
Speaking task	role-play a debate.

MEDICINE

UNL**O**CK YOUR KNOWLEDGE

Work with a partner. Discuss the questions below.

1 What are some common illnesses or medical problems? How are they treated?

2 How do illnesses usually spread from person to person?

3 The child in the photo is being given a vaccine to avoid getting a disease. Which diseases have vaccines? Which diseases do not?

4 Do you think vaccines are a good idea? Why / Why not?

PLUS

WATCH AND LISTEN

 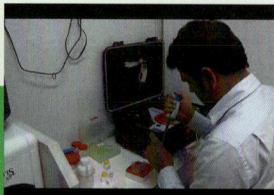  

PREPARING TO WATCH

ACTIVATING YOUR KNOWLEDGE

1 Work with a partner and answer the questions.

1 How long does it usually take to get results of a medical test, for example, of a blood test?

2 How and where are your medical records stored?

3 What do you think is the most important recent innovation in healthcare? Why do you think it is?

PREDICTING CONTENT USING VISUALS

2 Look at the pictures from the video. Which statements do you agree with?

1 Technology can improve healthcare for everyone.

2 In general, wealthy people receive better healthcare than poor people.

3 It's probably impossible to reach all the people who need medical care.

4 Access to a local clinic can be more important than advanced technology in a large hospital far away.

GLOSSARY

diagnostic tests (n) examinations to identify diseases or medical conditions

pre-natal screening (n) test to identify any problems with a pregnancy or the developing baby

the cloud (n) a computer network where files can be stored

underprivileged (adj) without the money, education or opportunities that the average person has

brainchild (n) an original idea or invention

the masses (n pl) ordinary people

trickle down (phr v) to flow gradually from a high place to a lower place in society, an organization or a school

GDP (abbr) Gross Domestic Product; the value of all goods and services produced in a country in a year

WHILE WATCHING

UNDERSTANDING MAIN IDEAS

3 ▶ Watch the video. Write *T* (true) or *F* (false) next to the statements below. Correct the false statements.

_____ 1 The Health Tablet provides test results very quickly.

_____ 2 The Health Tablet can store patient records.

_____ 3 The clinic provides healthcare for equal numbers of rich and poor people.

_____ 4 There are thousands of similar clinics, all over India.

_____ 5 Dr Kahol believes that innovations should benefit poor people first.

_____ 6 India invests heavily in its healthcare system.

UNDERSTANDING DETAIL

4 ▶ Watch again. Complete the notes.

1 The Health Tablet is _____
to poor people's lives in India. It can give people
_____ 33 tests along with
_____ .

2 Dr Kanov Kahol wants to improve healthcare for the poor. He says most healthcare innovations are _____ .
In contrast, he wants to develop them for the poor first because these devices will have to _____ .

3 For many people in India, good healthcare is not available. India only spends under _____ .
Every year, many people are forced into poverty because of
_____ .

MAKING INFERENCES

5 Work with a partner. Discuss the questions. Give reasons for your answers.

1 What do you think is the most valuable feature of the Health Tablet?

2 Why do you think India spends under 1.5% of its GDP on healthcare?

3 Dr Kahol says it makes sense to design innovations for the masses because they will "have to work in conditions and environments that are not necessarily very friendly". Explain what you think he means.

4 What other affordable healthcare technology might make a difference for the poor?

DISCUSSION

6 Work with a partner and answer the questions.

1 Do you use any technology to maintain or improve your health and fitness? Describe it.

2 Do you think that technology can close the gap between rich and poor in healthcare? How? If not, why wouldn't this work?

3 Are there some healthcare or medical problems that cannot be solved by technological innovation? What are they?

LISTENING

PREPARING TO LISTEN

1 You are going to listen to a seminar about pandemics. Before you listen, read the sentences and write the words in bold next to the definitions.

1 Doctors and nurses must be careful when treating patients. Sometimes they can **contract** the same diseases as the patients they are treating.

2 Cost is an important **factor** in deciding whether to pay for a vaccine.

3 In winter, it is common for people to become **infected** with viruses like the flu or a cold.

4 Doctors state that most colds **occur** after someone touches a surface that has the cold virus on it.

5 The Ebola **outbreak** was unexpected and spread very quickly to thousands of people. Now there is a vaccine in development.

6 **Prevention** of the flu focuses on washing your hands often and getting a flu vaccination every year.

7 It takes a long time to **recover** from surgery. My aunt was tired and felt some pain for several weeks before she felt normal again.

8 Juan is receiving **treatment** for his back pain. He says it is helping because his back does not hurt as much as before.

a _____ (v) to happen

b _____ (v) to become completely well again after an illness or injury

c _____ (v) to catch, or become ill with, a disease

d _____ (adj) having a disease as a result of organisms such as bacteria or viruses entering the body

e _____ (n) the act of stopping something from happening

f _____ (n) a sudden appearance of something, especially of a disease or something else dangerous or unpleasant

g _____ (n) something that you do to try to cure an illness or injury, especially something suggested by a doctor

h _____ (n) a fact or situation that influences the result of something

2 Read the text and look at the map. Then answer the questions below.

A pandemic is when a contagious disease spreads through the human population in a large region. This could be across multiple countries, or even the whole world. Throughout history there have been a number of pandemics, such as flu and cholera. A disease must be infectious (passed directly from person to person) for it to be considered a pandemic.

Risk of influenza pandemics across the globe

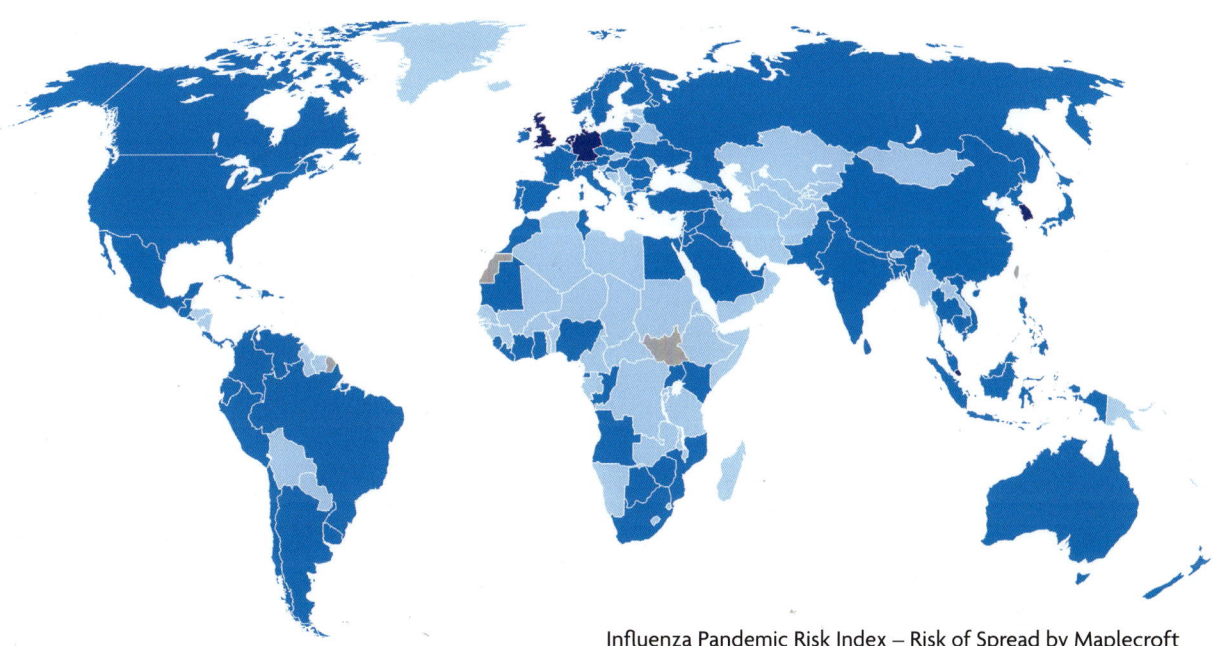

Influenza Pandemic Risk Index – Risk of Spread by Maplecroft

1 What are the factors in the spread of a disease? How can it be prevented from spreading?

2 What would make a country at high risk for a pandemic? Think about:
- size of population
- number of international airports
- density of population
- borders with other countries
- size of cities
- number of hospitals

3 Look at the map. Which colour do you think represents countries at high risk for pandemics? Which colour represents countries at low risk? What is the risk level in your country?

WHILE LISTENING

3 🔊 3.1 Listen to the seminar and check your answers to Exercise 2.

4 🔊 3.1 Listen to the seminar again. Take notes as you listen and focus on these questions. What might cause a pandemic? What factors make a country at high risk for a pandemic?

5 Compare your notes with a partner and write down any missing information.

SKILLS

Identifying contrasting opinions

In a discussion, a group considers and explores different ideas. Key phrases such as *In my opinion, ...* and *As far as I'm concerned, ...* indicate opinions and can help you separate facts from what somebody thinks. Most phrases are used at the beginning of a sentence to let the listener know that it is the speaker's opinion.

As far as I'm concerned, all parents should vaccinate their children.

Other phrases used at the beginning of a sentence include:

| I think ... | As I see it, ... | To me, ... |
| I believe ... | It seems to me that ... | From my perspective, ... |

6 🔊 3.1 Listen again and complete the student's notes with the different opinions. Then compare your answers with a partner.

idea for stopping the spread of disease	opinion 1	opinion 2
Governments must make sure populations are in good health and have good living conditions.	There's a limit to what governments can do in times of economic difficulty.	Governments don't always have the power to say exactly how everyone should live.
Everyone should be forced to have vaccines.	(1) A vaccine that worked well last year _____ .	(2) A lot of people don't want to have a vaccine that _____ .
People with diseases shouldn't be allowed into the country.	(3) People spread diseases _____ .	(4) It would be impossible to _____ .
All flights from countries with a pandemic should be stopped.	(5) It would _____ .	(6) It could _____ .

PRONUNCIATION FOR LISTENING

Intonation in tag questions

A tag question is a small question that is attached to the end of a statement. Tag questions can be used either to ask for agreement or to ask a 'real' question (for things, help or more information). It is the intonation which tells you what the speaker wants. When speakers use tag questions with rising intonation, usually they are uncertain their statement is true. When speakers use tag questions with falling intonation, usually they expect the listener to agree with them. Listening for these differences in intonation can help you understand a speaker's meaning.

Well, people who have the flu should stay at home from school or from work, shouldn't they? ↗ (expressing uncertainty)

Well, people who have the flu should stay at home from school or from work, shouldn't they? ↘ (expecting agreement)

7 🔊 **3.2** Listen to the sentences. Is the speaker expressing uncertainty or requesting agreement? Write *U* (uncertainty) or *A* (agreement).

1 __U__   3 _____   5 _____   7 _____
2 __A__   4 _____   6 _____   8 _____

LISTENING FOR ATTITUDE

POST-LISTENING

8 🔊 **3.3** Listen to the tag questions from the listening. What does the speaker mean? Choose the best answer.

1 **a** People should have to get vaccines.
  b People should not have to get vaccines.
2 **a** We should stop all flights from countries that are affected.
  b We should not stop all flights from countries that are affected.
3 **a** It would have a terrible effect on the economy.
  b It would not have a terrible effect on the economy.

DISCUSSION

9 Work with a partner. Discuss the questions.

1 Do you think your country is prepared to deal with a pandemic? Why / Why not? Look at the list of factors on page 63 to help you.
2 What could you do in a pandemic to protect yourself from contracting a disease?
3 How do you think people act when there is a pandemic? How do you think you would act?

HEALTH SCIENCE VOCABULARY

1 Read the sentences (1–8). Choose the word or phrase (a–b) that is closest in meaning to the bold word.

1 Doctors from the organization Doctors Without Borders provide **aid** where it is really needed. For example, many of the doctors work in poor countries.
   a help
   b equipment

2 Maha has a bad infection, so her doctor gave her an **antibiotic**.
   a a medicine that kills bacteria
   b a vaccine that prevents disease

3 Most doctors agree that having a vaccine is the best **prevention**.
   a way to stop a disease from infecting people
   b way to get better if you have a disease

4 This type of flu is very strong; it takes weeks for people to **recover**.
   a get better
   b get worse

5 Some doctors have a personal touch; they prefer to **treat** the person, not just the disease.
   a give food to
   b give medical care to

6 The new drug went through several **trials** to check its results before it became available for use by doctors.
   a operations
   b tests for effectiveness

7 The pandemic is growing quickly, and the government says the situation is **urgent** because many people could catch the disease.
   a not requiring immediate attention
   b requiring immediate attention

8 The researcher is studying a **virus** that is carried by mosquitoes.
   a an organism that causes disease
   b harm or damage to a body part

PLUS

CONDITIONALS

The third conditional

You can use the third conditional when you imagine a different past where something else happened, and there was another result. It describes something that was possible, but did not happen.

The *if*-clause expresses the past unreal condition (the situation that was untrue in the past). The main clause describes an imagined result. Use the past perfect in the *if*-clause. Use *would have* in the main clause to express a predicted result.

if-clause	*predicted result*

If she had gone to school that day, she **would have caught** the flu.

Use *could have* or *might have* in the main clause to express something possible or doable.

if-clause	*possible result*

If you had gone on your trip, you **might have caught** the virus.

The *if*-clause usually comes before the main clause, but it may also follow the main clause. Remember to use a comma after the *if*-clause when it comes first in the sentence.

possible result	*if-clause*

The government **could have prevented** a pandemic **if it had acted** in time.

You can use the third conditional to express regrets or sadness.
If I had had a flu jab in October, **I wouldn't have caught** the flu this winter. (But I didn't, and I regret it.)

---

2 Complete the interview with a scientist who studies the flu. Use the third conditional with the verbs in brackets.

Reporter: Today I'm talking to Dr Kayoko Niikura, an expert on pandemics. Dr Niikura, we're all fascinated by the Spanish flu of 1918 1919, I think, because no other pandemic has claimed as many lives – that's at least 40 million people worldwide. What happened?

Dr Niikura: Well, one problem was that the real cause of the flu was unclear, so there was no flu vaccine at the time. If scientists (1)_____ (develop) a flu vaccine back then, the pandemic (2)_____ (might / not / happen).

Reporter: So, 40 million people (3)_____ (might / survive) if scientists (4)_____ (find) the real cause of the flu?

PLUS

Dr Niikura: That's right. In fact, many experts believed that the flu was caused by bacteria, not a virus. So, they focused on developing vaccines for other illnesses caused by bacteria. If they (5)_____ (not / focus) on other illnesses, they (6)_____ (could / discover) more effective ways to prevent the flu. And if more scientists (7)_____ (question) the idea that bacteria was the cause, they (8)_____ (would / realize) the flu was caused by a virus much sooner.

Reporter: Why was it called the 'Spanish' flu?

Dr Niikura: Well, many countries wouldn't let newspapers report about illnesses and death at the time. But Spain did, so there were a lot more reports there. When King Alfonso XIII got sick, the entire world knew about it. That's why everyone thought the virus was from Spain. If other countries (9)_____ (allow) newspapers to report on it, people (10)_____ (would / not / call) it Spanish flu.

Review of the second conditional – unreal situations

Use the second conditional to describe present or future situations that are not true or are imagined. Use the past simple in the *if*-clause. Use the modals *could*, *might* or *would* in the main clause.

If people **stopped** having vaccines, there **would be** pandemics.
If people **got** vaccinated, they **could avoid** many illnesses.

Notice that in more formal English, speakers use *were* for the verb *be* with all subjects.
If I **were** president, I **would require** everyone to get vaccinated.
If the vaccine **were** available everywhere, fewer outbreaks **would occur**.

PLUS

3 Complete the sentences about the flu with your own ideas. Use the second conditional. If you are writing a main clause, use the modals in brackets.

1 The flu virus changes every year. If it stayed the same, <u>people wouldn't become ill every year</u> . (wouldn't)

2 The medicine isn't approved yet. _____ _____ , I would be able to take it and feel better.

3 There is a warning about a virus outbreak, so people are afraid to travel overseas right now. _____ , they wouldn't be afraid to go on holiday.

4 The virus is not in this country yet, so we don't need a vaccine. If there were an outbreak, _____ . (might)

5 Ada doesn't have health insurance, so she is worried about becoming ill. If she had health insurance, _____ . (would)

PREPARING TO LISTEN

1 Read the definitions. Complete the sentences with the correct form of the words in bold.

> **clinical** (adj) related to medical treatment and tests
> **controlled** (adj) limited
> **data** (n) information or facts about something
> **in favour of** (adj) on the side of or in support of
> **precaution** (n) an action that is taken to stop something bad from happening
> **prove** (v) to show to be true
> **researcher** (n) a person who studies a subject in detail to discover new information about it
> **trial** (n) a test to find out how effective or safe something is

1 Before a new vaccine can be released, experts must _____ that it is safe for public use.
2 First, scientists set up tests in a _____ environment that is appropriate for medical tests. This is often in a laboratory or a hospital with advanced medical tools.
3 Then the _____ start to conduct tests on the vaccine.
4 A lot of _____ are taken to make sure the tests are as safe as possible.
5 Some people are _____ making donations to help fund vaccine studies.
6 The tests need to be conducted in _____ conditions, without variations, so that the results are consistent.
7 The researchers then analyze the _____ collected during the tests.
8 Finally, _____ are conducted with volunteers to test the vaccine before it is released for public use.

2 You are going to listen to a debate about the flu vaccine on a radio programme. Before you listen, work with a partner and choose the answers that you think are correct.

1 Experts *agree / don't agree* about whether flu vaccines are necessary.
2 Experts *believe / have proved* that the flu vaccine saves lives.
3 Experts *have / haven't* shown that the flu vaccine is unsafe.
4 *Some / Almost all* of the public choose to get a flu vaccine.

WHILE LISTENING

3 🔊 3.4 Listen to the introduction and check your answers to Exercise 2.

4 🔊 3.5 Listen to a debate on a radio programme. Create a T-chart with one column for Dr Sandra Smith and one column for Mark Li. Take notes on each speaker's opinions about the flu vaccine. Use the questions to guide your notes.

- Is the flu vaccine a good idea?
- Do vaccines need to be tested each year?
- Is the flu vaccine helpful or harmful?
- Should people have the flu vaccine? If yes, who?

5 Compare your notes with a partner.

6 🔊 3.5 Write *T* (true) or *F* (false) next to the statements. Then correct the false statements. Listen to the debate again to check your answers.

_____ 1 Millions of people get severely ill from the flu every year.

_____

_____ 2 The majority of the population receives the flu vaccine.

_____

_____ 3 Dr Smith has had the flu vaccine.

_____

_____ 4 Mr Li is against all forms of vaccination.

_____

_____ 5 There is scientific evidence that the flu vaccine might not work.

_____

_____ 6 There is scientific evidence that the flu vaccine makes people ill.

_____

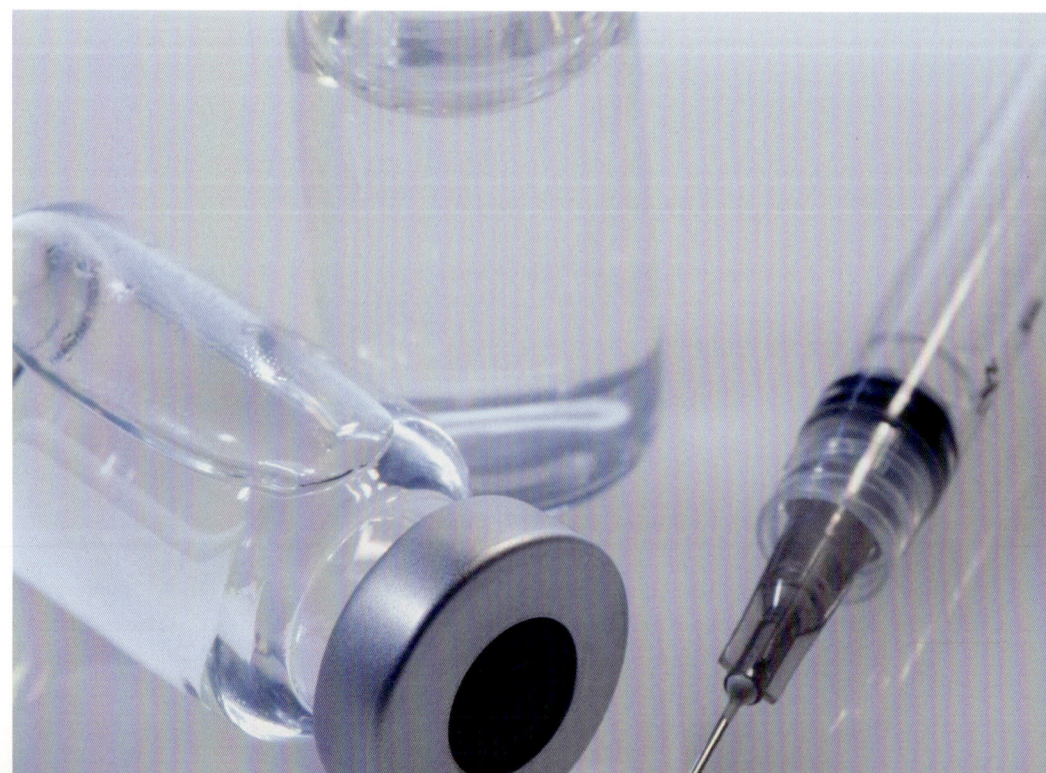

TAKING NOTES ON MAIN IDEAS

LISTENING FOR DETAIL

POST-LISTENING

Strengthening points in an argument

When speakers want to agree or disagree with someone and show that they are right in an argument, they can strengthen or support their point through various techniques, such as:

- offering additional information Let me **tell you more** about …
- returning to an earlier reference The study **which I mentioned before** was conclusive.
- repeating the other person's point and saying it is correct **You are right that** this vaccine is …
- giving a personal example **I have had this treatment myself**.
- using logic … **it doesn't mean** that all people vaccinated will become ill.

7 Match each speaker's point (1–5) to the technique (a–e) used to strengthen it.

1 All of my colleagues have had the vaccine. None of us have caught the flu. _____

2 Dr Smith is absolutely right that many vaccines work very well and that millions of lives have been saved by vaccination. _____

3 I'd definitely like to challenge the idea that there's no scientific basis for our work. I disagree with Mr Li on that point. Let me tell you more about my work in that area. _____

4 If people are vaccinated and then they happen to become ill, that doesn't logically mean the vaccine caused the illness. _____

5 Well, I'm sure Dr Smith is a very good doctor, but I think the flu vaccine package I mentioned earlier is clear. _____

a offering additional information
b returning to an earlier reference
c repeating the other person's point and saying it is correct
d giving a personal example
e using logic

DISCUSSION

8 Work with a partner. Use information from Listening 1 and Listening 2 to discuss the following questions.

1 Are vaccines routinely given in your country? Why / Why not?
2 When are they given? Who receives them?
3 Based on the debate, has your opinion changed about having the flu vaccine? Why / Why not?
4 Are you for or against vaccines in general? Why / Why not?

SPEAKING

CRITICAL THINKING

At the end of this unit, you are going to do the speaking task below.

> Role-play a debate between representatives from an international aid organization and representatives from a drug company. Discuss whether or not healthcare should be free for everyone.

SKILLS

Analyzing background and motivation

You can understand more about a speaker's point of view if you know about the person's background, personal and professional motivations and role in society. This information can also help you prepare your own arguments.

 ANALYZE

1 Work with a partner. Read the information about Dr Sandra Smith and Mark Li, who debated vaccination in Listening 2, and discuss the questions.

Dr Sandra Smith is a medical doctor who researches the flu virus at a national university. Some of her research has been paid for by drug companies that manufacture flu vaccines.

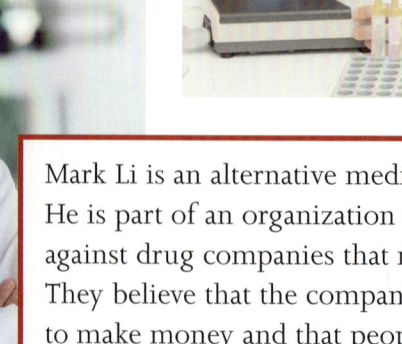

Mark Li is an alternative medicine practitioner. He is part of an organization that campaigns against drug companies that make flu vaccines. They believe that the companies create the vaccines to make money and that people don't need them.

1. How much do you think the differences in background and motivation between Dr Smith and Mark Li affect their work? In what ways?
2. Whose views are closer to your own?
3. Who do you think makes more money? Do you think that how much money someone has can influence what they think?
4. Think back to Listening 1 and Listening 2. Should governments require citizens to have vaccines? If yes, for what diseases? When should they be given? If vaccines are not required, how should governments protect their citizens?

2. Compare your answers with another pair. Did you have the same ideas? Why / Why not?

3. Read the statements. Who do you think said each one?
Write M (Mark Li) or S (Sandra Smith).

   1. People who eat the right foods don't need doctors or medicine. _____
   2. Modern medicine is one of the greatest achievements of science. _____
   3. One day, we'll have a vaccine for the common cold. _____
   4. Illness is the body's way of telling you to change your lifestyle. _____
   5. Drug companies make too much money from flu vaccines. _____
   6. Not giving a patient medicine would be against everything I believe. _____

4. Compare your answers with a different partner. Do you agree?

5. Work with a partner. Discuss what Mark Li and Sandra Smith might think of the topics below. Would they have the same opinions on any of the topics? Support your answer.

   1. alternative medicine
   2. treating diseases with food rather than medicine
   3. drug companies advertising their products on television
   4. doing exercise to promote health
   5. giving a child medicine to reduce a fever or other symptoms of illness
   6. free healthcare for everyone

APPLY

6 Work in groups:

Group A: You work for an international aid organization that sends doctors to help people in developing countries. You believe that healthcare should be free for everyone.

Group B: You work for a large pharmaceutical company. You believe that healthcare should not be free for everyone.

In your groups, discuss your background, motivation and opinions for your side of the issue. Write notes in the table below. Use the following ideas to help you:

- availability of medical care in urban and rural areas
- different types of diseases in certain regions
- the fact that drug companies are businesses and have to make a profit
- issues of fairness for drug companies, individuals and countries

7 Discuss what you think the other group's background, motivation and opinions might be. Write notes in the table below.

	group A	group B
background		
motivation		
opinions		

CREATING PERSUASIVE ARGUMENTS

When you want to make listeners understand and agree with your point of view, you use persuasive language. This calls attention to your main opinions and invites listeners to think about and agree with your point of view. It also makes it more difficult for speakers to disagree with you. Persuasive language can take many forms: giving personal examples, asking challenging questions, presenting support for a position and addressing the opposing argument. You can also use persuasive words or phrases, such as *How would you feel if*, or strong adverbs or adjectives (*obviously, a lot of*).

Giving personal examples

I've had patients who were healthy, then had the flu vaccine and became ill.

In my experience, patients often become ill after having the flu vaccine.

Asking challenging questions

Let me ask you this: has the flu vaccine been properly tested?

Presenting support for a position

The packaging on this flu vaccine clearly states that '**No controlled trials have been performed that demonstrate that this vaccine causes a reduction in influenza**'. It's here in black and white.

Addressing the opposing argument

Let me start by saying that I'm not against all vaccines. **Dr Smith is absolutely right that many vaccines work very well and that millions of lives have been saved by vaccination.**

SKILLS

1 Match the headings (1–5) to the examples (a–e) in the table.

1 give a personal example _____
2 ask challenging questions _____
3 use specific persuasive words and phrases _____
4 give information to support your position _____
5 address the other person's argument _____

a	Have there been proper clinical trials to prove that it works, that it stops infection?
b	However, the flu can cause severe illness or worse for a small percentage of the people who get it. It may not sound like a lot, but actually this is hundreds of thousands of people around the world each year. There isn't one single scientific study that proves that this year's flu vaccine works.
c	So while Mr Li is right – we don't do clinical trials of the flu vaccine in the way that we do trials for other medicines – that doesn't mean we aren't scientific in our methods.
d	All of my colleagues have had the vaccine. None of us have caught the flu. Let me tell you more about my work in that area.
e	*Obviously*, we want to do everything in our power to stop the infection from spreading. *Supposing* you gave your children the vaccine and it made them worse rather than better? *How would you feel* if someone in your family did not have the vaccine and then became really ill? *It's obvious* that the vaccine hasn't been properly tested.

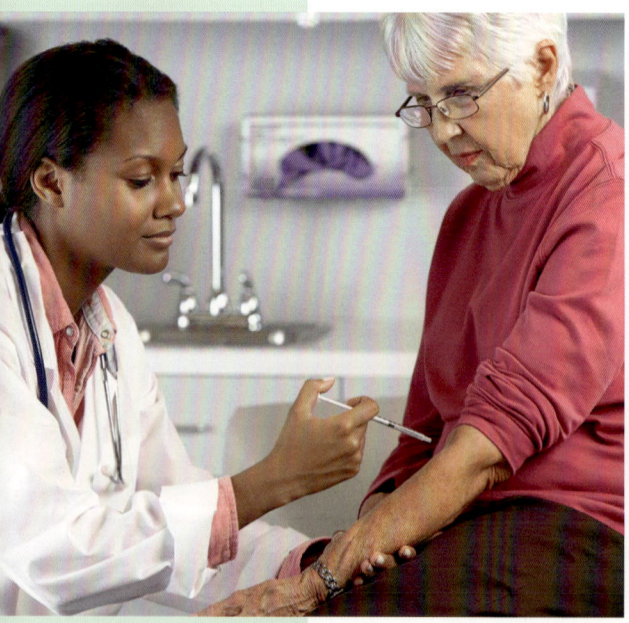

2 Work with a partner. Rewrite the facts as persuasive statements. Use the strategy in brackets to help you.

1 Some big pharmaceutical companies spend more money on advertising than on research and development. (support for a position)

_____

_____

2 The cost of developing a new vaccine is £153 million – £280 million. (use persuasive words and phrases)

_____

_____

3 It takes years of study to become a doctor, which is why they are among the highest-paid professional workers. (give a personal example)

_____

_____

4 The top five global drug companies are wealthier than many of the world's nations. (ask challenging questions)

_____

_____

5 Malaria is an easily preventable disease, but people still contract it because they can't pay for a vaccine. (address the opposing argument)

_____

_____

6 Only a small number of people in developing countries are able to afford basic, life-saving treatments for common illnesses. (use persuasive words and phrases)

_____

_____

3 Read your statements to another pair. Are their statements persuasive? Why / Why not? If not, work together to rewrite the statements and make them more persuasive.

PLUS

SPEAKING TASK

Role-play a debate between representatives from an international aid organization and representatives from a drug company. Discuss whether or not healthcare should be free for everyone.

PREPARE

1 Separate into your two groups. Look back at your notes on each group's background, motivation and opinions in Critical thinking. Add any new information.

2 Prepare an opening statement for the debate to introduce your viewpoint. Review the language in Preparation for speaking to express your opinions. Practise your opening statement in your group. Make sure each person makes at least one comment.

3 Think about the other group's views and make notes about how they might respond to your opening statement. Make notes of persuasive language that you might use to counter their arguments. Remember to:

- give personal examples and opinions (if possible)
- ask challenging questions
- give information to support your viewpoint

4 Prepare for the debate.

- Be ready to make notes on what the other group says, as you will need to respond to their views in your counter-argument.
- Use your ideas from Exercise 3 to help you.
- Use the following format for the debate:

Group A: Announce the topic: *Healthcare should be free for everyone.*
Group A: Opening statement in favour
Group B: Opening statement against
Group A: Counter-argument in favour
Group B: Counter-argument against

5 Refer to the Task checklist below as you prepare for your debate.

TASK CHECKLIST	✔
State and support your position in the debate clearly.	
Ask challenging questions.	
Give personal examples.	
Address the other group's argument.	
Use persuasive arguments.	

DISCUSS

6 Have the debate with another group.

7 Answer these questions.

1 What did you like about the way arguments were presented?
2 What could be improved?
3 Which argument do you think was the most persuasive? Why?

OBJECTIVES REVIEW

1 Check your learning objectives for this unit. Write *3*, *2* or *1* for each objective.

3 = very well   2 = well   1 = not so well

I can ...

watch and understand a video about a device which provides instant results to 33 tests.   _____

identify contrasting opinions.   _____

strengthen points in an argument.   _____

analyze background and motivation.   _____

use the third conditional.   _____

use the second conditional for unreal situations.   _____

create persuasive arguments.   _____

role-play a debate.   _____

2 Use the *Unlock* Digital Workbook for more practice with this unit's learning objectives.

UNLOCK
ONLINE

WORDLIST

aid (n)	in favour of (adj)	recover (v)
antibiotic (n)	infected (adj)	researcher (n)
clinical (adj)	occur (v)	treat (v)
contract (v)	outbreak (n)	treatment (n)
controlled (adj)	precaution (n)	trial (n)
data (n)	prevention (n)	urgent (adj)
factor (n)	prove (v)	virus (n)

= high-frequency words in the Cambridge Academic Corpus

LEARNING OBJECTIVES

IN THIS UNIT YOU WILL ...

Watch and listen	watch and understand a video about cloning endangered species.
Listening skills	distinguish main ideas from details; take notes on main ideas and details.
Critical thinking	organize information in a presentation.
Grammar	use multi-word prepositions; use the past perfect.
Speaking skills	give background information and explain a problem; use signposting language in a presentation.
Speaking task	give a problem and solution presentation.

THE ENVIRONMENT

UNL**O**CK YOUR KNOWLEDGE

Work with a partner. Discuss the questions.

1 What is deforestation?

2 What are its causes and effects?

3 Other than deforestation, what things do people do that affect the environment?

4 How can people use natural resources without harming the environment?

PLUS

WATCH AND LISTEN

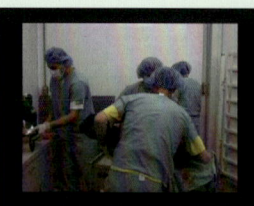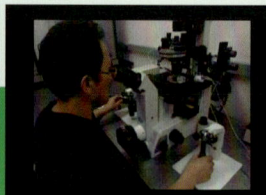

PREPARING TO WATCH

ACTIVATING YOUR KNOWLEDGE

1 Work with a partner. Discuss the questions.

1 Can you think of any animals that have disappeared or are endangered?
2 What role do humans play in making an animal extinct or endangered?
3 What can people do to prevent more animals from becoming extinct?

PREDICTING CONTENT USING VISUALS

2 Look at the pictures from the video. Discuss the questions with your partner.

1 What type of animal do you see in the first picture?
2 What do you think the doctors and scientists are doing?
3 What animal do you think is behind the TV reporter? What do you know about it?

GLOSSARY

clone (v) to produce a cell or organism that has the same chemical patterns in its cells as the original from which it was artificially produced

skin cell (n) the smallest unit of an animal which makes up the skin

genetic (adj) relating to the biological process by which the characteristics of living things are passed from generation to generation

euthanize (v) to kill an animal because it is very old or sick

astonishing (adj) very surprising

counterpart (n) a person or thing that has the same role or purpose as another person or thing in a different organization or place

WHILE WATCHING

3 ▶ Watch the video. Which sentence best summarizes the main idea?

UNDERSTANDING
MAIN IDEAS

 a Bantengs, which are endangered, have been cloned by using the cells of an animal that died 23 years earlier.

 b We now have the technology to clone endangered species, but many people are concerned that we aren't dealing with the real problem.

 c While certain animals cannot be cloned at this time, it is possible that we may be able to clone them in the future.

4 ▶ Watch again. Answer the questions.

UNDERSTANDING
DETAIL

 1 Why do scientists believe that they are closer to protecting endangered species?

 _____

 2 How were scientists able to clone the banteng?

 _____

 3 What worries some conservationists about cloning?

 _____

5 Work with a partner. Discuss the questions.

MAKING INFERENCES

 1 Based on the information in the video, how successful is cloning? Explain your answer.

 2 Do you think cloned animals are able to thrive in the wild? Why / Why not?

 3 What are the dangers of cloning?

 4 How might cloning affect the environment?

DISCUSSION

6 Work in a small group. Discuss the questions.

 1 Are there any endangered species in your country or region? Which ones?

 2 What are people currently doing to help save these animals?

 3 In your opinion, is cloning a good method to save endangered species? Why / Why not?

 4 In addition to trying to protect endangered species, what other ways are people in your community helping the environment?

LISTENING

PREPARING TO LISTEN

UNDERSTANDING KEY VOCABULARY

1 You are going to listen to a lecture about habitat destruction. Before you listen, read the words and definitions. Then complete the sentences with the correct form of the words in bold.

> **adapt** (v) to adjust to different conditions
> **coastal** (adj) on or related to land by the sea or ocean
> **conservation** (n) the act of being careful not to waste water, energy, etc.
> **exploit** (v) to use something in a way that helps you (or unfairly for an advantage)
> **habitat** (n) the natural surroundings where a plant or animal lives
> **impact** (n) the strong effect something has on a situation or person
> **modify** (v) to change something, usually to improve it or make it more acceptable
> **waste** (n) unwanted substances or material

1 The _____ of water is important, to make sure all people have enough clean drinking water.

2 One of the natural _____ of the brown bear is the mountains of the United States.

3 Recycling programmes are important, because less _____ goes to landfill.

4 Many tourists like to visit _____ regions because they like to be near the ocean.

5 Some animals have learned to _____ to a new environment as temperatures continue to rise.

6 Humans cannot continue to _____ Earth's natural resources, like coal or oil; sooner or later they will run out.

7 A simple act of turning off the lights can make a big _____ when trying to save energy.

8 We can _____ our behaviour to prevent further climate change.

Distinguishing main ideas from details

Speakers often support their main ideas with details. Details give you more information and help to illustrate the main ideas. To determine if a speaker's words are main ideas or details, ask yourself: is this an important point, or does it support an important point? Distinguishing main ideas from details helps you to understand the organization of the speaker's ideas.

2 Match the details (a-j) to the main ideas in the table.

Details

a In Australia, Europe, Japan and North America, foxes live in urban areas, even big cities such as London.

b Part of this environmental change is due to natural, rather than human, causes.

c It destroyed around 800 square kilometres of farmland and a huge area of forest.

d One other animal that is as at home in the city as in the countryside is the raccoon.

e In 1991, a volcano in the Philippines erupted and killed many people and animals.

f In Africa and Asia, monkeys live in cities alongside people and exploit the human environment by stealing food or eating things that humans have thrown away.

g Today this is around 10%, as the Earth has been warming since that time.

h In Singapore, the 1,500 wild monkeys that live in and around the city have become a tourist attraction.

i Just 10,000 years ago, about half of the planet was covered in ice.

j It also caused severe floods when rivers were blocked with volcanic ash.

Planet Earth is dynamic and always changing.	Habitat destruction hasn't been bad news for all animals.

WHILE LISTENING

3 🔊 4.1 Listen to the lecture and check your answers.

LISTENING FOR MAIN IDEAS

SKILLS

Taking notes on main ideas and details

One way to take notes is to list main ideas on one half of the paper and details that support them on the other side of the paper. You do not need to write complete sentences. You should listen for key words and important information.

4 🔊 **4.1** Listen to the lecture again and complete the notes with details you hear.

Earth is always changing	10,000 years ago, about half of Earth covered in ice; now only (1)_____ is covered in ice. Changes are in part due to (2)_____ rather than human causes.
Natural forces can destroy the environment	1991 – volcano in the Philippines erupted and killed many people and animals; destroyed (3)_____ of farmland and a huge area of forest Caused severe floods when (4)_____ by volcanic ash
Humans are also responsible for habitat destruction	Originally more than (5)_____ square kilometres of rainforest worldwide; (6)_____ today Deforestation: approximately 160,000 square metres per year In Europe, only about 15% of land not modified by humans Some places have habitat broken into parts, e.g. separated by roads – called (7)_____ – can cause serious problems
Humans have affected the land, animals and sea	Pollution from coastal cities has damaged the ocean; destroyed habitat of (8)_____
Animals are feeling at home in the city and in the countryside	Monkeys live alongside humans in (9)_____ In (10)_____, foxes in urban areas Leopards in (11)_____ Number of city raccoons increased Have different (12)_____ depending on their environment; common foods include (13)_____; raccoons in cities eat (14)_____
Not everyone feels that ecotourism is helping the environment	Tourists travel long distances by aeroplane, create (15)_____ Resorts use local (16)_____ such as water and produce (17)_____ that creates pollution in the local environment

5 Use your notes from Exercise 4 to complete the text.

The Earth always changes. (1)_____ years ago, half of it was covered in ice. Humans have changed the Earth; originally there were more than 16 million square kilometres of (2)_____ , today there are less than (3)_____ million. Each year, about (4)_____ square metres are destroyed. Foxes and raccoons exploit the city environment by eating (5)_____ . Critics of ecotourism say air travel and waste from hotels cause (6)_____ .

POST-LISTENING

6 Read each extract (1–3) from the lecture. Choose the statement (a–c) that best matches the lecturer's opinion.

1 'Part of this environmental change is due to natural, rather than human, causes.'
   a Natural causes result in some environmental change.
   b Natural causes result in most environmental change.
   c Human causes result in most environmental change.
2 'Habitat destruction hasn't been bad news for all animals.'
   a The destruction of animal habitats is always a bad thing.
   b The destruction of animal habitats is not necessarily negative.
   c The destruction of animal habitats is inevitable.
3 'We tend to think of human activity as always having a negative impact on the environment.'
   a It's common to think that humans only negatively affect the environment.
   b It's wrong to think that humans only negatively affect the environment.
   c It's correct to think that humans only negatively affect the environment.

PRONUNCIATION FOR LISTENING

Pauses in prepared speech

Prepared speech, such as in lectures and presentations, often has different intonation to natural speech. In a prepared speech, the speaker often pauses at clause boundaries, which are usually where punctuation marks are placed.

7 🔊 4.2 Listen to an extract from the lecture. Notice where the speaker pauses (/ /) when speaking.

> In some places / /, habitats haven't been destroyed / /, but they have been broken into parts / /, for example / / separated by roads / /. This is called fragmentation / /. If animals are used to moving around throughout the year / / and a road is built through the middle of their habitat / /, fragmentation can cause serious problems.

8 🔊 4.3 Listen and mark the pauses in the extract from the lecture.

> One other animal that is as at home in the city as in the countryside is the raccoon. In fact, raccoons are so at home in the city that the number of city raccoons has increased. Raccoons have different diets depending on their environment. Common foods include fruit, plants, nuts and rodents. Much like the foxes of London, raccoons living in the city are known to eat rubbish out of bins, steal food from people's homes and occasionally bite people.

9 Practise saying the paragraphs with a partner.

DISCUSSION

10 Work with a partner. Discuss the questions.

1 How have people changed habitats in the country you live in?
2 Think of an environment you know. Which animals live there naturally? Do any animals live there that are originally from somewhere else?

MULTI-WORD PREPOSITIONS

GRAMMAR

> *Multi-word prepositions* are two- or three-word phrases that function like one-word prepositions (*of, on, by*). Multi-word prepositions include:
>
> - two-word phrases (*apart from, according to*)
> - three-word phrases (*by means of, as well as*)
>
> Like one-word prepositions, multi-word prepositions are followed by nouns, noun phrases and gerunds. They show the relationship between two things. For example, *in front of* shows location.

PLUS

1 Match the multi-word prepositions (1–5) to the functions (a–e).

1 according to, based on
2 owing to, due to
3 apart from, except for
4 together with, as well as
5 rather than, instead of

a making an exception
b giving a source
c giving another choice
d including
e giving a reason

2 Choose the correct multi-word preposition to complete each sentence.

1 *Based on / Apart from* research that I carried out in Ethiopia, I can conclude that the destruction of deserts can be reversed.
2 Visitors rarely go to the research station, *according to / due to* its extremely remote location.
3 *According to / Rather than* the latest *Economist Magazine*, share prices fell sharply last month.
4 The engineers decided to use solar power *owing to / instead of* conventional batteries.
5 The doctors used strong medication *as well as / except for* lots of liquid to help cure the patients.
6 The phone is assembled almost entirely by machines, *instead of / except for* the outer case.

3 Write your own sentences based on the information in brackets. Use a multi-word preposition.

1 (giving a source – news website)
   <u>According to the news website I read this morning, ...</u>

2 (giving a reason – wild animals moving into cities)
   _____

3 (giving another choice – between two reactions to climate change)
   _____

4 (including – two animals which have adapted to living in cities)
   _____

5 (making an exception – not recycling certain items)
   _____

THE PAST PERFECT

The *past perfect* is used to describe a completed event or time period that happened before another event in the past. Use the past simple to describe the later event or time period.

Police officers spotted a young leopard in the streets of Mumbai. The leopard **had moved** into the city from the nearby forest.

(First, the leopard moved into the city from the forest; then the police spotted it.)

Form the past perfect with *had* + the past participle of the main verb. Form the negative by adding *not* after *had*. The form is the same for all subjects.

cover → had covered / had not covered (hadn't covered)

You can use the prepositions *before, by* and *until* to introduce the later time period.

Until these natural resources were discovered, of course, changes to desert habitats **had not** really **affected** people very much.

People often use the past perfect to give reasons or background information for later events.

Before people started settling in the Arctic, much of the land **had been untouched.**

4 🔊 **4.4** Listen to an excerpt from a student's essay on Rachel Carson. Complete the text with the past simple or past perfect verbs you hear.

Before she (1)_____ her influential book *Silent Spring* in 1962, Rachel Carson (2)_____ years working for the US government at environmental agencies like the US Bureau of Fisheries and the US Fish and Wildlife Service. During her time there, she (3)_____ her own personal research and writing. By 1955, Carson (4)_____ already _____ several books on environmental research when she (5)_____ to do research full-time. One subject that she was particularly interested in was the effects of pesticides[1] on the environment and on human health. During World War II, the government (6)_____ the pesticide DDT to protect people against diseases caused by pests. After the war, farmers (7)_____ large amounts of DDT into the air to protect their crops. Carson (8)_____ that the chemical was making people ill with cancer and was causing animals to die, so she (9)_____ to do scientific research on the subject and publish it as a book, to warn people about the risks. After Carson (10)_____ *Silent Spring*, the pesticide industry (11)_____ her for her research. However, the US government (12)_____ by banning the use of DDT in the United States. Soon her book was translated into several languages and was published around the world.

[1]**pesticides** (n) chemicals used to kill pests like insects and small animals

Rachel Carson

5 Complete the sentences with the past perfect or the past simple form of the verbs in brackets.

1 Before people _____ (settle) in the northernmost parts of the Arctic, the area _____ (be) mostly empty.

2 Before the city _____ (begin) developing the area for new residential buildings, people _____ (use) it as a park.

3 We _____ (not/notice) foxes coming into this neighbourhood until we _____ (see) news reports about them on TV.

4 By the time the volcano _____ (erupt), the government _____ (evacuate) everyone from the area.

PLUS

VERBS TO DESCRIBE ENVIRONMENTAL CHANGE

6 Read the definitions. Complete the sentences with the correct form of the words in bold.

> **adapt** (v) to adjust to different conditions
> **affect** (v) to have an influence on something
> **decline** (v) to gradually become less, worse or lower
> **exploit** (v) to use something in a way that helps you (or unfairly for an advantage)
> **extract** (v) to remove or take out something
> **impact** (v) to have an influence on something
> **occur** (v) to happen
> **survive** (v) to continue to live or exist

1 Foxes have _____ to living in cities, and now they are doing well there.
2 Extinct species could have _____ if people had taken more care to protect them.
3 The number of wild birds in Europe has _____ sharply over the last 30 years.
4 Resources have been _____ from endangered habitats without destroying them.
5 Humans have _____ the environment quite negatively by destroying forests and using dangerous chemicals.
6 Changes to the environment can negatively _____ animals.
7 Many environmental changes have _____ because of people's actions.
8 Urban foxes have _____ their new habitat by finding food in people's rubbish bins.

PREPARING TO LISTEN

1 Work with a partner. Discuss the questions.

USING YOUR
KNOWLEDGE

1 What is a desert?
2 Are there any desert areas in your country? If so, where are they?
3 What kinds of plants, animals or products do you find in the desert?

2 You are going to listen to a talk about desert habitats. Before you listen, read the sentences and write the words in bold next to the definitions.

UNDERSTANDING
KEY VOCABULARY

1 Antarctica usually has a **harsh** winter with extremely cold temperatures.
2 Alaska is the last great **wilderness**. There is still so much land that has not been used or built on, and is kept in its natural state.
3 Researchers collected **minerals** to find out more about what is in the soil.
4 **Diamond** is the hardest naturally occurring substance on Earth.
5 The electrical company installed **copper** wires in the new building.
6 Many countries use **natural gas** found below the Earth's surface to heat their homes.
7 The government has banned coal **mining** in certain areas where it could be extremely dangerous to the environment.

a _____ (n) the industry or activity of removing valuable substances from the earth
b _____ (n) fuel for heating or cooking that is found underground
c _____ (n) valuable or useful chemical substances that are formed naturally in the ground
d _____ (n) a transparent, extremely hard precious stone that is used in jewellery, and in industry for cutting hard things
e _____ (adj) severe and unpleasant
f _____ (n) a place that is in a completely natural state without houses, industry, roads, etc.
g _____ (n) a reddish-brown metal, used in electrical equipment and for making wires and coins

PLUS

WHILE LISTENING

3 🔊 **4.5** Listen to the talk. Complete the notes on the main ideas.

Topic: (1)_____
Humans have learned to (2)_____ the resources of
the desert
The desert is an (3)_____ that supports a variety of plant
and animal life
If desert is destroyed:
    More (4)_____ will be in the air.
    Plants will (5)_____; as (6)_____ will be saltier,
    we'll lose a valuable food source.
Solutions: (7)_____ desert resources carefully instead of
abusing them; apply (8)_____ solutions

4 🔊 **4.5** Listen again. Number the details in the order you hear them.

a Bringing water into the desert to grow plants can make desert soil too salty. _____
b Computer technology can forecast how climate change will affect deserts. _____
c The Earth's deserts cover 33.7 million square kilometres. _____
d Scientists are using solar energy to produce water in deserts. _____
e The Topnaar people have an understanding of the natural world. _____
f Deserts provide many of the world's minerals and metals. _____
g There are over 2,200 desert plant species in Saudi Arabia. _____
h Desert surface temperatures in summer can reach 80°C. _____

5 🔊 **4.5** Answer the questions with a partner. Then listen again to check your answers.

1 What percentage of the Earth's surface is desert? _____
2 In which part of Africa do the Bedouins live? _____
3 What metals are found in the desert? _____
4 What conditions are needed for acacia trees to grow?
_____
5 What is one of the best-known desert animals in the Arabian Peninsula?
_____
6 What kind of energy are scientists in Saudi Arabia using to produce fresh water? _____

POST-LISTENING

LISTENING FOR TEXT ORGANIZATION

6 Match the parts of a presentation (1–3) to the sentences from the talk (a–c).

1 giving background information _____
2 explaining a problem _____
3 offering a solution _____

a The problem is that human activity is affecting modern deserts all over the world. According to the United Nations, traditional ways of life are changing as human activities such as cattle ranching, farming and large-scale tourism grow.

b The United Nations reports in *Global Deserts Outlook* that the Earth's deserts cover about 33.7 million square kilometres, or 25% of the Earth's surface.

c The UN gives the example of using the latest computer technology to help forecast how climate change will affect deserts, and using that information to prepare for these changes.

7 Read the three details. Which part of the talk do they come from? Write *background information, explain a problem* or *offer a solution*.

a Tribes such as the Topnaar, in southwest Africa, are known for their ability to survive in the desert due to their use of local plants and animals for food, medicine and clothing. _____

b According to a blog called *A Smarter Planet*, scientists in Saudi Arabia are already using solar energy to produce fresh water in the desert.

_____

c Data from the United Nations shows that every year nearly 2% of healthy desert disappears. _____

DISCUSSION

SYNTHESIZING

8 Work with a partner. Use your notes from Listening 1 and Listening 2 to discuss the following questions.

1 What natural habitats exist in your country?
2 What human activities take place in those habitats?
3 Do you use any products or foods that come from those habitats? Do you think this might cause any damage to those habitats?

SPEAKING

CRITICAL THINKING

At the end of this unit, you are going to do the speaking task below.

▶ Give a presentation about a change in the environment and discuss possible solutions.

SKILLS

Organizing information in a presentation

Understanding the organization of information in a presentation can help you understand the development of the speaker's ideas. An outline is a general plan of the features you will include in a presentation. Outlines are useful ways to show the connection between main points, specific examples and details.

 REMEMBER

1 Look back at your notes from Listening 2. Complete the outline for Listening 2 with the phrases from the box. Then compare with a partner.

> Human survival   Desert environment and wildlife   People in cities
> Desert plants   People in deserts   Desert animals
> Use wind and solar energy   Plant and animal survival

Topic: Decline and destruction of deserts
Introduction (background information): _____
I. Main idea: _____
   A. Detail: _____
      a. Example: Topnaar
      b. Example: Bedouins
   B. Detail: _____
II. Main idea: _____
   A. Detail: _____
      a. Example: Acacia tree
   B. Detail: _____
      a. Example: Arabian oryx
Solutions: Manage desert resources carefully instead of abusing them; apply technological solutions; _____ to provide clean energy in existing desert cities

2 Look at the outline again and write *T* (true) or *F* (false) next to the statements.

The outline ...

_____ 1 shows clear connections between the presentation topic, main ideas, examples and supporting details.

_____ 2 shows the order of the parts in the presentation.

_____ 3 tells the speaker exactly what to say in the presentation.

_____ 4 includes irrelevant details that do not belong in the talk.

3 Create an outline for a talk on one of the topics below. Choose a topic, do some research online and prepare an outline. Use the outline from Exercise 1 as a model. Be sure to include two or three main ideas with details and examples in your outline. You will use this outline for the speaking task at the end of this unit.

CREATE

The increase in 'superstorms' (extreme hurricanes) around the world

Ice melting in the Arctic

The destruction of the Amazon rainforest

4 Think of some possible solutions to the problem you chose in Exercise 3. Write notes about them in your outline.

5 Share your work with a partner. Provide feedback to each other.

PREPARATION FOR SPEAKING

GIVING BACKGROUND INFORMATION AND EXPLAINING A PROBLEM

Background information is often necessary to put a problem in context. In other words, you need to say *why* it is a problem. One way of structuring this background information is to give main ideas, examples of those ideas and details to clarify the examples:

Let's begin by looking at some background information from the United Nations Environment Programme. The United Nations reports in Global Deserts Outlook that ...

Humans have learned to exploit the resources of the desert for survival and profit by adapting their behaviour, culture and technology to its harsh environment. To give you an example, tribes such as the Topnaar ...

1 Match the sentences (1–6) with their functions (a–f).

1 According to the Food and Agriculture Organization of the United Nations, millions of people around the world survive by eating fish. _____

2 Data shows that the amount of manufactured chemicals in the oceans is increasing. Eighty percent of ocean pollution comes from human activity on land. _____

3 If we continue to pollute the world's oceans, marine plants and animals will not survive. _____

4 Oceans are essential for life on Earth. People rely on them for survival. _____

5 All of us who rely on the oceans for food will then have to find different food sources. _____

6 Human activity is destroying oceans all over the world. The two main problems are pollution and overfishing. _____

a introduces the background information
b gives a specific detail that illustrates the background information
c says what the main problem is
d gives details that explain the problem
e explains the consequences of the problem
f says how the problem might affect the audience personally

SIGNPOSTING LANGUAGE IN A PRESENTATION

Speakers *signpost* by using transitional words and phrases in lectures and presentations. This helps them guide the listener through what they are saying now, and what they will say next. You can use signposting throughout your talk to help the audience understand the talk's structure, such as when you are giving an example, starting a new topic or making a conclusion. Here are examples of signposting language:

- to give an example: *For example, To illustrate*
- to start a new topic: *Next, Now I'm going to talk about*
- to make a conclusion: *In conclusion, To sum up*

2 Look at the signposting language below. Match the phrases in bold (1–8) to the purpose they serve in the presentation (a–h).

1 But **what does this mean** for the rest of the world? _____
2 **To put it another way**, we will all be affected. _____
3 **Moving on now to** the typical desert environment, _____
4 **A good example of this** is Egyptian cotton. _____
5 **That's all I have to say** on that point. _____
6 **Let's begin by** looking at some background information from the United Nations Environment Programme. _____
7 **To summarize**, deserts are not only important to the people who live in them. _____
8 **The topic of my talk** is the decline and destruction of the world's deserts. _____

a introducing the topic
b giving an overview
c finishing a section
d starting a new section

e querying and analyzing
f giving examples
g paraphrasing and clarifying
h summarizing and concluding

3 Match the phrases below to the purpose that they serve in the presentation in Exercise 2 (a–h).

1 That concludes this part of the talk … _____
2 To give you an example … _____
3 Let's turn now to … _____
4 I'd like to recap … _____
5 Today I'm going to talk about … _____
6 Let's consider this in more detail … _____
7 So what I'm saying is … _____
8 I have three main points to make … _____

PLUS

SPEAKING TASK

▎ Give a presentation about a change in the environment and discuss possible solutions.

PREPARE

1 Look back at the outline for the research you did in Critical thinking. Add any new information you would like to include.

2 Prepare a short introduction. Make notes based on your research from Critical thinking. Think about what kind of background information to include in your introduction in order for the audience to understand the problems in your presentation. Use language from Preparation for speaking to help you.

3 Look back at your proposed solutions in your outline. What kind of information could you include in your conclusion? Use signposting language from Preparation for speaking to help you.

4 Refer to the Task checklist below as you prepare your presentation.

TASK CHECKLIST	✔
Use signposting language to help guide the audience.	
Give background information.	
Explain the problem and possible solutions.	
Stress words for emphasis.	

PRESENT

5 Form a group and take turns giving your presentations. Take notes as you listen to your classmates' presentations. Ask questions at the end of each presentation.

6 Were the other students' presentations similar to your own? Why / Why not?

OBJECTIVES REVIEW

1 Check your learning objectives for this unit. Write *3*, *2* or *1* for each objective.

3 = very well   2 = well   1 = not so well

I can ...

watch and understand a video about cloning endangered species.   _____

distinguish main ideas from details.   _____

take notes on main ideas and details.   _____

organize information in a presentation.   _____

use multi-word prepositions.   _____

use the past perfect.   _____

give background information and explain a problem.   _____

use signposting language in a presentation.   _____

give a problem and solution presentation.   _____

2 Use the *Unlock* Digital Workbook for more practice with this unit's learning objectives.

UNLOCK ONLINE

WORDLIST		
adapt (v) ⊙	exploit (v) ⊙	mining (n) ⊙
affect (v) ⊙	extract (v) ⊙	modify (v) ⊙
coastal (adj) ⊙	habitat (n) ⊙	natural gas (n)
conservation (n) ⊙	harsh (adj) ⊙	occur (v) ⊙
copper (n) ⊙	impact (n) ⊙	survive (v) ⊙
decline (v) ⊙	impact (v) ⊙	waste (n) ⊙
diamond (n)	mineral (n) ⊙	wilderness (n)

⊙ = high-frequency words in the Cambridge Academic Corpus

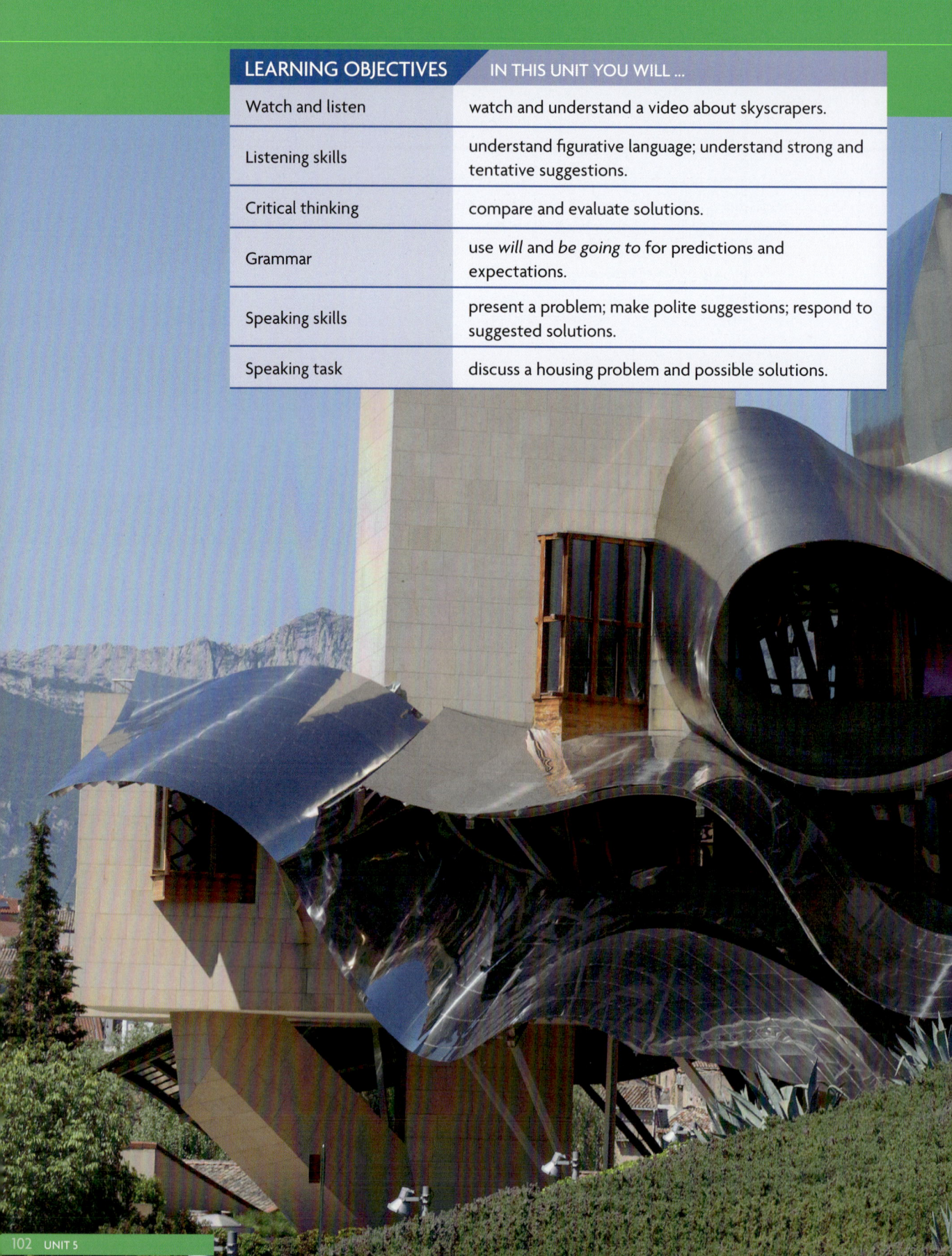

LEARNING OBJECTIVES	IN THIS UNIT YOU WILL ...
Watch and listen	watch and understand a video about skyscrapers.
Listening skills	understand figurative language; understand strong and tentative suggestions.
Critical thinking	compare and evaluate solutions.
Grammar	use *will* and *be going to* for predictions and expectations.
Speaking skills	present a problem; make polite suggestions; respond to suggested solutions.
Speaking task	discuss a housing problem and possible solutions.

UNLOCK YOUR KNOWLEDGE

Work with a partner. Discuss the questions.

1 Where do you think this building is?

2 Who do you think might use the building? What is it used for?

3 What do you think the advantages of the building are? The disadvantages?

PLUS

WATCH AND LISTEN

PREPARING TO WATCH

ACTIVATING YOUR KNOWLEDGE

1 Look at the example in the table. Think of three more famous buildings or structures and use them to complete the table. Then compare your answers with a partner.

building / structure	location	features
The Eiffel Tower	Paris, France	tall, beautiful, romantic

PREDICTING CONTENT USING VISUALS

2 Look at the pictures from the video. Discuss the questions with your partner.

1 Compare and contrast the buildings in the first photo and in the second photo.
2 How have buildings changed since the first skyscrapers were built?
3 Which view do you prefer, the view in the third photo or the view in the fourth photo? Why?

GLOSSARY

stately (adj) formal in style and appearance

consumer (n) a person who buys goods or services for their own use

market (n) the business of buying or selling a particular product or service

skyline (n) the shape of objects against the sky, especially buildings in a city

bar chart (n) a graph in which different amounts are represented by vertical or horizontal rectangles that have the same width but different heights or lengths

WHILE WATCHING

3 ▶ Watch the video. Write *T* (true) or *F* (false) next to the statements below. Correct the false statements.

_____ 1 Skyscrapers originated in New York City.

_____

_____ 2 Louis Sullivan is credited with creating the skyscraper.

_____

_____ 3 The first skyscraper was completed in 1898.

_____

_____ 4 The skyscraper is considered a symbol of American consumerism in the world economy.

_____

_____ 5 Skyscrapers have changed the appearance of cities around the world.

_____

4 ▶ Watch again. Complete the notes.

Architects began to experiment with new buildings after:
(1)_____

Where Louis Sullivan lived and worked: (2)_____

Where Auditorium Building is located: (3)_____

In 1920, 100 million consumers were served by: (4)_____

_____

Tall buildings represent: (5)_____

5 Work with a partner and discuss the questions.

1 How have other disasters influenced building and building styles?
2 What other factors affect a building's design?
3 What do you think inspires great architects like Louis Sullivan?

DISCUSSION

6 Discuss the questions with your partner.

1 Are there skyscrapers near where you live? How are they similar to or different from the skyscrapers in the video?
2 What materials are often used in skyscrapers?
3 Is there a famous building that represents the culture of your country? What does it symbolize to you?

LISTENING 1

PREPARING TO LISTEN

UNDERSTANDING KEY VOCABULARY

1 You are going to listen to a conversation between two property developers. Before you listen, read the sentences and write the correct form of the words in bold next to the definitions.

1 Selina prefers houses from the eighteenth century, but I prefer **contemporary** houses that have a lot of windows and glass.
2 A lot of **potential** buyers came to look at the building today. They seemed really interested in the building and the neighbourhood it is in.
3 Euan said he could **transform** the old house into something that looks like new with just a few small renovations.
4 Sandra **obtained** ownership of the building after paying the previous owner £1.5 million.
5 The building has some beautiful architectural **features**, such as tall columns and very old statues on the roof.
6 The construction did not start well. A part of the new wall **collapsed** and had to be rebuilt.
7 I **anticipate** that the houses will rise in value in the next ten years.

a _____ (v) to completely change the appearance, form or character of something
b _____ (v) to fall down suddenly
c _____ (adj) happening now; modern
d _____ (n) a noticeable or important characteristic or part
e _____ (v) to expect that something will happen
f _____ (adj) possible when the necessary conditions exist
g _____ (v) to get something, especially by a planned effort

USING YOUR KNOWLEDGE

2 Work with a partner. Discuss the questions.

1 Do you prefer older or more contemporary buildings? Explain your reasons.
2 Describe a building that you like. Why do you like it?

WHILE LISTENING

3 🔊 **5.1** Listen to the conversation. What two problems are discussed?

1 _____

2 _____

LISTENING FOR MAIN IDEAS

4 🔊 **5.1** Listen again. Complete the notes on the proposed solutions to the problems. Then compare answers with a partner.

TAKING NOTES ON DETAIL

Solutions

1 Nearby _____ and renovation will _____ the area

2 Knock down the original building

3 _____ the building; it has lots of _____

4 Transform _____ with a _____ building

5 Design new building with _____ features

6 Add _____ landmark made of _____ and _____

7 Include _____ and red _____ from old _____ as part of new _____

8 Put _____ on the ground floor and _____ or _____ above

5 Use your notes from Exercise 4 to correct the statements.

1	At the beginning of the conversation, both developers think a building development in Westside is a good idea.
2	There isn't any development going on in Westside.
3	There has been a lot of investment in the area in the past 20 years.
4	The developers think the best idea is to knock down the warehouse.
5	The developers need to choose between a contemporary building style and a traditional one.
6	The building can't offer floor space for any shops.
7	Shops would have to be on the second floor.
8	Renovation would mean removing all the original features of the building.

POST-LISTENING

Understanding figurative language

Figurative language refers to using words or expressions in a different way from their usual, literal meaning. For example, speakers may use comparisons or exaggerations instead of simple facts to make their point more interesting or dramatic. *The room was as cold as ice* is an example of figurative language and means that the room was very cold, although probably not literally freezing.

6 Match the figurative phrases in bold (1–4) to their meanings (a–d).

1 I'm afraid we might be **biting off more than we can chew**. _____
2 I think it's **a potential goldmine**. _____
3 That building is more **like a prison** than a potential shopping centre. _____
4 We could give the old building **a new lease of life**. _____

a a fresh beginning
b trying to do a bigger job than we can realistically do
c a building that no one wants to visit
d an opportunity to make a lot of money

7 Which figurative phrases from Exercise 6 support knocking the old building down? Which support converting and modernizing it? Why?

Supports knocking the building down:

_____

_____

Supports converting and modernizing it:

_____

_____

8 Work with a partner. Use the figurative language from Exercise 6 to complete these sentences. Use your own ideas.

1 I bit off more than I could chew when I _____

_____

_____ .

2 _____ is a potential goldmine.
3 _____ seems like a prison.
4 I got a new lease of life when I _____

_____

_____ .

9 Share your sentences with a partner. Ask follow-up questions.

PRONUNCIATION FOR LISTENING

Emphasis in contrasting opinions

When you state an opinion that is different from somebody else's, you can emphasize your opinion by stressing the words or information that is different from theirs.

A: I think the original building has <u>a lot of</u> potential.

B: I think we really want to <u>transform</u> the area with something <u>modern</u>.

10 🔊 5.2 Listen to the short conversations. Underline the words or phrases that Speaker B stresses.

1 A: It has some beautiful original features.
   B: It looks as though it's about to collapse!

2 A: Acquiring such an old building could be a huge mistake.
   B: Really? I think the project is going to be a great success.

3 A: It would be more of a transformation if we built a modern building made of materials like steel and glass.
   B: Couldn't we do both? We'll maintain more of a connection to the past if we include the old building as part of the new one.

11 Work with a partner. Practise saying the sentences in Exercise 10 with the underlined words stressed. What is the difference in meaning if you do not stress these words?

DISCUSSION

12 Work with a partner. Discuss the questions.

1 Do you think it is a good idea to add modern features to historical buildings? Why / Why not?

2 Think of an old building that you are familiar with. Do you think it is better to knock it down, restore it to how it was originally or add new features to it? Why?

FUTURE FORMS

GRAMMAR

Will and *be going to* for predictions and expectations

You can use *will* and *be going to* to express predictions or expectations.

This part of the city **will** look better after the old buildings are modernized.

A lot of people **are going to** move into the luxury flats that are being built in the city centre.

You can use adverbs to show different degrees of certainty in predictions. Use *certainly, definitely, possibly* and *probably* after *will* or *be* in *be going to*. Use adverbs before *won't*. Use them before or after *be* in *be not going to*.

I'**ll definitely** consider buying a house.

I **certainly won't** consider living in a city.

A lot of people **are probably going to** be interested in the new shops after they open.

We'**re probably not going to** buy a house. / We **probably aren't going to** buy a house.

Use *maybe* and *perhaps* at the beginning of sentences.

Perhaps I'**ll** study Architecture, so I can work to restore old buildings to their former glory.

Maybe I'**ll** do an Architecture course to learn more about building materials.

Use *be going to* for predictions when there is present evidence.

The building is old and has cracks in the bricks. It'**s going to** collapse during the next earthquake.

There is no money in the budget to build a fountain. We'**re not** / We **aren't going to** build it.

PLUS

1 Complete the sentences by inserting the adverbs.

1 The building I want to move into was bought by a developer. It's going to be renovated before I move there. (definitely)

2 The construction team isn't going to begin work until next month. (probably)

3 The supporting walls are already up. The developers will complete the building soon. (probably)

4 The developer is drawing up his plans now. He will send me the plans for the flats on Friday. (maybe)

5 I will help you with your Architecture assignment now. (certainly)

6 Farah is off work on Friday. She will help you study for the Architecture test. (perhaps)

2 Answer the questions about the future so that they are true for you. Use *will* or *be going to* and adverbs to show certainty.

1 What kind of building will you live in five years from now?

_____

2 Do you think you will buy any property? Why / Why not?

_____

3 Do you think your classroom building will be around much longer? Why / Why not?

_____

4 How do you think the buildings in this town or city will be different ten years from now?

_____

5 How do you think your home will look ten years from now?

_____

ACADEMIC VOCABULARY FOR ARCHITECTURE AND TRANSFORMATION

3 Read the paragraph and write the verbs in bold next to the correct definitions.

ARCHITECTURE AND TRANSFORMATION

Architecture can **transform** the way people interact with the world, so architects must **anticipate** how a building will impact the local area. If the design of a building includes a lot of large windows, the people working inside **maintain** a connection with nature because they can see the sky. When people **abandon** old warehouses, which are left to collapse, this creates an opportunity for developers to **acquire** such properties and **convert** them into shops, flats and offices. Developing an old building can **contribute** to the improvement of a whole neighbourhood, but suitable sites can be difficult to identify as cities **expand**.

1 _____ (v) to be one of the reasons why something happens
2 _____ (v) to completely change the appearance, form or character of something
3 _____ (v) to continue to have, or keep in existence
4 _____ (v) to increase, or cause to increase, in size, number or importance
5 _____ (v) to expect that something will happen
6 _____ (v) to leave something forever
7 _____ (v) to change something from one thing to another
8 _____ (v) to buy or get something

4 Complete the sentences with the correct form of the verbs from Exercise 3.

1 We need to _____ the amount of retail space available.
2 We could _____ the local area with a new retail complex.
3 The new public transport system has _____ to the improvement of the city centre.
4 We _____ that the shopping area will bring £30 million in profit over the year.
5 The developer's plan to _____ a warehouse to a block of flats was a major success.
6 It may be difficult to _____ a piece of land within the city.
7 We can't _____ this project just because of a few setbacks.
8 We will _____ the number of houses in the new development, not increase it.

PLUS

LISTENING 2

PREPARING TO LISTEN

UNDERSTANDING
KEY VOCABULARY

1 You are going to listen to a housing development meeting. Before you listen, read the sentences and write the words in bold next to the definitions.

1 We're **concerned** about the size of the building. Doesn't it look a bit too big for the area?
2 The old building is **adequate** and is in no danger of collapsing.
3 The **existing** decorations need to be changed completely to something more modern.
4 We need something that is **appropriate** for the local area.
5 The plan is very **sympathetic** to the local neighbourhood and will leave the historical area as it is now.
6 A building of that size could be **controversial** because it is taller than all the others and might block everyone's view.
7 The plan is very **ambitious**; I'm not sure the developers will be able to finish on time.

a _____ (adj) that exists or is being used at the present time
b _____ (adj) causing a lot of disagreement or argument
c _____ (adj) enough or satisfactory for a specific purpose
d _____ (adj) agreeing with or supporting
e _____ (adj) not easily done or achieved
f _____ (adj) suitable or right for a specific situation or occasion
g _____ (adj) worried or anxious

PLUS

2 Work with a partner. Look at the pictures of plans for a new development in Exercise 6 on page 114. Discuss your opinions of the plans. Try to use words from Exercise 1.

3 Work with a partner. Discuss possible solutions to the potential problems in the housing development plan.

USING YOUR KNOWLEDGE

potential problems	possible solutions
1 There is a tall building blocking the light for another block of flats in the development.	
2 The modern design of the development doesn't fit in with the traditional buildings in the area.	
3 The undeveloped area they plan to build on is woodland, and residents want to retain it.	

4 Present your ideas to another pair. Did you identify the same solutions or different ones? Whose solutions are better?

WHILE LISTENING

5 🔊 5.3 Listen to the housing development meeting between Maria and John (the clients) and Jamal and Tom (the developers). Use the T-chart in Exercise 3 to take notes on the solutions to the problems. Then compare your notes with a partner.

TAKING NOTES ON MAIN IDEAS

6 🔊 5.3 Match the descriptions to the correct pictures. Then listen again to check your answers.

1 The proposed building site _____
2 The developers' proposal _____
3 The clients' preferred proposal _____
4 A proposal not discussed in the meeting _____

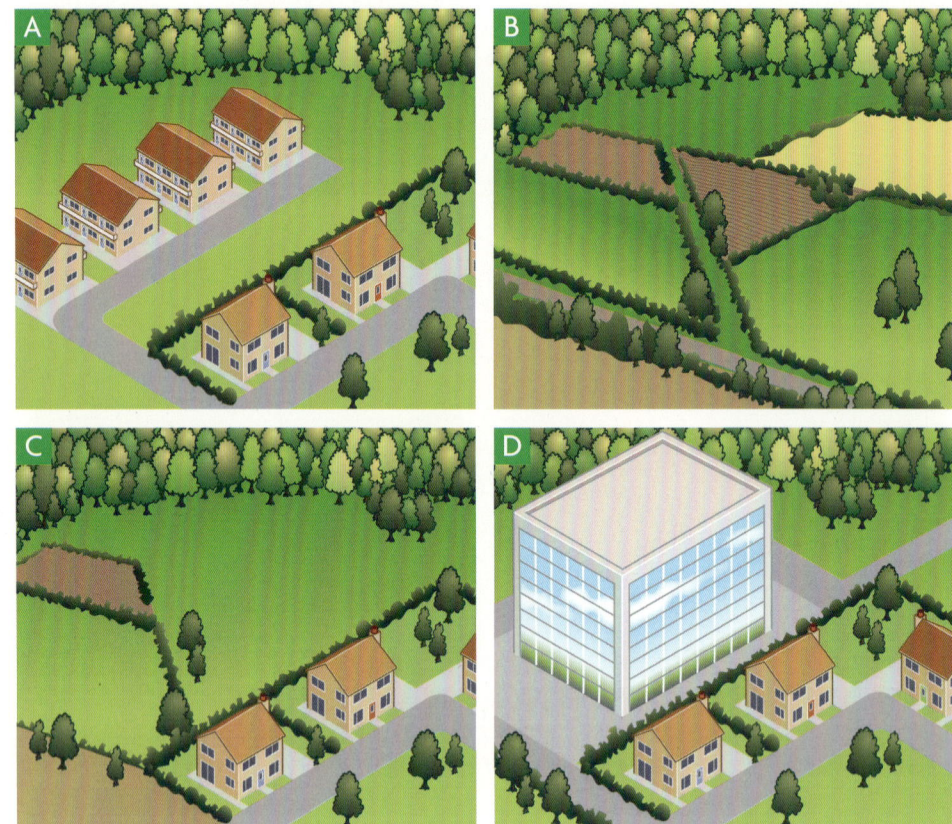

7 Who said the statements below? Write *D* (developers) or *C* (clients).

1 One of the biggest benefits of this plan is that it will create housing for as many as 200 people. _____
2 We could consider using reflective glass. _____
3 You described the natural area you'd like to build on as waste ground, but actually, that's a woodland. _____
4 As it stands, this plan ... would be very controversial. _____
5 What about more, smaller, lower buildings? _____
6 Lots of glass is a great idea but, in my view, the only viable option is to use brick. _____
7 How about we position the new buildings near the edge of the woods? _____
8 I feel confident we can come up with a good plan over the next two weeks. _____

POST-LISTENING

SKILLS

Understanding strong and tentative suggestions

When making suggestions, speakers use different language to emphasize their point, depending on how strongly they feel. To make a strong suggestion, speakers may use words like *only* or *strongly*. To make a tentative suggestion, speakers may use polite expressions like *We could* and *Wouldn't it be better if ...* . They may also state the suggestion as a question or use words like *maybe* or *probably*.

8 🔊 **5.4** Listen to the speakers. Are they making strong or tentative suggestions? Write *T* (tentative) or *S* (strong).

1 What about more, smaller, lower buildings? _____

2 In my view, the only viable option is to use brick. _____

3 We need to think about what will be appropriate with the existing houses. _____

4 I strongly recommend that you reconsider this. _____

5 Wouldn't it be better if we used this first design you have supplied to identify a few priorities? _____

6 I like your thinking. I completely agree. _____

LISTENING FOR ATTITUDE

DISCUSSION

9 Work with a partner. Use your notes from Listening 1 and Listening 2 to discuss the following questions.

1 Do you think it is better to live in a flat or a house? Why?

2 Would you prefer to live in an old or a new building? What do you look for in a living space?

3 Should new houses or developments be built on existing sites or in new green areas?

4 If you were designing a block of flats for an urban area, where would you build it – in an old part of the town or in a new part of the town? How many people would live there? What features would it have?

SYNTHESIZING

SPEAKING

CRITICAL THINKING

At the end of this unit, you are going to do the speaking task below.

> An oil company owns a block of flats where 200 single workers and 50 families who work for the company live. The flats are cramped, uncomfortable and too far away from international schools and the workers' main offices. The company needs the workers to move out of the current block one year from now. It has £3.8 million to spend. Discuss the problem and possible solutions.

 **ANALYZE**

1 Work with a partner. In the table, list the problems mentioned in the speaking task. Then make a list of project requirements for the new block of flats.

problems	project requirements	solution A	solution B	solution C
crowded flats	must have more space			

Comparing and evaluating solutions

Some projects have specific requirements which will influence the solution you identify. Think carefully about each idea so that you get the best results.

2 Look at the three housing solutions below. Compare your list of project requirements to each housing solution and answer the questions.

1 Which project requirements does each solution meet? Write ✔ in the table for solutions that meet each requirement.

2 Which project requirements does each solution not meet? Write ✘ in the table for those that don't meet the project requirements.

3 What needs to change for the solutions to better fit the project requirements?

Solution A: Al Qasim Tower

- Available in six months
- Eight-storey office building made of glass and steel
- Offices could be converted to bedrooms
- Toilets would be shared
- Shower rooms could be added on each floor
- Could accommodate up to 180 single workers and 40 families
- Located 3 kilometres from offices/factory
- Near subway line for 8 kilometre journey to international school
- No facilities (parks, green spaces) for children nearby
- Price: £3.2 million
- Conversion cost: £600,000

Solution B: Iqbal House Hotel

- Available now
- 1920s hotel made of brick
- Could accommodate up to 210 single workers and 30 families
- Lots of traditional architectural features
- Hotel was abandoned 10 years ago
- Located 4 kilometres from offices/factory
- Located 10 kilometres from international school by road
- Plenty of open space for children to play and for adults to walk, cycle, etc.
- Price: £1.6 million
- Conversion cost: £2.4 million

Solution C: Land purchase

- Land available now
- Would need to complete government planning process before building (about 3 months; building would take another 3 months)
- Could accommodate up to 250 single people and 60 families in up to 6 blocks of flats, option to build more accommodation in future
- Located 6 kilometres from offices/factory
- Located 12 kilometres from international school by road, bus and train
- Plans could include full recreational facilities for adults and children
- Land price: £1.1 million
- Estimated building costs: £3 million

3 Work with another pair. Compare your responses to Exercise 2 and answer the questions.

1 Which solution do you think best meets the project requirements?

_____

_____

2 What points does each plan have that might impact your decision?

_____

_____

3 Can you reach a group decision? Why / Why not?

_____

_____

PREPARATION FOR SPEAKING

PRONUNCIATION FOR SPEAKING

Emphasizing a word or idea to signal a problem

Emphasizing or stressing a word in a sentence can help listeners understand its importance. Changing the emphasized or stressed word also changes the important piece of information in that sentence, and can be used to signal a problem.

1 🔊 5.5 Listen. Underline the stressed word in each sentence. The first one is done for you.

1 The <u>main</u> issue is that most retailers don't want to do business here.
2 The main issue is that most retailers don't want to do business here.
3 The main issue is that most retailers don't want to do business here.
4 The main issue is that most retailers don't want to do business here.

2 Match the explanations with the sentences from Exercise 1.

a There are other types of business that will be happy to do business here, but retailers don't want to. _____
b There are other issues, but this is the most important one. _____
c Retailers are happy to put up advertising here, but they don't want to open shops in this area. _____
d There are aspects of the project that aren't issues, but this particular fact is a problem. _____

IDENTIFYING PROBLEMS AND SUGGESTING SOLUTIONS

SKILLS

Presenting a problem

When presenting a problem, speakers often use phrases that signal there is an issue, such as *The problem is ...* , *The main issue is ...* , and *We need to find a way around ...* .

Speakers use these phrases to let the audience know what they are going to focus on and emphasize that they have considered it and have a possible solution in mind.

3 Put the words in order to make sentences.

1 of / prices / We / a / high / need / problem / to / the / find / around / way / .

_____

2 time / The / is / problem / enough / we / that / have / don't / .

_____

3 issue / main / The / is / people / that / our / don't / design / like / .

_____

4 a / around / way / find / need / We / to / problem / the / attracting / business / of / .

_____

5 the / is / building / The / issue / main / that / is / collapsing / .

_____

6 problem / that / The / is / no one / to / wants / area / in / live / the / .

_____

Making polite suggestions

Making a suggestion in the form of a question can be more polite than using a direct statement such as *I think* … or *We have to* … . This approach to making suggestions is more common when people are brainstorming and exploring a variety of ideas. Using it means the speaker is less likely to offend anyone. It is also a more formal and professional way of speaking.

PLUS

4 Write six suggestions using the structures in the box.

1 Could we … 2 Can I suggest we … 3 Why don't we …	increase	the budget?
4 Should we consider … 5 How about … 6 Have you thought about …	increasing	

5 Work with a partner. Take turns making suggestions for each of the problems. Use the structures from Exercise 4 to help you.

1 There is very little space for parking in the local area. (build car park)
   <u>Could we build a car park?</u>

2 The planned building is too high. (reduce height)
   _____

3 There isn't enough outdoor space. (turn the waste ground into a park)
   _____

4 There isn't any space for gardens around the block of flats. (build a rooftop garden)
   _____

5 The shop units are too small to attract large retailers. (have more, larger units)
   _____

6 We won't be able to attract businesses to this area. (offer lower rents)
   _____

6 Work with a partner. Make suggestions for each topic.

1 plans for the weekend
   _____
   _____

2 ways to improve the school or class
   _____
   _____

3 helping the environment
   _____
   _____

RESPONDING TO SUGGESTED SOLUTIONS

7 Read the responses. Does the speaker accept or reject the solution? Tick (✔) the correct box.

	accept	reject
1 That's a great idea, but I'm not sure it addresses the problem.		
2 I like your thinking. I agree completely.		
3 I think that's a great idea.		
4 We thought that might be an option at first, but now we realize it won't work.		
5 That seems like an obvious solution, but it doesn't address the issue of cost.		
6 Let's do it.		

8 Work with a partner. Practise saying the sentences below. Take turns making the suggestion and accepting or rejecting it, using phrases from Exercises 4 and 7.

   1 How about building four smaller blocks of flats rather than one large one?
   2 Should we include a community garden in the new development?
   3 Can I suggest we reduce the size and scale of this development?

SPEAKING TASK

▶ An oil company owns a block of flats where 200 single workers and 50 families who work for the company live. The flats are cramped, uncomfortable and too far away from international schools and the workers' main offices. The company needs the workers to move out of the current block one year from now. It has £3.8 million to spend. Discuss the problem and possible solutions.

PREPARE

1 Work in groups of four. Look at the list of project requirements that you wrote in Critical thinking. As a group, choose one solution to focus on.

2 Split into two pairs. One pair are the project developers. The other pair are the project clients.

> **Project developers:** You will present your solution to your clients. You need to highlight the positive aspects of your solution. Think about any of the project requirements which the solution does not address. How will you deal with them? How could you respond?

> **Project clients:** You will listen to a presentation from the project developers. You need to ask questions about any information that they don't mention in their solution, or anything you aren't sure about. What problems might you need to identify?

3 In your pairs, look again at the table in Exercise 1 and the answers to the questions in Exercises 2 and 3 in Critical thinking. Add any new information.

4 Refer to the Task checklist below as you prepare for your discussion.

TASK CHECKLIST	✔
Identify problems and suggest solutions.	
Emphasize words and ideas to signal problems.	
Make polite suggestions.	
Respond to suggested solutions.	

PRACTISE

5 Practise your presentation/questions with your partner. Use your answers to Exercise 3 in Critical thinking to help you. Revise and make changes to your presentation/questions as necessary.

DISCUSS

6 Discuss the problem and solution as a group.

OBJECTIVES REVIEW

1 Check your learning objectives for this unit. Write *3*, *2* or *1* for each objective.

3 = very well   2 = well   1 = not so well

I can ...

watch and understand a video about skyscrapers.   _____

understand figurative language.   _____

understand strong and tentative suggestions.   _____

compare and evaluate solutions.   _____

use *will* and *be going to* for predictions and expectations.   _____

present a problem.   _____

make polite suggestions.   _____

respond to suggested solutions.   _____

discuss a housing problem and possible solutions.   _____

2 Use the *Unlock* Digital Workbook for more practice with this unit's learning objectives.

UNLOCK ONLINE

WORDLIST

abandon (v) ⊙	concerned (adj) ⊙	feature (n) ⊙
acquire (v) ⊙	contemporary (adj) ⊙	maintain (v) ⊙
adequate (adj) ⊙	contribute (v) ⊙	obtain (v) ⊙
ambitious (adj) ⊙	controversial (adj) ⊙	potential (adj) ⊙
anticipate (v)	convert (v) ⊙	sympathetic (adj) ⊙
appropriate (adj) ⊙	existing (adj) ⊙	transform (v) ⊙
collapse (v) ⊙	expand (v) ⊙	

⊙ = high-frequency words in the Cambridge Academic Corpus

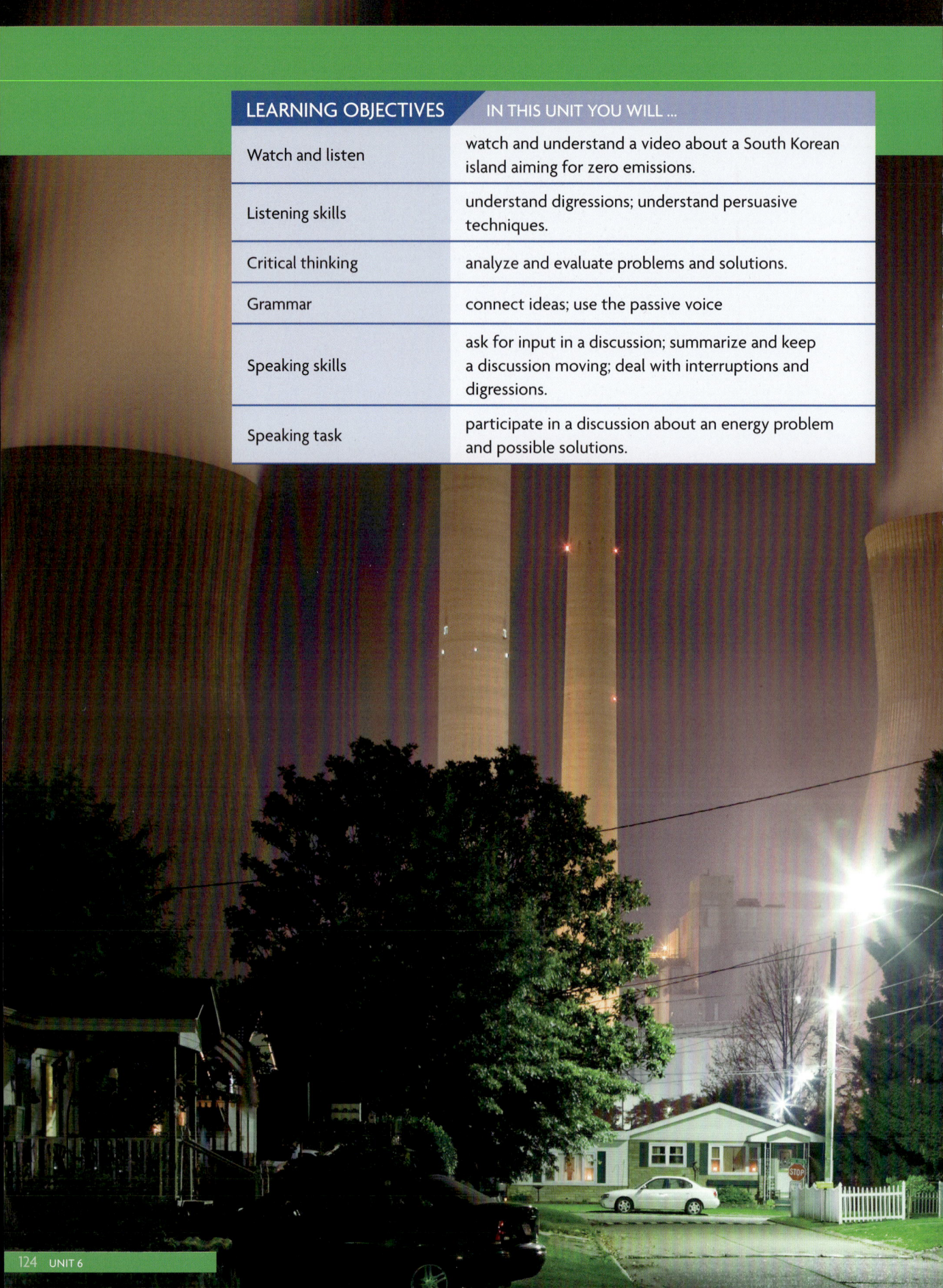

LEARNING OBJECTIVES	IN THIS UNIT YOU WILL ...
Watch and listen	watch and understand a video about a South Korean island aiming for zero emissions.
Listening skills	understand digressions; understand persuasive techniques.
Critical thinking	analyze and evaluate problems and solutions.
Grammar	connect ideas; use the passive voice
Speaking skills	ask for input in a discussion; summarize and keep a discussion moving; deal with interruptions and digressions.
Speaking task	participate in a discussion about an energy problem and possible solutions.

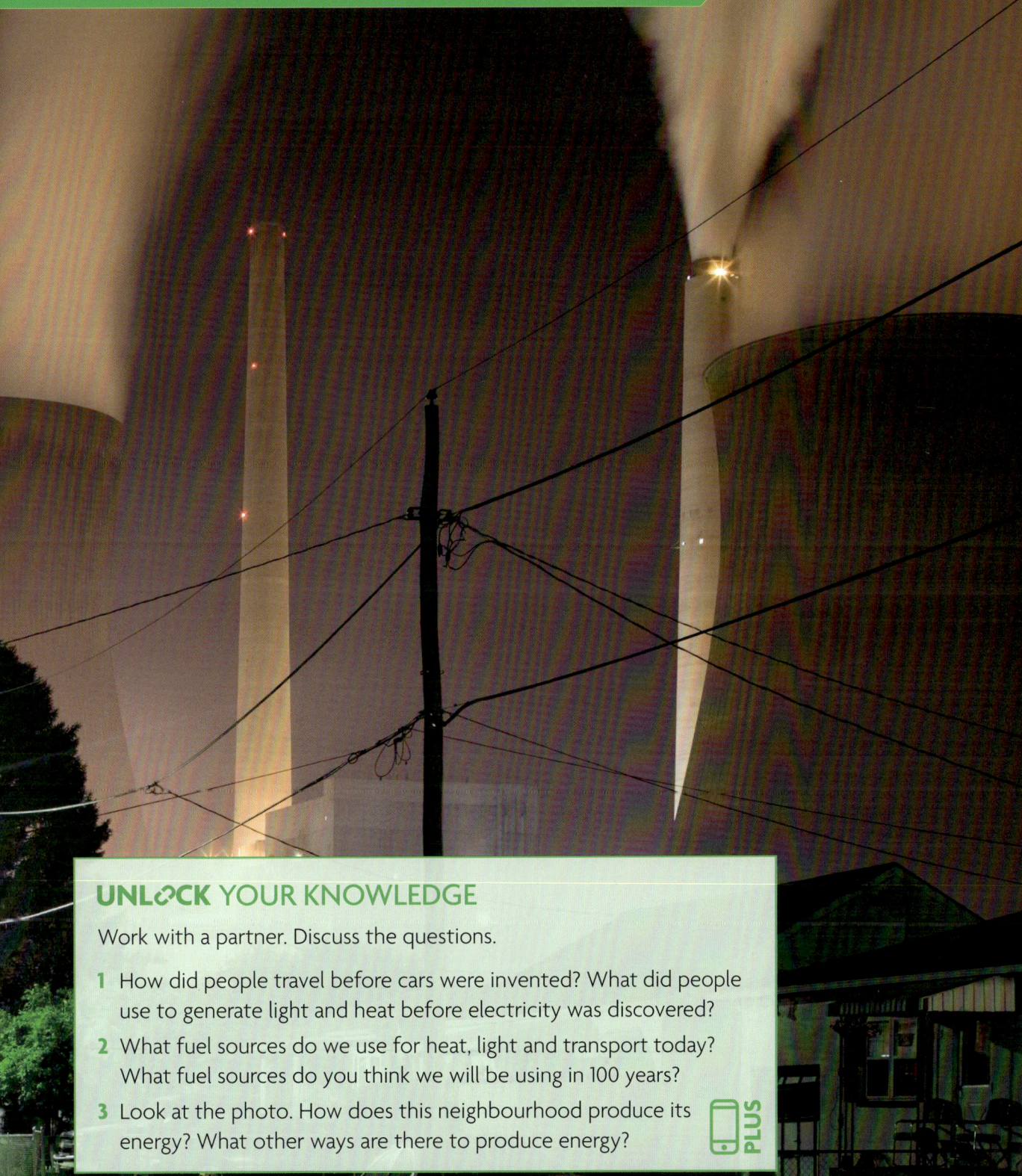

UNL♻CK YOUR KNOWLEDGE

Work with a partner. Discuss the questions.

1 How did people travel before cars were invented? What did people use to generate light and heat before electricity was discovered?

2 What fuel sources do we use for heat, light and transport today? What fuel sources do you think we will be using in 100 years?

3 Look at the photo. How does this neighbourhood produce its energy? What other ways are there to produce energy?

PLUS

PREPARING TO WATCH

ACTIVATING YOUR KNOWLEDGE

1 Work with a partner and answer the questions.

1 What fuel sources are used to make the electricity we use at home today? What fuels do vehicles use?
2 What alternative energy sources are available today? Are they renewable?
3 What do you think will be our main sources of power in 50 years? What will they be in 500 years?

PREDICTING CONTENT USING VISUALS

2 Look at the pictures from the video. Discuss the questions with a partner.

1 What kinds of energy sources do the pictures show?
2 What are the advantages and disadvantages of each type of energy?
3 In what parts of the world do you think each type of energy is used the most?

GLOSSARY

in accordance with (phr) in the way described by a rule, law or wish

stunning (adj) extremely beautiful

sparkling (adj) shining brightly

lush (adj) filled with lots of healthy trees and plants

preserve (v) to keep something as it is

ideal (adj) perfect; the best possible

WHILE WATCHING

UNDERSTANDING MAIN IDEAS

3 ▶ Watch the video. Write *T* (true) or *F* (false), or *DNS* (does not say) next to the statements below. Correct the false statements.

_____ 1 A country that achieves carbon neutrality will have no carbon emissions.
_____ 2 The South Korean island of Jeju wants to achieve zero emissions.
_____ 3 Jeju is famous for its natural beauty.
_____ 4 Jeju island will be the first community in Asia to be carbon-free.
_____ 5 Only electric cars are permitted on Jeju Island at the moment.
_____ 6 Jeju hopes to attract eco-tourists.

4 ▶ Watch again. Complete the summary with words from the box.

> zero   balance   charge   solar   neutrality
> 2030   electric   emissions   trees   wind

Countries that signed the Paris Climate Agreement are trying to reduce their carbon ¹_____ . Many are trying to achieve carbon ²_____ . In other words, they hope to ³_____ their emissions with other actions, for example, planting ⁴_____ . Jeju is going further; it is trying to achieve ⁵_____ emissions by the year ⁶_____ . To accomplish this, the government is promoting three types of alternative energy, all from renewable sources: (1) ⁷_____ power, (2) ⁸_____ power, and (3) ⁹_____ vehicles. Jeju is the perfect place for electric cars because you can drive around the whole island on only one ¹⁰_____ .

5 Work with a partner. Write *T* next to the statements that are true according to the video.

_____ 1 Most countries will reach their carbon emission goals by 2030.
_____ 2 The continued use of fossil fuels could spoil Jeju's natural beauty.
_____ 3 The South Korean government hopes that its action to help the environment will promote tourism.
_____ 4 Without help from the government, people on Jeju might not buy solar panels or electric cars.
_____ 5 Solar and wind power will provide more energy for the island than traditional energy sources.

DISCUSSION

6 Discuss the questions with your partner. Compare your answers with another pair.

1 Would you like to visit Jeju? Why / Why not? What would you do there?
2 Would you like to live on a carbon-free island like Jeju? What do you think would be the best part? What parts of life might be difficult?
3 What forms of renewable energy are used in your city or country? Is their use increasing?

LISTENING

LISTENING 1

PREPARING TO LISTEN

UNDERSTANDING KEY VOCABULARY

1 You are going to listen to a radio interview about the island of El Hierro in Spain. Before you listen, read the definitions. Complete the sentences with the words in bold.

> **capacity** (n) the amount that something can produce
> **consistent** (adj) always acting in a similar way
> **cycle** (n) a set of events that repeat themselves regularly in the same order
> **element** (n) one part of something
> **generate** (v) to produce
> **mainland** (n) the biggest or primary part of a country, not including the islands around it
> **network** (n) a system of parts that work together
> **reservoir** (n) a natural or artificial lake that stores and supplies water

1 A solar panel is one _____ needed to make the office more energy efficient. Another is special lightbulbs.
2 The president has a _____ voting record; he always supports alternative energy sources.
3 The _____ stores enough water to supply the entire town for a year.
4 The _____ may have a lot of petrol cars, but the islands around it have more electric cars.
5 The engineer set the batteries to recharge on a 24-hour _____ .
6 The _____ allows all the computers in the office to communicate with each other.
7 The temperature needs to be higher in order to _____ enough heat to warm the building.
8 The wind turbines are operating at full _____ and should be able to produce electricity for the entire city.

2 Before you listen to the radio interview, complete the fact file with the words from the box.

USING YOUR
KNOWLEDGE

area   government   mainland   population

FACT FILE: *The Island of* EL HIERRO

(1)_____ : part of Spain
(2)_____ : 11,000
(3)_____ : 268 km²
Distance to the (4)_____ :
400 km
Claim to fame: energy independent

3 Work in pairs. Answer the questions.

1 What do you think life is like on El Hierro?
2 What would probably need to be imported from the mainland?
3 What sort of energy supply do you think is available there?
4 What do you think *energy independent* means?

WHILE LISTENING

4 🔊 6.1 Listen to the radio interview about El Hierro. Choose the ending for each sentence.

LISTENING FOR
MAIN IDEAS

1 The people of El Hierro …
   a need to buy all of their oil.
   b need to buy 30% of their oil.
   c don't need to buy any oil.
2 El Hierro's energy is provided by …
   a wind and hydroelectric power.
   b solar and wind power and imported oil.
   c solar and hydroelectric power.
3 The system also provides water for …
   a a small lake filled with fish.
   b a water park.
   c drinking and agriculture.

5 🔊 **6.2** Listen to the first part of the radio interview again. Complete the student's notes about Pedro Rodriguez with the missing details.

Pedro Rodriguez
- owns a (1)_____
- has lived there (2)_____
- lived in (3)_____ for a lot of his life
- city life is (4)_____ ; island life is
  (5)_____

What's great about El Hierro
- sound of (6)_____
- peace and (7)_____
   - in the city, everyone hurries everywhere
   - you are surrounded by (8)_____ , can never relax
   - career was in (9)_____
- energy (10)_____
- before, power came from (11)_____
   - shipped over (12)_____ barrels from the
   (13)_____ every year
   - cost (14)_____ a year

6 🔊 **6.3** Now listen to the second part of the radio interview again. Complete the student's notes about wind and hydroelectric power with the missing details.

Wind power
- wind blows (1)_____ hours a year
   - (2)_____ % of the year
- generate energy by using wind (3)_____
   - capacity of (4)_____ megawatts
   - enough to power (5)_____ homes
Hydroelectric power
- when energy of moving (6)_____ is converted
  into electricity
   - usually from a river with a (7)_____
   - theirs is from a reservoir inside a (8)_____
   - reservoir holds over (9)_____ cubic metres
   - is 700 metres above (10)_____

- water flows in a (11)_____
  - pumped up the (12)_____ by the wind power
  - released when it's needed
- provides (13)_____ water
- provides water for (14)_____
- comes from (15)_____
  - desalination plant
  - parts come from (16)_____

POST-LISTENING

LISTENING FOR TEXT ORGANIZATION

SKILLS

Understanding digressions

Speakers sometimes digress or move away from the main topic in a conversation. Sometimes they do this to add an interesting piece of information or an anecdote, even if it is not directly related to the topic. Other times they do this because they haven't prepared answers to, or aren't thinking about, the question they have been asked. Recognizing when someone is digressing can help you move the focus back to the main topic of a conversation.

7 Read the topics Pedro talks about during the interview. Write *R* (relevant) or *D* (digression).

1 Peace and quiet _____
2 Traffic in Madrid _____
3 The fast pace of city life _____
4 The sound of the sea _____
5 The banking profession _____
6 Freedom on the island _____

8 Match the questions (1–3) with the relevant answers (a–c). Then check your answers with a partner.

1 What is the most important power source on El Hierro? _____
2 Can life be hard on El Hierro? _____
3 What do you miss about living on the mainland? _____

a Having easy access to facilities, like cinemas and a variety of restaurants.
b Probably the wind turbines. Without them we wouldn't be able to power the pump system for the water.
c It can be difficult in the winter, when the sea is rough. Basic supplies often take several days longer to arrive.

9 Now read the digressions. What questions from Exercise 8 do you think the speakers heard?

    a My children think it's boring here, but I wanted them to grow up with the freedom to explore outside. _____

    b I didn't like living in my old city. It was too noisy and the buildings were too tall. _____

    c We've thought about installing solar panels to generate extra electricity on the island. _____

PRONUNCIATION FOR LISTENING

Intonation related to emotion

Intonation is the rise and fall of pitch in a person's voice. Intonation can tell you how a speaker feels at that moment or about the topic.

10 🔊 6.4 Listen to the same question spoken with four different emotions. Then practise saying them with a partner.

    You don't like it here, then?

    1 bored   3 surprised

    2 sarcastic   4 encouraging

11 🔊 6.5 Listen to the sentences. Write the emotion expressed in the sentences. Use the words from Exercise 10.

    1 It's a real challenge living here. _____

    2 El Hierro is completely energy independent. _____

    3 It must be difficult sometimes. _____

    4 You can't drink saltwater … _____

    5 You're a long way from everything out here, aren't you? _____

12 Work with a partner. Take turns saying the sentences with different emotions. Can your partner guess which emotion you're expressing?

DISCUSSION

13 Work with a partner. Discuss the questions.

    1 What alternatives to fossil fuels are you familiar with? What are their advantages and disadvantages?

    2 What kinds of energy would work best in your community? Explain.

CONNECTING IDEAS

GRAMMAR

Transition words and phrases

Remember, you can connect ideas using transition words and phrases to show different relationships between sentences, such as giving extra information, comparing and contrasting and explaining a result.

We're a long way from the mainland, **so** delivery of anything takes at least a few days. (explaining a result)

Yes, that's right. **What's more,** the system also provides our drinking water and water for use in agriculture. (giving extra information)

It's a real challenge living here. **On the other hand,** we all love it. (comparing and contrasting)

1 Complete the tables with the transition words and phrases from the box.

> and as a result   Moreover,   Furthermore,   In addition,
> Even so,   Nevertheless,   therefore

giving extra information		
Yes, that's right.	What's more,	the system also provides our drinking water and water for use in agriculture.

comparing and contrasting		
It's a real challenge living here.	On the other hand,	we all love it.

explaining a result		
We're a long way from the mainland,	so	delivery of anything takes a few days.

2 Work in pairs. Use the words and phrases from the middle columns in Exercise 1 to connect the sentences.

1 City life is stressful. Island life is relaxing. (comparing and contrasting)

_____

2 The houses use solar energy. They have water-recycling systems. (giving extra information)

_____

3 Dams can damage habitats. They have to be planned carefully. (explaining a result)

_____

4 The wind blows for 35% of the year. That isn't enough to provide all of the island's electricity. (comparing and contrasting)

_____

5 This electric car can go just over 99 km per hour. The battery can be charged using solar power. (giving extra information)

_____

6 The system requires that water moves from a high place to a lower place. We've placed a water tank on a hill. (explaining a result)

_____

THE PASSIVE VOICE

GRAMMAR

Use the passive voice when the result of an action is more important than who or what made it happen (the agent). It puts emphasis on the object of the verb instead of the subject. Form the passive voice by using the appropriate form of the auxiliary verb *be* + the past participle.

Hydroelectric power is when the energy of moving water **is converted** into another form. (Note: It is not important to know who or what converts the energy.) Different machines **are used** to convert the energy.

Speakers usually omit the agent when they talk about a process or to report news events. The listener needs to focus on the action and not on who performed the action.

However, use a *by* + agent phrase if the agent is important or if the meaning of the sentence would be unclear without it.
The water **is pumped** up the hill <u>by the wind power.</u>

When using modals with the passive voice, use a modal + *be* + past participle of the main verb. *Not* comes after the modal in the negative form.
Hydroelectric power **can be used** as a cheap alternative to fossil fuels.
Nuclear power plants **should not be built** near communities.

3 🔊 **6.6** Listen to each statement. Write *A* (active) or *P* (passive). Then compare your answers with a partner.

1 _____   3 _____   5 _____
2 _____   4 _____   6 _____

4 Complete the paragraph below, using the passive voice for the verb in brackets.

Geothermal energy (1)_____ (use) in many countries around the world because it is one of the few truly renewable energy sources. It (2)_____ (create) by the heat from the Earth. The main sources of this heat can range from the shallow ground to the hot water and hot rock that (3)_____ (find) beneath the surface of the Earth. This energy can also (4)_____ (extract) even deeper below the Earth's surface, where extremely hot temperatures (5)_____ (cause) by magma and molten rock. In many locations around the world, wells (6)_____ (drill) into underground reservoirs in order to generate electricity. At some power plants, power (7)_____ (supply) by steam from a water-powered generator. Hot water near the surface of the Earth (8)_____ (can / use) to provide heat for buildings, for growing plants in greenhouses, drying crops, heating water at fish farms and pasteurizing milk.

5 Write passive sentences using the words provided. The first one has been done for you as an example.

1 energy / generate / wind turbines
   Energy is generated by wind turbines.

2 water / pump / up the hill
   _____

3 salt / take out of / the seawater
   _____

4 supplies / transport / from the mainland
   _____

5 in the past, all the power / produce / oil
   _____

6 wind turbines / blow / the wind
   _____

📱 PLUS

ACADEMIC VOCABULARY FOR NETWORKS AND SYSTEMS

6 Read the article. Write the words in bold next to the definitions.

With the steady **decline** in supplies of coal and oil, exploring the **potential** of alternative energy sources has increased in recent decades. Installing an alternative-energy **generation** system to power an entire town is a huge **challenge**. A single energy **source**, such as solar or wind power, rarely has the **capacity** to do this. Engineers and designers therefore need to come up with a **network** of technologies to provide a consistent power supply from a variety of sources. Each **element** of the system must take advantage of a natural resource when it is available. Wind turbines need a certain amount of wind to produce electricity, so when the wind slows or stops, another part of the system needs to be able to perform the same task.

1 _____ (n) the production of energy in a particular form
2 _____ (n) one part of something
3 _____ (n) the ability to do something in particular
4 _____ (n) the origin or place something comes from
5 _____ (n) something requiring great effort to do successfully
6 _____ (n) a system of parts that work together
7 _____ (n) the amount that something can produce or contain
8 _____ (n) a decrease in something

LISTENING 2

PREPARING TO LISTEN

USING YOUR KNOWLEDGE

1 You are going to listen to a meeting about saving energy in an office. Before you listen, look at the picture and discuss the questions with a partner.

1 What things in an office environment use energy?
2 How could energy be saved in an office environment?
3 What benefits could saving energy have in an office environment?

2 Read the text. Write the words in bold next to the definitions.

Simple measures to reduce energy **consumption** can cut office energy bills by up to 20%, such as reducing the **volume** of rubbish. Some businesses, however, are going further to be environmentally friendly. The **function** of large energy-saving plans is to save a lot of money as well as the environment, but there are **limitations**. One **drawback** of making an office more **efficient** is that it is expensive in the beginning, although money is saved over time. Large, complex energy-saving projects can also have a **maintenance** cost that often isn't factored in, which can be expensive, especially when the new technology is still **experimental**.

1 _____ (n) the act of using, eating or drinking something
2 _____ (n) the work needed to keep something in good condition
3 _____ (adj) new and not tested
4 _____ (adj) producing good results without waste
5 _____ (n) a situation that restricts something
6 _____ (n) a role or purpose
7 _____ (n) the number or amount of something
8 _____ (n) a disadvantage or negative part of a situation

PLUS

WHILE LISTENING

3 🔊 6.7 Listen to a meeting about saving energy at an office. Complete the notes on the speakers' proposed solutions to the office energy problem. Tick (✔) the ideas that the speakers identify as 'large-scale'.

speaker	proposed solutions	large-scale
Zara	Install (1)_____ on the roof	
Allen	Change to (2)_____ lightbulbs	
Abdul	Clean dirty windows to get more (3)_____	
	Turn off (4)_____ when get up from desk	
Zara	Turn off (5)_____ when it isn't hot	
	Get rid of one (6)_____	
	Install a solar (7)_____ heating system	

4 🔊 **6.7** Listen to the meeting again. Complete the sentences with the words or phrases you hear.

1 One alternative energy source is to install _____ on the roof.
2 Energy-efficient lightbulbs pay for themselves _____ .
3 _____ the windows will let more natural light in.
4 They don't really need _____ photocopiers.
5 They could also turn off computer screens and _____ .
6 _____ is a problem, and they would need to pay an engineer to do repairs.
7 They could market themselves as a _____ business.
8 They want to immediately start making _____ changes and look into more complex changes later.

5 Choose the correct answer.

1 Energy-efficient bulbs *are / aren't* hugely expensive to install.
2 Energy-efficient bulbs are *expensive / inexpensive*.
3 Being a green business would be *good / bad* publicity.
4 They can get rid of *one / both* of their photocopiers.
5 The solar energy system will have a *low / high* operating cost.
6 If the solar energy system doesn't produce a lot of power, it could *cost / save* money

POST-LISTENING

Understanding persuasive techniques

When giving an opinion or a suggestion in a discussion, speakers often use persuasive language to try to convince listeners that they are right, that their suggestions are good ideas, or that there is a problem with someone else's idea. This can be a useful technique, but you should not use it too much. When you are listening, make sure to focus more on *what* is said, rather than *how* it is said. Here are examples of sentences that use different persuasive techniques:

I see your point. Even so, I think solar panels are the best idea. (challenging a point)
Don't you think that solar panels are a good idea? (asking a question)
Trust me when I say that solar panels are the best idea. (reassuring)
You also need to consider the cost of solar panels. (adding information)
By and large, I see what you're saying, but solar panels are just more efficient. (expressing reservations)

6 Match the persuasive techniques (a–e) to the sentences from the meeting (1–5).

1 Well, if we really want to do something to save on electricity costs long-term, why don't we consider an alternative energy source? _____

2 No, I really like that idea because once it's installed, the system will have a low operating cost, and it's an environmentally friendly way to generate electricity, which are two big positive points, but there are other considerations. For example, we'd have to look at the generating capacity of the system. _____

3 The fact is, both systems Zara mentioned are technically complex and expensive to install. _____

4 I can't help but feel that a solar energy project would be too ambitious. _____

5 I can assure you that the company wouldn't do anything unsafe or illegal. _____

a challenging a point
b asking a question
c reassuring
d adding information
e expressing reservations

7 Work with a partner. Match the sentences to the persuasive techniques (a–e) in Exercise 6.

1 On that point, we could employ a window cleaner at a relatively low cost. _____

2 I don't think we need to worry about the cost of installing a system until we find one that would work for us. _____

3 I'm not convinced that we get enough sunshine here to make a solar power system effective. _____

4 Have you thought more about my idea of getting rid of a photocopier? _____

5 I see what you mean, but consider the fact that sometimes we do need to leave our computer screens on. _____

DISCUSSION

SYNTHESIZING

8 Work with a partner. Use your notes from Listening 1 and Listening 2 to discuss the following questions.

1 What other reasons can you think of for using alternative energy sources at home or in the workplace?

2 Would it be possible to make your home more energy efficient, like El Hierro or the office you heard about in Listening 2? If so, what ideas would be appropriate? If not, why not?

SPEAKING

CRITICAL THINKING

At the end of this unit, you are going to do the speaking task below.

> How can we save energy in our place of work / study?

1 Work with a partner. Look back at your notes from Listening 2, Exercise 3. What solutions were proposed in the meeting? What were the large-scale solutions?

REMEMBER

2 With your partner, brainstorm some possible problems with energy use at a university or workplace. Think of as many as you can. Make a list.

ANALYZE

lights left on at night

3 Choose the three biggest problems and write them in the top row of the table.

EVALUATE

problems	1	2	3
possible solutions			

Analyzing and evaluating problems and solutions

SKILLS

Try to really understand the reasons for a problem. Understanding the reasons for the problem can help you think of effective solutions. Then you can assess which solutions are best.

4 Think of possible solutions to each problem and add them to the table. Include at least two large-scale solutions (alternative sources of energy) and at least two small-scale solutions (ways of reducing consumption) for each problem. You will use this table again for the speaking task at the end of this unit.

PREPARATION FOR SPEAKING

KEEPING A DISCUSSION MOVING

> #### Asking for input, summarizing and keeping a discussion moving
>
> In some discussions, such as meetings in a committee or in an office, someone usually manages the meeting and leads the discussion points and is called the 'chair'. The chair usually asks participants to provide input on the discussion, summarizes main points and keeps the discussion moving. There are certain words and phrases a chair might use to ask for input, summarize or keep a discussion moving.
>
> **asking for input**
> What do you think?
> Does anyone have anything to add?
>
> **summarizing**
> To summarize the key points …
>
> **keeping a discussion moving**
> We'd better move on to the next point.
> Let's finish this point and then move on.
>
> Do we all agree that … ?

SKILLS

1 Match the speaker's sentences (1–3) to the functions (a–c).

1 Sorry, but that's not really what we're discussing right now. _____
2 Does anyone have anything to say about this idea? _____
3 I'd just like to recap the key points so far. _____

a asking for input
b keeping the discussion moving / on topic
c summarizing

**PLUS**

2 Complete the conversation with the expressions from the box.

> a Does anyone have anything to say
> b Sorry, but that's not really what we're
> c To summarize the key points

A: (1)_____ : we agree that we want to reduce energy consumption, and we want to consider an alternative energy source. (2)_____ about a solar energy system?

B: I'm more concerned about our water usage.

A: (3)_____ discussing right now.

3  6.8 Listen and check your answers.

Dealing with interruptions and digressions

During a discussion, participants sometimes need to deal with interruptions or digressions from the topic. When speaking firmly to someone, you can still be polite by beginning phrases with *Sorry, but ...* or *Excuse me, but ...* and using expressions such as *Could you possibly ...* and *Would you mind ...* . For example:

Excuse me, but I'd just like to finish this point.
Sorry, but if you give me one more minute, I'm about to finish.
Could you possibly give me one more minute?
Would you mind if I finish this last point?

4 Work with a partner and practise making the sentences more polite.

1 Wait. I haven't finished speaking.
2 I don't understand. Explain.
3 That's off the topic.
4 Stop talking. We can't hear what Tom is saying.

PRONUNCIATION FOR SPEAKING

Using a neutral tone of voice

When you feel excited, upset or angry, your tone of voice can sound argumentative. Maintaining a neutral, relaxed tone of voice can help stop a request for clarification on a point from sounding like a challenge or argument.

5 🔊 6.9 Listen to the sentences. How does the speaker sound? Write *A* (argumentative) or *N* (neutral).

1 Sorry, but could you hold that thought until Abdul has finished, please? __A__
2 Sorry, but could you hold that thought until Abdul has finished, please? __N__
3 So are you saying you're against using solar power? _____
4 Could I just clarify something here? Are we talking about solar power or wind power? _____
5 Do you mean this is completely new technology? _____
6 Could I just clarify something here? Could we even use a solar power system on the roof of the building? _____

6 Work with a partner. Take turns saying the sentences in Exercise 5. Use either a neutral or an argumentative tone. Can your partner guess which tone you're using?

SPEAKING TASK

How can we save energy in our place of work / study?

Work in groups of three or four. Have a meeting using the agenda below. Each student should lead the discussion for one item on the agenda.

Agenda
1 Current problems with energy consumption
2 Possible alternative sources of energy (large-scale ideas)
3 Other ways of reducing consumption (small-scale ideas)
4 Summary and conclusions

PREPARE

1 Discuss the main problems with energy consumption in your place of work / study. Review the table of problems and possible solutions you created in Exercise 3 in Critical thinking. Add any new ideas.

2 Each member of the group picks two or three ideas to raise for each agenda point in the discussion. Work on your own and make notes on the language you might use to raise your point.

3 Make notes on language that you might use to keep the discussion on topic.

4 Refer to the Task checklist below as you prepare for your discussion.

TASK CHECKLIST	✔
Ask for opinions on the topic.	
Use a neutral tone of voice.	
Clarify information.	
Deal with interruptions and digressions from the topic.	
Summarize what's already been discussed.	

DISCUSS

5 Have the discussion. Take turns leading the discussion. Try to agree on a ranking for your solutions and choose the three best ones to implement.

6 Did you come to any conclusions at the end? Why / Why not?

OBJECTIVES REVIEW

1 Check your learning objectives for this unit. Write *3*, *2* or *1* for each objective.

3 = very well   2 = well   1 = not so well

I can ...

watch and understand a video about a South Korean island aiming for zero emissions. _____

understand digressions. _____

understand persuasive techniques. _____

analyze and evaluate problems and solutions. _____

connect ideas. _____

use the passive voice. _____

ask for input in a discussion, summarize and keep a discussion moving _____

deal with interruptions and digressions. _____

participate in a discussion about an energy problem and possible solutions. _____

2 Use the *Unlock* Digital Workbook for more practice with this unit's learning objectives.

UNLOCK ONLINE

WORDLIST		
capacity (n) ⊙	efficient (adj) ⊙	mainland (n) ⊙
challenge (n) ⊙	element (n) ⊙	maintenance (n) ⊙
consistent (adj) ⊙	experimental (adj) ⊙	network (n) ⊙
consumption (n) ⊙	function (n) ⊙	potential (n) ⊙
cycle (n) ⊙	generate (v) ⊙	reservoir (n)
decline (n) ⊙	generation (n) ⊙	source (n) ⊙
drawback (n)	limitation (n) ⊙	volume (n) ⊙

⊙ = high-frequency words in the Cambridge Academic Corpus

LEARNING OBJECTIVES	IN THIS UNIT YOU WILL ...
Watch and listen	watch and understand a video about the African contemporary art market.
Listening skills	infer opinions; distinguish fact from opinion.
Critical thinking	use debate statements and responses; prepare for a debate.
Grammar	use relative clauses.
Speaking skills	express contrasting opinions; restate somebody's point; use language for hedging.
Speaking task	participate in an informal debate.

ART AND DESIGN

UNIT 7

UNL⟲CK YOUR KNOWLEDGE

Work with a partner. Discuss the questions.

1 Do you think the sculpture in this photo is art? Why / Why not?

2 What do you think makes something art?

3 What kind of art is popular in your country? What kind of art do you like?

PLUS

WATCH AND LISTEN

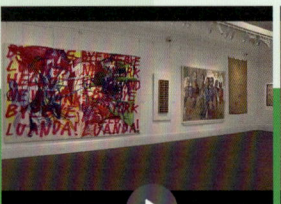   

PREPARING TO WATCH

ACTIVATING YOUR KNOWLEDGE

1 Work with a partner and answer the questions.

1 Who are some famous artists that you are familiar with?
2 What kind of art do they create?
3 What are their most famous works of art?
4 How do you define art?

PREDICTING CONTENT USING VISUALS

2 Look at the art in the pictures from the video. Write two adjectives in the table to describe the art.

picture	adjectives
1	
2	
3	
4	

GLOSSARY

heat up (phr v) become more active

auction house (n) a company that sells art and other items to the person who will pay the highest price

young market (n) the buying or selling of something which people started buying and selling recently

discarded objects (n phr) things that have been thrown away

UNDERSTANDING MAIN IDEAS

3 ▶ Watch the video. Circle the correct answer.

1 Which statement best describes the contemporary African art market?
  a It covers a wide range of media types.
  b It has been very popular for over ten years.
  c It is expensive compared to other art markets.
2 Why did Sotheby's decide to have a contemporary African art auction?
  a African art is more profitable than art from other countries.
  b There is no place for these works of art in their other auctions.
  c There is a growing interest among museums and private buyers.

3 What is the best description of El Anatsui's work?
  a a mix of traditional and modern themes
  b the most popular of the African art works
  c a continuation of his father's work

4 ▶ Watch again. Use the words in the box to complete the summary.

SUMMARIZING

> demand   an auction   collectors
> discarded   contemporary   media

Sotheby's has great confidence in the ¹_____ African Art market. More and more museums and private ²_____ want to buy these works. In response to this ³_____ , Sotheby's held ⁴_____ of 80 works by 60 different African artists. These works of art cover a wide range of ⁵_____ , including painting, sculpture, photography and textiles. The sale was a great success. The most expensive piece, a painting by Irma Stein, sold for £728,750. A textile work by the Ghanaian artist, El Anastui, made from ⁶_____ bottle caps and cans, sold for almost half a million pounds.

5 Work with a partner. Discuss the questions and give reasons for your answers.

MAKING INFERENCES

  1 Why do you think there is increasing interest in contemporary African art?
  2 Do you think that interest will continue to grow?
  3 Irma Stein's painting, *Sunflowers*, looks very different from many of the other pieces in the auction. What might be a reason for that difference?
  4 Do you think there is anything specifically African about these works?

DISCUSSION

6 Discuss the questions with your partner. Compare your answers with another pair.

  1 Would you go to an exhibition of these works? Why / Why not?
  2 Which of the works did you like the best? Why?
  3 Do you prefer traditional works of art or more contemporary work? Why?

LISTENING 1

PREPARING TO LISTEN

1 You are going to listen to a radio report about the work of a graffiti artist. Before you listen, read the sentences and write the words in bold next to the definitions.

1 **Vandalism** is a common crime in this city. A lot of the buildings have been spray-painted, and several cars have broken windows.

2 The artist sees her paintings as a form of **self-expression**. She shows a different part of her personality in every painting.

3 Many artists carefully consider the **composition** of their paintings, especially where people are placed in relation to other objects.

4 The newspaper review contained a lot of **criticism** about the artist's work.

5 Police officers discovered the **identity** of the graffiti artist when he was caught on camera painting on an office building.

6 The journalist will **comment** on the new paintings in the gallery when he writes about them in his next article.

7 Some people believe that all artists have the **right** to paint wherever they want, without being punished.

8 The unusual colours and shapes in the painting showed the artist's **creativity**.

a _____ (n) who someone is; the qualities that make a person different from others

b _____ (n) a person's opportunity to act and be treated in particular ways that the law promises to protect for the benefit of society

c _____ (n) the crime of intentionally damaging property belonging to other people

d _____ (n) how someone expresses their personality, emotions or ideas, especially through art, music or acting

e _____ (v) to express an opinion

f _____ (n) the way that people or things are arranged in a painting or photograph

g _____ (n) the ability to produce original and unusual ideas, or to make something new or imaginative

h _____ (n) the act of saying that something or someone is bad

2 Look at the photo. Discuss the questions in pairs.

graffiti

1 Describe the image. Where do you think it might be found?
2 Who do you think might have painted it? Why?

WHILE LISTENING

3 🔊 7.1 Listen to the radio report. Then answer the questions.

1 Where is this piece of graffiti?
   a at an art gallery
   b on a person's house
   c on an office building
2 What is the reporter trying to learn?
   a people's opinion about the graffiti
   b if graffiti is art or a crime
   c what the laws are regarding graffiti
3 Do these people who are interviewed like the graffiti? Circle *yes* or *no*.
   a Alex   *yes   no*
   b office worker   *yes   no*
   c police officer *yes   no*
   d Simone   *yes   no*
   e Joseph   *yes   no*

4 🔊 7.1 Listen again. Complete the table with the different opinions of each person interviewed.

person	opinions
Alex	
office worker	
police officer	
Simone	
Joseph	

POST-LISTENING

5 Use your notes from Exercise 4 to match the speakers (1–5) to their statements (a–j). Then compare answers with a partner.

1 Alex   3 police officer   5 Joseph
2 office worker   4 Simone

a We remove all graffiti because it's the law. _____
b I don't really like it. It's just graffiti, isn't it? _____
c I just think it's cool – it has a distinctive style. _____
d The people who own this building didn't ask for this, did they? _____
e I think he or she could make a lot of money. _____
f It's something interesting to look at, and it looks good, doesn't it? _____
g I think this type of art is a really good way of expressing your ideas. _____
h The artist is communicating a message about how young people feel. _____
i The colour scheme and the composition work very well together. _____
j I actually really like it, despite the fact that it's illegal. _____

6 Work with a partner. Tell your partner which of the people in Exercise 5 you agree with. Who do you disagree with? Do you have the same opinion as your partner?

Inferring opinions

Sometimes when people speak, they try to sound neutral or conceal their opinion about a topic, usually to appear fair and professional. However, the words and phrases used can often reveal different, more personal opinions.

7 Look at the words each person used to describe the graffiti painter and the graffiti. Answer the questions.

police officer	this artist, very creative, a piece of art, artistic, expressive, artwork, vandalism
reporter	the area's mystery graffiti artist, our illegal painter, this piece of vandalism

1 Which words and phrases in the table have positive connotations?
2 Which words and phrases have negative connotations?
3 Which person do you think likes the painting more? Does this surprise you? Explain.

PRONUNCIATION FOR LISTENING

Stress in word families

Changing the form of a word sometimes changes the stress, too.
Say the stressed syllable in a longer, louder way than the other syllables.
The stressed syllables in these words are underlined.

ap-<u>ply</u> (v)   ap-pli-<u>ca</u>-tion (n)

8  7.2 Listen and underline the stressed syllable in each word. The first two are underlined for you.

verb	noun
1 <u>de</u>-co-rate	de-co-<u>ra</u>-tion
2 com-<u>pose</u>	com-po-<u>si</u>-tion
3 com-mu-ni-cate	com-mu-ni-ca-tion
4 cre-ate	cre-a-tion
5 ex-hib-it	ex-hi-bi-tion
6 re-com-mend	re-com-men-da-tion

noun	adjective
7 ac-tiv-i-ty	ac-tive
8 ar-tist	ar-tis-tic

9 Work with a partner. Practise reading the word pairs from Exercise 8 with the correct stress.

DISCUSSION

10 Work with a partner. Discuss the questions.

1 Is there street art where you live? If so, what do you think of it?
2 Would you like to have street art outside your home? Why / Why not?
3 Do you think street art and graffiti should be illegal? Why / Why not?

PLUS

RELATIVE CLAUSES

GRAMMAR

Relative clauses can define, describe or add extra information about nouns. Most relative clauses begin with a relative pronoun (*who, that, which, whose*) or a relative adverb (*where* or *when*). In the example, the relative pronoun *who* introduces more information about the subject.

(The person) **who painted the graffiti** is very creative.

Use *who* or *that* for people.
The artist **who/that** painted the wall is unknown.

Use *which* or *that* for things or ideas.
The sculpture **which/that** was just placed in the park was created by my cousin.

Use *when* for time.
I went to the gallery on Thursday **when** the new exhibition opened.

Use *where* for places.
The artist is speaking at the university **where** she got her degree in Fine Art.

Use *whose* for possession.
The graffiti artist **whose** name I have forgotten just painted on my wall!

A relative clause must include a verb. When the relative pronoun is the object of the verb, you can omit it from the clause.

She paints in a style **which** is modern and colourful. (*which* is the subject of the verb *be* in the relative clause. It can't be omitted.)

The work (**which**) he is most famous for is hanging in our new gallery. (*which* is the object of the verb *be* in the relative clause. It can be omitted.)

1 Complete the sentences with the correct relative pronoun or adverb in brackets. Underline the noun that each relative clause refers to.

1 Ray Noland, _____ is better known as 'CRO', is a well-known street artist in Chicago. (who / whose / which)

2 The people _____ houses are covered in graffiti are worried about their property values. (who / whose / where)

3 The museum _____ the *Mona Lisa* is displayed is in Paris. (that / which / where)

4 It is sometimes better to visit museums on Mondays _____ fewer tourists are there. (that / where / when)

📱 PLUS

Defining and non-defining relative clauses

Defining relative clauses give *essential* information about the nouns they describe. This information often identifies or distinguishes the noun.

Art **that is painted illegally on city buildings** is called graffiti. (The information identifies a particular type of art – not all types of art.)

My sister **who lives in Bristol** loves street art. (The information distinguishes this sister from others; it implies there is more than one sister.)

Non-defining relative clauses add *extra, non-essential* information about the nouns they describe. In writing, use commas before and after the clause. In speaking, use a short pause before and after the clause.

Graffiti, **which is often painted on city buildings without permission,** is a big topic of debate right now. (The information does not identify the type of graffiti; it gives more information about it.)

My sister, **who lives in Bristol,** loves street art. (The information is extra, non-essential; it also implies the speaker has only one sister.)

You cannot omit the relative pronoun in a non-defining clause.

2 Underline the relative clauses and write D (defining) or ND (non-defining). Discuss why the clauses are defining or non-defining with a partner.

1 The painting *Liberty Leading the People*, <u>which hangs in the Louvre</u>, was painted by Eugène Delacroix. ____ND____

2 The painting includes the figure of Marianne, who represents the victory of the French Republic over the monarchy. _____

3 The painting that Botticelli painted on the walls of the Tuscan Villa Lemmi is located in the same room as Luini's *Adoration of the Magi*. _____

4 Marianne, whose image appears on small stamps and euro coins, is also depicted as a statue at the Place de la République in Paris. _____

5 People who visit the Louvre can use cameras and video recorders, but not flash photography. _____

6 The Louvre is the museum where *The Da Vinci Code* was filmed. _____

3 Complete these sentences using the words or phrases and type of clause in brackets. The first one has been done for you as an example.

1 Art (wall, mural) (D)
 Art that is painted on a wall is called a mural.

2 The Prado museum (in Madrid, a collection of paintings by El Greco) (ND)

_____

3 I like art (bright, colourful) (D)

_____

4 *The Mona Lisa* (Da Vinci painted it around 1503, the Louvre) (ND)

_____

5 Pieces of art (famous, expensive) (D)

_____

4 Answer these questions with a partner. Use relative clauses in your discussions, using the examples as a model.

1 What does a painting need to include for you to consider it beautiful?
A painting which is considered beautiful must be ...

2 Do you like contemporary art or do you prefer classical or more traditional art?
Art which is ...

3 What is a famous piece of art you know? Do you know where it is displayed? What is special about that place?

4 How much money should an artist receive for a piece of work? Do you think artists can earn enough money to make a living from their work?

LISTENING 2

PREPARING TO LISTEN

1 Read the definitions. Complete the sentences with the words in bold.

> **analyze** (v) to study something in a systematic and careful way
> **appreciate** (v) to recognize how good or useful something is
> **display** (v) to show something in a public place
> **focus on** (phr v) to give a lot of attention to one particular person, subject or thing
> **interpret** (v) to describe the meaning of something, often after having examined it in order to do so
> **reject** (v) to refuse to accept or believe something
> **restore** (v) to return something to an earlier condition
> **reveal** (v) to show something that was previously hidden or secret

1 I don't think you fully _____ the talent of the artist. He is much more innovative than you think.

2 We should scientifically _____ the painting to determine its age.

3 I hope the artist's speech will _____ the inspiration for his work.

4 I would proudly _____ the artwork in my gallery.

5 It would be difficult to correctly _____ the symbolism in the painting.

6 I firmly _____ the idea that the graffiti artist is a criminal. That is simply not the case.

7 Some artists work to _____ old or damaged art to its original condition.

8 The artist's name is secret; the gallery owner will _____ the identity at the grand opening.

2 You are going to listen to an informal debate about public art. Before you listen, discuss the questions with a partner.

1 Is it right for local government to spend money on sports and leisure?
2 Should they spend any money on public art?
3 If you were in charge of the budget, which of these areas would you prioritize or make most important? Which do you think are more important for a community? Why?

WHILE LISTENING

3 🔊 7.3 Listen to the informal debate. Take notes on the participants and their opinions.

	opinions
Robert	
Bilal	
Ahmad	
Azra	
Sandra	
Claudia	

4 Tick (✔) the opinions mentioned in the discussion. Use your notes from Exercise 3 to help you.

1 Maintaining the sculpture costs too much money. ☐
2 Public buildings could be sold instead of the sculpture. ☐
3 Art is an important part of any culture. ☐
4 Removing public art could cause big problems in the city. ☐
5 The sculpture is a safety concern. ☐
6 Public art could become a tourist attraction. ☐
7 A private donation has been made that will pay for a leisure centre. ☐
8 A balance needs to exist between leisure activities and public art. ☐

5 🔊 **7.3** Listen to the debate again and complete the notes. Then compare notes in pairs.

Statement 1: Public art is a waste of money.

Response 1.1: Art is an important part of any culture.

Response 1.2: Art can have a very positive effect on people.

Response 1.3: We don't know if we can sell the sculpture.

Decision 1: We need to find out (1)_____ and get an art expert to (2)_____ .

Statement 2: If we don't commission public art, we need to put something in its place.

Response 2.1: Build the leisure centre instead.

Response 2.2: We'd need to (3)_____ .

Decision 2: Let's put together (4)_____ .

Statement 3: The public art causes a public safety issue.

Kids (5)_____ .

Response 3.1: I wonder if it's (6)_____ that's the problem.

Response 3.2: Moving it might solve the problem. It is just costing us money for repairs.

Decision 3: We should consider moving the sculpture to (7)_____ .

Statement 4: What if the city does not commission more art or build the leisure centre?

Response 4.1: The money would be put back into the budget, and we'd have to (8)_____ .

Response 4.2: Our children need to (9)_____ . We need to balance art and leisure in the lives of our children.

Decision 4: We need to (10)_____ in more detail.

Kodomo no Ki (Tree of Children)
by Taro Okamoto, Aoyama, Japan

POST-LISTENING

SKILLS

Distinguishing fact from opinion

A fact is a piece of information that is known to be true. An opinion is an individual's ideas or beliefs about a subject. Ideally, in a debate everyone agrees on the facts so that the debate can focus on opinions.

The identity of world-famous graffiti artist Banksy is a mystery. (fact)
Graffiti ruins the city landscape. (opinion)

6 Are these sentences facts or opinions? Write *F* (fact) or *O* (opinion).

1 The total bill for cleaning and repairs has come to more than £7,000. _____
2 Constantly cleaning and restoring a piece of art is not an appropriate way to spend public money. _____
3 We had 400,000 visitors to our city art gallery and museum last year.
   _____
4 We don't know exactly how much the art is worth. _____
5 We can replace the art with something that will be popular. _____
6 I don't think we'll be able to find anything that everyone likes. _____
7 Kids have been damaging the sculpture almost every night. _____
8 The shopping centre will be a great place to display public art. _____

7 Work with a partner. Write one opinion about each fact.

1 There is graffiti on the sculpture.
   _____

2 Kids climb on the existing sculpture.
   _____

3 The town is building a leisure centre.
   _____

4 Repairing and restoring the sculpture costs thousands of pounds.
   _____

DISCUSSION

8 Work with a partner. Use your notes from Listening 1 and Listening 2 to discuss the following questions.

1 Which places near where you live display public art? What do you think of this artwork? Do you think most people have the same view as you?
2 Why do you think these places have put art on display?
3 Some cities pay artists to paint graffiti on their buildings. What makes this different from the graffiti mentioned in Listening 1?

SYNTHESIZING

SPEAKING

CRITICAL THINKING

At the end of this unit, you are going to do the speaking task below.

▶ Have an informal debate about whether or not public money should be spent on public art.

Debate statements and responses

In a debate, a *statement* is an expression of a position, opinion or suggestion on the topic. A *response* is a reaction to the statement that has been made. Participants in a debate respond to an initial statement and any further responses before a decision can be reached.

 **UNDERSTAND**

1 Look back at Exercise 5 from Listening 2. Notice how the debate is structured. Then match the parts of a debate (1–4) to the sentences from the debate (a–d).

1 Statement
2 Response 1
3 Response 2
4 Decision

a Public money should be used to buy public art.
b I don't think public money should buy art because not everyone likes it.
c Let's put together a proposal.
d You could say that, but I think we could probably find some piece of art that would be popular.

Preparing for a debate

In a debate, you need to be prepared to give reasons and evidence for your position. You will also need to think about how you can prove that the opposing side's reasons are weak or illogical. When you prepare for a debate, be sure to do some research beforehand and take notes on the following:

1. Your statement
   a. Find reasons to support your statement.
   b. Find facts or examples to support your reasons.
2. The opposing statement
   a. Think of reasons that the opposing side may use to support their statement.
   b. Find weaknesses in the opposing side's reasons – facts or examples that weaken or disprove them.

Coming to a debate with well-researched notes will help you remember the information you need to support your statement and weaken the opposing side's position.

2 Work with a partner. Think of four more reasons to support each statement in the table. Write the reasons next to the numbers.

Statement 1: Public money *should* be spent on public art.	Statement 2: Public money *should not* be spent on public art.
1 Public art can attract tourists and boost the local economy.	1 There are more important things to spend public money on, like the police and other emergency services.
2	2
3	3
4	4
5	5

3 Evaluate your reasons from Exercise 2. Decide which statement and reasons you agree with the most. Write the statement as an opinion:

Public money should / should not be spent on public art because

_____ .

This will be the opinion you defend in the speaking task at the end of this unit.

4 With your partner, think of facts and examples to use as evidence to support the reasons you wrote for your statement. Write them in the table.

5 Look back at the reasons you wrote for the opposing statement in Exercise 2. With your partner, think of some facts or examples you could use to weaken or disprove these reasons. Write them in the table.

LANGUAGE FOR DEBATES

Expressing contrasting opinions

In a debate or discussion, people may state opinions that you disagree with. If you want to persuade people that your opinion is correct or that what the other person said is untrue, you can introduce the opposing opinion and then express your own contrasting opinion using the expressions below.

Opinion the speaker disagrees with

At first glance, it looks/seems as if ...　　*It looks like ...*
Many people think (that) ...　　*We take it for granted that ...*
People tend to believe (that) ...　　*Some people say ...*
We assume (that) ...　　*It seems like ...*

People tend to believe that graffiti is a crime.
We assume that photography is just an everyday hobby.
It seems like art is only for the rich and educated.

Speaker's opinion

But in fact, ... / The fact is ...　　*In reality, ...*
However, ...　　*The truth/fact of the matter is ...*
Actually, ...　　*Nevertheless, ...*
But actually, ...　　*Even so, ...*

However, graffiti is a legitimate form of artistic expression.
In reality, photography is a form of fine art like painting or sculpture.
The truth of the matter is anyone can enjoy art, regardless of their financial or educational backgrounds.
At first glance, it looks as if graffiti is on the rise in our city, **but actually**, it is on the decline.

1 Read the example sentence and answer the questions.

This looks like spray painting **but, in fact**, it's a very artistic piece of work.

  1 What does the speaker think of the work?
  2 Which expression in bold signals the opinion that the speaker disagrees with?
  3 Which expression in bold signals the speaker's opinion?

2 Work in pairs. Take turns saying the example sentence in the explanation box, replacing the bold phrases with other phrases from the box.

SKILLS

3 Work in pairs. Take turns giving contrasting opinions. Use the words in brackets to help you.

1 Statement 1: A lot of money is spent on public art.
Statement 2: Only 0.5% of public money is spent on art. (We assume that ... ; but in fact)

We assume that a lot of money is spent on public art, but in fact only 0.5% of public money is spent on art.

2 Statement 1: Public art has no long-term cost.
Statement 2: Cleaning and maintenance need to be considered. (Many people think that ... ; However)

3 Statement 1: The new sculpture is very popular.
Statement 2: A thousand people have signed a petition to have it removed. (It seems like ... ; but actually)

4 Statement 1: The government wasted a lot of money on the sculpture.
Statement 2: It was donated to the city. (It looks like ... ; The fact of the matter is)

SKILLS

Restating somebody's point

In an informal debate or discussion, speakers sometimes restate another person's point, either because they aren't sure they've understood it and they want to clarify it or because they want to call attention to it and argue against it.

4 Read the conversations. Does speaker A feel speaker B is asking for clarification? Write *Y* (Yes) or *N* (No).

1 **A:** I think we should start over again.
B: Start over again? Do you mean reject all three of the applications?
A: No, I think we should consider them all, but let's take a break first. _____

2 **A:** It's clear to me that we shouldn't invest in art right now. We don't have the money.
B: We don't have the money? So what you're saying is that public art isn't important.
A: That's not exactly what I meant; art is important, but there just isn't any money in the budget right now. _____

3 **A:** That painting is nothing but graffiti.
B: Nothing but graffiti? In other words, you don't think it's art.
A: Exactly. Art is in museums, not in public spaces. _____

4 **A:** We can spend £10,000 a year on art for the next three years.
B: £10,000 a year? So, if I understand you correctly, our total artwork budget is £30,000, then?
A: Yes, that's right. _____

5 Work in pairs. Take turns reading the statements below and restating them, either to clarify the statement or argue against it. Use the expressions in Exercise 4 to help you.

1 Pablo Picasso is the greatest artist the world has ever seen.
2 Fashion designers are artists and clothes are works of art.
3 I don't think the government should spend any money on public art.

SKILLS

Language for hedging

Hedging makes speakers sound less direct and more polite when responding to a statement that they do not agree with. Hedging reduces the risk of someone arguing with you because you are weakening your statements. You can add modals like *may, might, can* and *could* for hedging.

A: Public art is a waste of time and money.
B: Well, **I'm not an expert, but** I have heard that some professional psychologists say that art **might** benefit your health.

Speaker B hedges by clearly stating that he or she is not an expert before giving an opinion, and uses the modal *might* to weaken the statement.

Here are some other hedging phrases you can use to make a statement or respond.

Hedges for making a statement	Hedges for responding
Personally, I'm not really sure ...	*You could say that; however, ...*
I'm not an expert, but ...	*That's true in part, but I think ...*
All I know is, ...	*You may be right, but I wonder if ...*
For me, ...	*I see what you're saying, but maybe ...*

PLUS

6 Work with a partner. Look at the opinions and responses in the table. Take turns giving opinions and responding. Use hedging language to make the opinions and responses more polite.

	Student A: opinions	Student B: responses
1	I don't think this picture represents anything important.	I disagree. It gives us something to think about.
2	Making art isn't as important as making money.	I disagree. Making art is an important form of human expression.
3	We shouldn't install this sculpture.	I disagree. It would be very popular with the students.
4	Painting graffiti is a crime.	Not all graffiti-style painting is a crime.

PRONUNCIATION FOR SPEAKING

SKILLS

Stress in hedging language

When using hedging language, the speaker usually stresses two elements in a sentence. One is the expression that acknowledges the other speaker's statement. When a modal is used to acknowledge the other speaker's original opinion, it is usually stressed. The other statement is the speaker's opinion, where often the pronoun *I* or *me* is stressed.

That might be true in part, but I think ...

7 🔊 7.4 Listen to the hedging language. Underline the stressed words or phrases. The first one is done for you.

1 Personally, I'm not really sure ...
2 I'm not an expert, but ...
3 All I know is, ...
4 For me, ...
5 You could say that; however, actually ...
6 That's true in part, but I think ...
7 You may be right, but I wonder if ...
8 I see what you're saying, but maybe ...

8 Work with a partner. Using the phrases from Exercise 7, take turns giving opinions about art (1-4) and responding with hedging language (5-8). Be sure to stress the underlined words.

SPEAKING TASK

Have an informal debate about whether public money should be spent on public art.

PREPARE

1 Look back at the table in Critical thinking. Add any new reasons or evidence. Highlight your three strongest reasons – you will use them during the debate.

2 Look at the reasons and evidence you wrote for the opposing side in Critical thinking. Think of ways to show that you disagree with those ideas. Write sentences using language for expressing contrasting opinions or hedging.

3 Refer to the Task checklist below as you prepare for your debate.

TASK CHECKLIST	✔
Express contrasting opinions.	
Use hedging language while giving opinions and when responding to other people's opinions.	
Restate other speakers' points if relevant.	

PRACTISE

4 Work with a partner who chose the same side as you. Practise giving your statements and reasons.

DISCUSS

5 Work with two people who chose the opposite side. Have the debate. Take notes in the table to help you address other people's points. Could you come to any decisions or identify any next steps in your debate? Why / Why not?

Public money *should* be spent on public art.	Public money *should not* be spent on public art.
1	1
2	2
3	3
Group decision:	

OBJECTIVES REVIEW

1 Check your learning objectives for this unit. Write *3*, *2* or *1* for each objective.

3 = very well   2 = well   1 = not so well

I can ...

watch and understand a video about the African contemporary art market.   _____

infer opinions.   _____

distinguish fact from opinion.   _____

use debate statements and responses.   _____

prepare for a debate.   _____

use relative clauses.   _____

express contrasting opinions.   _____

restate somebody's point.   _____

use language for hedging.   _____

participate in an informal debate.   _____

2 Use the *Unlock* Digital Workbook for more practice with this unit's learning objectives.

WORDLIST		
analyze (v) ⊙	display (v) ⊙	reveal (v) ⊙
appreciate (v) ⊙	focus on (phr v)	right (n) ⊙
comment (v) ⊙	identity (n) ⊙	self-expression (n)
composition (n) ⊙	interpret (v) ⊙	vandalism (n)
creativity (n) ⊙	reject (v) ⊙	
criticism (n) ⊙	restore (v) ⊙	

⊙ = high-frequency words in the Cambridge Academic Corpus

LEARNING OBJECTIVES	IN THIS UNIT YOU WILL ...
Watch and listen	watch and understand a video about a Japanese woman who designed a mobile app at the age of 82.
Listening skill	understand specific observations and generalizations.
Critical thinking	analyze and use data from a line graph.
Grammar	use verbs with infinitives or gerunds.
Speaking skills	reference data in a presentation; explain details and trends in a graph; explain causes and effects.
Speaking task	give a presentation using graphical data.

UNIT 8

AGEING

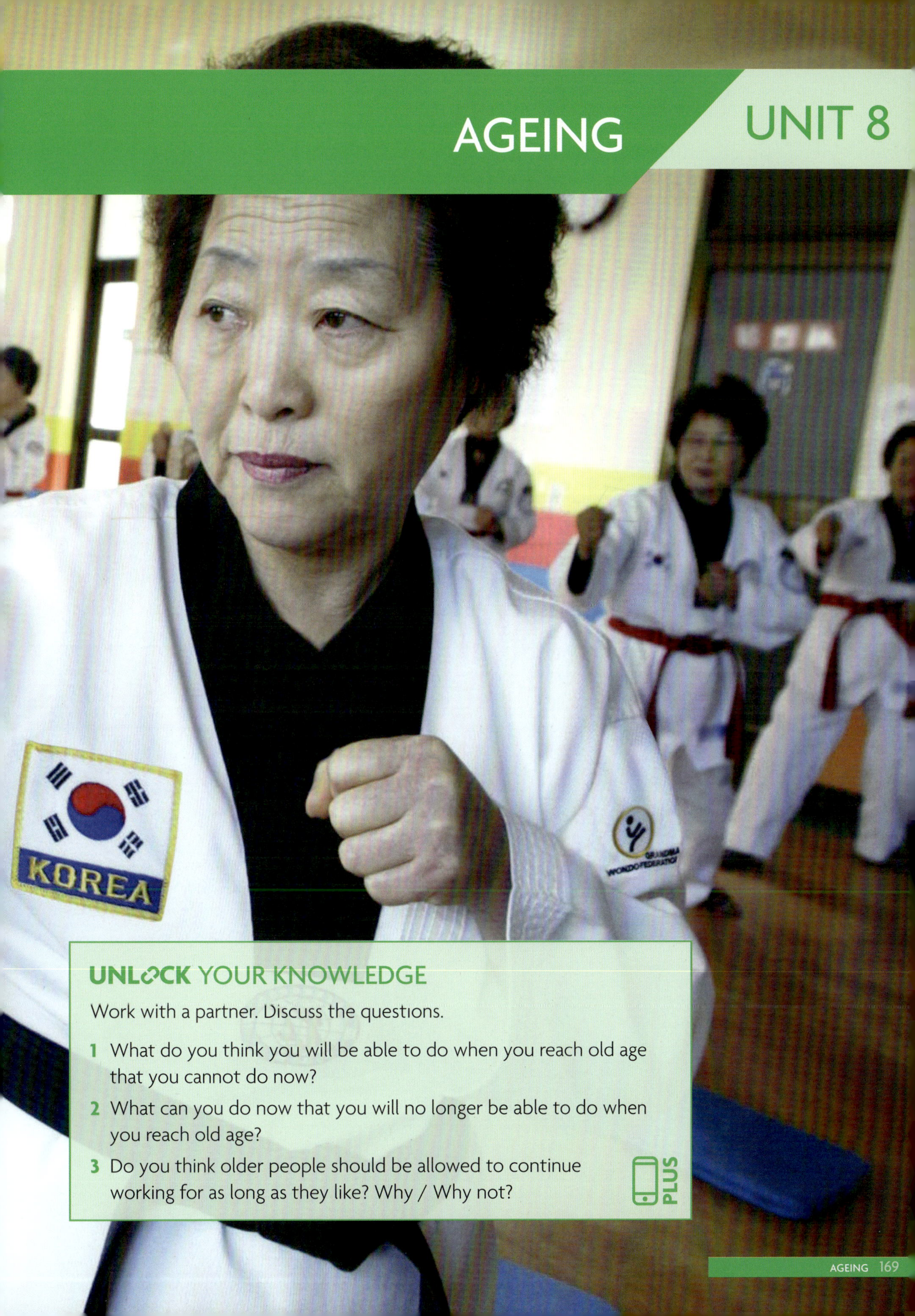

UNLOCK YOUR KNOWLEDGE

Work with a partner. Discuss the questions.

1 What do you think you will be able to do when you reach old age that you cannot do now?
2 What can you do now that you will no longer be able to do when you reach old age?
3 Do you think older people should be allowed to continue working for as long as they like? Why / Why not?

PLUS

WATCH AND LISTEN

PREPARING TO WATCH

ACTIVATING YOUR KNOWLEDGE

1 Work with a partner and answer the questions.

1 What kinds of things do older people do after they retire?
2 Do you think it's good for people to keep working after they retire? Why / Why not?
3 How do the older people you know use new technology? How easy is it for them?
4 Do you like playing computer games or game apps on your smartphone? Why / Why not? Do you think they can be useful? How?

PREDICTING CONTENT USING VISUALS

2 Look at the pictures from the video. Answer the questions.

1 Do you think this woman is retired? Why / Why not?
2 Does she seem comfortable with technology? Give reasons for your answer.
3 What kind of app is shown in the second and third pictures?

GLOSSARY

begin a new chapter (phr) start to do something differently from what you did before

with something in mind (phr) thinking about it

coding language (n) a set of rules, words, etc. that are used for writing computer programs

impressed (adj) feeling admiration or respect

a sense of achievement (phr) a feeling that you have done something difficult or important

WHILE WATCHING

3 ▶ Watch the video. Write *T* (true) or *F* (false) next to the statements. Correct the false statements.

UNDERSTANDING MAIN IDEAS

_____ 1 Wakamiya worked in technology before she retired.

_____ 2 She always enjoyed working with computers.

_____ 3 Designers were not interested in creating games and apps for the elderly.

_____ 4 She taught herself Apple's coding language.

_____ 5 Wakamiya's app uses figures from science fiction.

4 ▶ Watch again. Complete the notes.

UNDERSTANDING DETAIL

Masako Wakamiya worked as a banker until she was [1]_____ years old. After she retired, she took care of [2]_____ . In order to keep her mind active, she [3]_____ . She tried different apps for her smartphone, but one thing that disappointed her was that they were [4]_____ . The app designers she contacted [5]_____ , so she decided to [6]_____ . She designed an app that used figures from [7]_____ in a game. When he saw Wakamiya's app, Tim Cook, the head of Apple, invited her to [8]_____ conference.

5 Work with a partner. Which statements can you infer from the video? Find quotes from the video that support your inferences.

MAKING INFERENCES

1 Masako Wakamiya has not led a traditional life.

2 App designers don't think that the elderly would be a very successful market for their products.

3 Wakamiya earned a lot of money from selling her app.

4 Tim Cook was very impressed with Wakamiya's work.

5 Wakamiya has inspired other older people to create their own apps.

DISCUSSION

6 Discuss the questions with your partner. Compare your answers with another pair.

1 What do you think is most difficult about new technology for elderly people?

2 Do you think elderly people will become more comfortable with technology in the future? Why / Why not?

3 What do you think you will do when you retire?

4 What do you think is the best way to stay active in retirement?

LISTENING

LISTENING 1

USING YOUR KNOWLEDGE

UNDERSTANDING KEY VOCABULARY

PREPARING TO LISTEN

1 You are going to listen to a finance podcast. Before you listen, discuss the questions in a group.

   1 At what age do older people usually stop working in your country? Do you think that is too old, too young or just right? Why?
   2 Do people in your country save money for when they stop working? How do they usually do it?

2 Read the definitions. Complete the sentences with the correct form of the words in bold.

> **asset** (n) something valuable that is owned by a person, a business or an organization
> **dependent** (n) a person who is financially supported by another person
> **ensure** (v) to make something certain to happen
> **generation** (n) all of the people of about the same age within a society or within a particular family
> **pension** (n) a sum of money paid regularly to a person who has stopped working because of old age
> **permit** (v) to allow something; to make something possible
> **property** (n) land and buildings owned by someone
> **retirement** (n) the point at which someone stops working, usually because of having reached a particular age

1 Many people look forward to _____ , when they stop working permanently and have more leisure time.
2 There were three _____ of my family at the party: my grandparents, my parents and me.
3 The management company for the retirement housing complex does not _____ people under the age of 55 to live there.
4 My brother has two _____ – his young son and his baby daughter.
5 One part of a nurse's job at a care home is to _____ that the residents get the medications they need.
6 My father will start receiving his _____ when he becomes 68 years old. The money will help him live comfortably without having to work.
7 Many people decide to buy a home rather than rent because they want to own _____ .
8 My grandparents have considerable _____ in Scotland. Their house is huge, they have an expensive car and they have a lot of sheep.

WHILE LISTENING

3 🔊 **8.1** Listen to the podcast about retirement and the elderly. Tick (✔) the topics discussed. Then compare with a partner.

LISTENING FOR MAIN IDEAS

1 a comparison of past and present retirement ☐
2 the financial and social problems of care for the elderly ☐
3 an example of an enjoyable retirement ☐
4 problems experienced travelling abroad ☐
5 the effects of increased health and fitness ☐
6 the role of pensioners in their grandchildren's lives ☐
7 a prediction about retirement ☐
8 advice on how to save money ☐

4 🔊 **8.1** Listen to the podcast again. Complete the notes with the numbers you hear.

TAKING NOTES ON DETAIL

Spending power of the over-60s in the UK:
Assets as a group – over (1) £_____
Last year – (2)_____ % of all consumer spending
Average married person aged 65–74 spends (3)_____ % of income on food and entertainment
Rick and Nadia Jones:
Retirement age – (4)_____
Value of home – about (5) £_____
Outlook for the next generation:
(6)_____ of parents plan to leave their home, but no money, to their children
(7)_____ % of Europeans 65 and over are still working

POST-LISTENING

SKILLS

Understanding specific observations and generalizations

Specific observations are statements about particular people, things or facts. *Generalizations* are broad statements about the way things usually are. A generalization is much easier to challenge because the evidence that supports it is likely to be less strong. Listening for whether something is a specific observation or a generalization can tell you if it is true only in the case the speaker is referring to, or in a large number of cases.

Pensioners are enjoying their retirement years. (generalization)
Pensioners interviewed at Willow House Retirement Home said they are enjoying their retirement years. (specific observation)

5 Read the sentences and write *S* (specific observation) or *G* (generalization).

1 We both retired at 65. __S__

2 People nowadays don't usually think of their sixties as old. __G__

3 According to one survey, 20 years ago most of today's older people believed they would work in the garden, read and babysit their grandchildren. _____

4 We've managed to save enough money to permit us to live the life we've always wanted. _____

5 Retired people now want to do more exciting things! _____

6 Since we retired, we've travelled a lot and have had years of fun and excitement. _____

7 Today's working generation is probably facing a more difficult retirement than their parents. _____

8 Pensions are getting smaller, many companies are no longer providing pensions at all and the average age of retirement is increasing. _____

PRONUNCIATION FOR LISTENING

SKILLS

Elision and intrusion

When speaking naturally, native speakers do not always pronounce each sound. They connect words, which may cause consonant sounds such as /t/ or /d/ to be dropped. This is called *elision*.

worst job ➝ 'worsjob'   and then ➝ 'anthen'

Native speakers may also join vowels, especially when one word ends with a vowel sound and the next word begins with a vowel sound. This joined vowel sound often sounds like /j/ or /w/. This is called *intrusion*.

go out ➝ go /w/ out   she arrived ➝ she /j/ arrived

6 🔊 8.2 Listen and tick (✔) the correct category for the words in bold.

	vowels joined with /j/	vowels joined with /w/	dropped /d/	dropped /t/
1 ... **and because** they worked hard and saved hard for their retirement, they have plenty of money to spend.				
2 According **to one** survey, 20 years ago most of today's older people believed they would work in the garden, read and babysit their grandchildren.				
3 They **understand that** the money is ours to spend.				
4 They **also understand** that as long as we're in shape and healthy, we might as well enjoy life.				
5 **We are** not planning on selling it, so they'll get that eventually.				
6 I think our parents' generation thought it was really important to save for the **next generation**.				
7 People who have exercised **and eaten** a good diet throughout their lives have plenty of energy to enjoy life, no matter what age they retire at.				

7 Work in pairs. Practise saying the sentences in Exercise 6 using elision and intrusion.

DISCUSSION

8 Work with a partner. Discuss the questions.

1 At what age should children be able to support themselves financially?
2 To what extent should grown children listen to their parents?
3 How can children help their parents as their parents get older?

VERBS WITH INFINITIVES OR GERUNDS

Some verbs can be followed by *to* + infinitive, some verbs can be followed by gerunds (verb + *-ing*) and some verbs can be followed by either.

Verbs followed by *to* + infinitive	Verbs followed by gerunds	Verbs followed by *to* + infinitive or gerunds
advise	avoid	begin
agree	consider	continue
arrange	enjoy	like
force	finish	prefer
manage	practise	hate
need	recommend	love
offer	suggest	start
promise		
refuse		
threaten		
want		

Example of a verb followed by *to* + infinitive:
We live close to our daughter and **offer to babysit** our grandchildren regularly.

After some verbs in active sentences, the object goes before the infinitive.
The government **advised** people **to pay** into a private pension.

Other verbs which follow this pattern are *allow, cause, enable, entitle* and *persuade*.

Example of a verb followed by a gerund:
We'll **consider travelling** after retirement, as we'll have more time.

Example of a verb which can be followed by either an infinitive or a gerund:
Alan **began to think** about when he would retire.
Alan **began thinking** about when he would retire.

GRAMMAR

1 Choose the correct verb forms to complete the sentences.

1 Juliana agreed *to visit / visiting* her grandchildren once a week after she retired.

2 James and Haley recommend *to go / going* to Bangkok to celebrate our retirement.

3 We arranged *to meet / meeting* a financial adviser to make sure we had enough money saved before retirement.

4 We were persuaded *to babysit / babysitting* our grandchildren after we stopped full-time work.

5 When Eric finishes *to work / working*, he is moving to Spain because the weather is warmer.

6 My grandmother enjoys *to garden / gardening* and can spend more time now in the garden than she could before she stopped working.

7 Tomás manages *to save / saving* an extra 100 euros a month; he wants to use the money to buy a house when he retires.

8 Annalise practises *to play / playing* the piano more, now that she is retired.

2 Correct the sentences.

1 We always advise our daughters enjoy life.

_____

2 We want encourage to other people to retire early.

_____

3 We managed for save enough money when we were working.

_____

4 Our friends recommended to spend our savings on a holiday.

_____

5 We refuse for spend our retirement at home.

_____

6 I won't force to my children take care of me.

_____

7 We do not need to delay to retire, because we saved a lot of money when we were working.

_____

8 The financial adviser wants that you work until you are 65 years old.

_____

3 Rewrite the sentences using the verbs in brackets. In some items, more than one answer is possible.

1 My children said they would support me when I'm old. (promise)
   My children promised to support me when I'm old.

2 Trina wanted to move to a new city. (consider)

   _____

3 Her financial consultant said that she should change her pension plan, so she could retire comfortably. (advise)

   _____

4 We would never leave our children without any inheritance. (threaten)

   _____

ACADEMIC VERBS FOR SUPPORT AND ASSISTANCE

4 Match the less formal words (1–8) to the academic words (a–h).

Less formal

1 give	5 help
2 allow	6 make sure
3 work together	7 show
4 give (oneself) to	8 take part

Academic

a permit	e assist
b devote (oneself) to	f cooperate
c contribute	g indicate
d ensure	h participate

5 Complete each sentence below with an academic word from Exercise 4. Sometimes more than one answer is possible.

1 Local care services need to _____ with each other to ensure government standards are met.

2 We should _____ elderly people to choose where they live.

3 The government should _____ that care for the elderly is high quality.

4 Retired people often want to _____ money to their grandchildren's education.

5 Families often _____ older members of the family so they can continue to live independently.

6 Recent statistics _____ that more elderly people now live in retirement homes.

7 People _____ themselves to their children and expect care in return.

8 Elderly people need to be able to _____ in local community activities.

PREPARING TO LISTEN

1 You are going to listen to two students give presentations about ageing in their countries. Before you listen, read the sentences (1–8) and choose the correct definition (a–c) for the words in bold.

1 Some children assume **responsibility** for their elderly parents.
   a the urge to reject someone you have known for a long time
   b the duty to take care of someone or something
   c the role of a young child of elderly parents

2 I want to visit Turkey because that is where my **ancestors** are from.
   a people related to you who lived a long time ago
   b your grandchildren
   c people who are not related to you, but who have a common interest

3 Juan's father is a good **provider**; he works hard to make sure his family has everything they need.
   a someone who takes money for personal use
   b someone who brings money and resources to a family
   c someone who teaches academic subjects

4 My brothers **contribute** half of their monthly salary to the household bills.
   a earn
   b take money away from someone
   c help by providing money or support

5 Residents of the retirement home can **participate** in a variety of activities and social events.
   a avoid taking part in something
   b think about doing something
   c become involved in an activity

6 Many adults **devote** their free time to helping their elderly parents.
   a avoid doing something because it is difficult, time-consuming, etc.
   b use time, energy, etc. for a particular purpose
   c forget to do something important

7 The **institution** where my grandfather lives has excellent nursing care.
   a a place where an organization looks after people for a period of time
   b a block of flats or other large building for accommodation
   c a government building used to help the elderly with specific medical requirements

8 Surveys **indicate** that more and more elderly people are moving into retirement homes.
   a make a false claim
   b keep information a secret from the public
   c show, point or make clear in another way

PLUS

2 Work with a partner. Discuss the questions.

1 What challenges do the elderly face in modern society?
2 What are the advantages of care homes for the elderly?
   The disadvantages?
3 What are the advantages of caring for elderly relatives at home?
   The disadvantages?

3 Compare your answers with another pair.

WHILE LISTENING

4 🔊 8.3 Listen to two students, Mika and Ahmet, give presentations on the situation for elderly people in their countries. Create a T-chart to take notes on the information each student presents.

5 Use your notes from Exercise 4 to answer the questions. Then compare answers with a partner.

1 Where is each speaker from?
   Mika: _____
   Ahmet: _____
2 Who focuses on the changing situation of the elderly? _____
3 Who focuses on how the elderly are cared for? _____
4 What are their main points?
   Mika: _____
   _____
   _____
   _____

   Ahmet: _____
   _____
   _____
   _____

6 🔊 **8.3** Use your notes from Exercise 4 to complete the details in the table. Then listen again to check your answers.

	Mika	Ahmet
country		
population today		
% 65 or older today		
% of households with older people	no information	
expected population in 2050		
expected % age 65 or older in 2050		

POST-LISTENING

7 Work in pairs. Are the situations following the bold words and phrases causes or effects? Write *C* (cause) or *E* (effect).

1 This increase will **result in** more elderly people that need care. _____
2 My grandparents live with us **because** they need more help than when they were younger. _____
3 When older relatives move in, it **leads to** a child's role changing from dependent to caregiver. _____
4 The population increase **stems from** the fact that people are living longer. _____
5 Living closely together **can raise** tensions. _____
6 Moving elderly people into care homes **allows** the younger generation to continue their lives unchanged. _____

DISCUSSION

8 Work with a partner. Use your notes from Listening 1 and 2 to discuss the following questions.

1 How are the elderly cared for in your country?
2 Has the way the elderly are cared for in your country changed in the past 20 years? If so, how? Do you think it will change in the next 20 years? Why / Why not?
3 What will you do after you retire? Who do you think you will live with? What will your lifestyle be like?

CRITICAL THINKING

At the end of this unit, you are going to do the speaking task below.

▶ Give a presentation on how ageing has changed a country's population over time and the impact this is likely to have on its society in the future.

Analyzing and using data from a line graph

When giving a presentation, it is not enough to simply describe data. You must also explain why it is important. For example, when using a line graph, you might talk about changes over time, significant or unusual features or the main data trends.

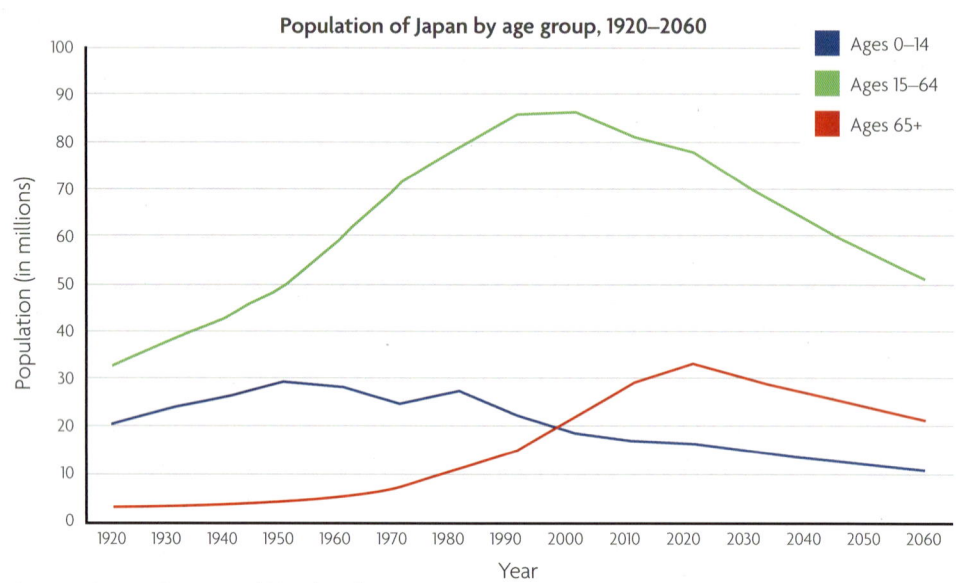

Source: Japan Statistical Yearbook

 **ANALYZE**

1 Look at the line graph. Answer the questions.

1 What was Japan's population over the age of 65 in the year 2010?

2 What was Japan's population under the age of 14 in 2010?

3 What will Japan's population over the age of 65 be in 2050?

4 Which population group will be the largest in 2050?

5 As of 2010, which population group was the lowest and will continue to decrease over time?

2 Look at the graph in Exercise 1 again. What might happen to the populations after 2060? Make three predictions.

Prediction 1: _____

_____

Prediction 2: _____

_____

Prediction 3: _____

_____

3 If your predictions are correct, what implications are there for the government of Japan?

EVALUATE

4 Split into three groups. Each group will look at one country: A, B or C. In your group, look at the graph for your country. Answer the questions and take notes.

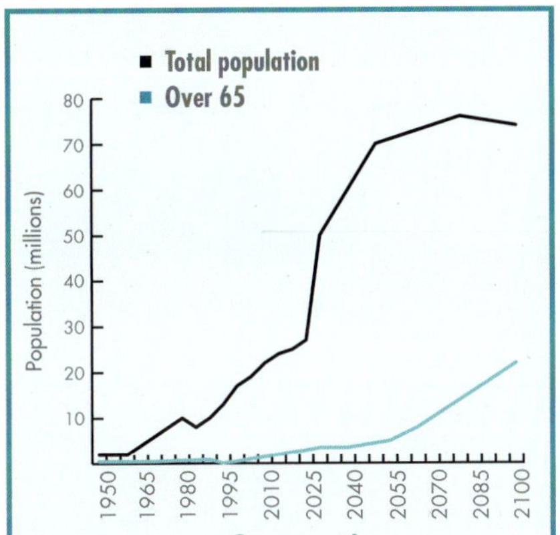

ANALYZE

Country A
Country B 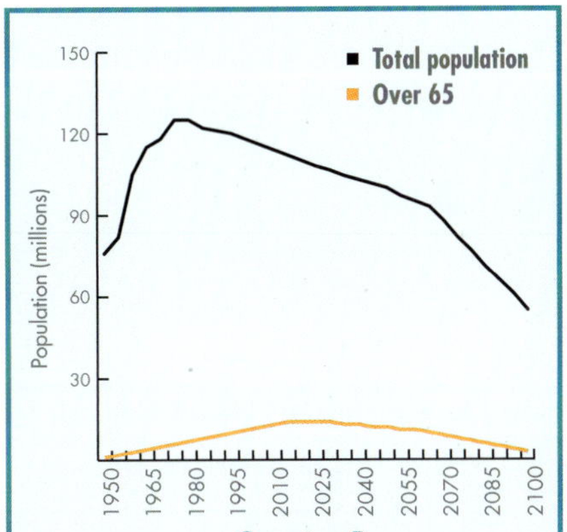
Country C 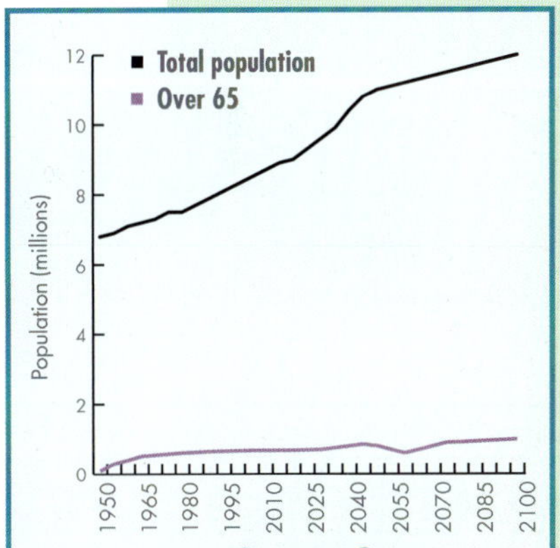

1 What are the main points or trends that your graph shows?

_____

_____

_____

_____

_____

2 Is there a relationship between any of the data in your graph (e.g. cause and effect)?

_____

_____

_____

_____

_____

5 Look at the additional information about your country below. Answer the questions in your group and take notes.

1 How does this information correspond with the data on the graph?

_____

_____

2 Is it supported by the main points that you found?

_____

_____

3 Is it supported by any significant or unusual features in the graph?

_____

_____

Country A

- In country A, many young people have recently begun moving to the city, so rural populations are becoming more elderly.
- At 2%, the percentage of the population aged over 65 is relatively small and almost all elderly people are cared for by their families.
- The government has no plans to provide institutions for elderly people.

Country B

- For people in country B, it is normal for adult children to leave home and live away from their parents.
- Most elderly people are cared for by institutions. This enables younger generations to continue working, knowing they are well-cared for.
- The government provides institutions for elderly people in order to help families who cannot afford to pay for their care.

Country C

- For people in country C, adult children usually settle near their parents so they can take care of them in old age.
- About 30% of elderly people are cared for by institutions.
- Because of a predicted increase in the population aged over 65 in the next 50 years, the government has started a programme to build institutions for elderly people.

6 With your group, make predictions about what might happen to the country's population after 2100.

_____

_____

_____

REFERENCING DATA IN A PRESENTATION

Explaining details and trends in a graph

You can use specific language to explain the types of details and trends shown in a graph. Using these phrases will help the listener understand the data better.

increases	**decreases**	**other movements**
skyrocket / spike	*decrease / fall*	*fluctuate*
peak at	*drop*	*stabilize*
a steady increase	*a steady decrease*	*remain steady*

1 Look at the line graphs. Match the descriptions to the correct country (Y or Z).

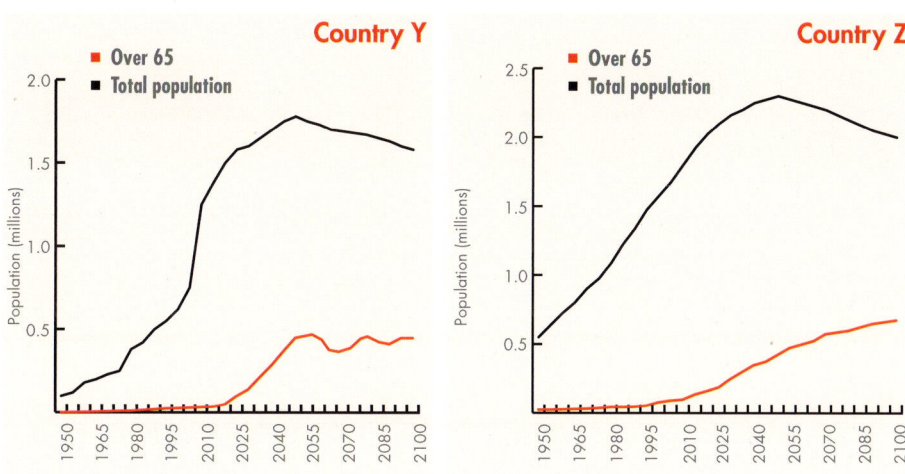

1 As you can see in the graph, between 2010 and 2085, the population of over-65s **will skyrocket** from 100,000 to 700,000 people. _____

2 If you look at the graph, you can see the population **peaks at** 1.78 million people in 2050. _____

3 Between 2055 and 2070, the population of over-65s **is probably going to drop** from 500,000 to 300,000. _____

4 If you look at the data provided, you can see that the growth in population **remains steady** from 1950 to 2050. _____

5 After peaking in 2055, the population of over-65s **will fluctuate and then stabilize** at about 450,000 people. _____

6 After **a steady increase** in population between 2010 and 2050, the population **is predicted to fall** slowly. _____

2 Work with a partner. Look at the phrases in bold in Exercise 1. These are different ways to describe details and trends in a graph. Use these phrases to describe other details and trends you may notice in the graphs.

After an increase in the population over 65, …

Explaining causes and effects

Explaining causes and effects to your audience helps them understand why information is important. Using cause and effect language shows the audience how different pieces of information are connected. Some common cause and effect language is:

was the result of	*was brought about by*
can be traced back to	*was due to*

When you use these words, the listener knows that one thing caused, or was the result of, the other.

*The higher cost of healthcare **was the result of** less government funding.*
*The crisis **was brought about by** a lack of understanding.*
*The older population in our country **can be traced back to** the fact that younger people are not starting families.*
*The decrease in pension plans **was due to** the financial crisis.*

3 Match the sentence halves. Use information from the graphs on page 185.

1 The steady increase in population between 1950 and 2000 was the result of … _____

2 The sharp rise in population between 2005 and 2010 was brought about by … _____

3 The predicted decrease in population from 2050 onwards can be traced back to … _____

4 The number of over-65s will increase steeply after 2020 because of … _____

5 Immigration and improvements in healthcare between 1950 and the present account for … _____

a families deciding to have fewer children today.
b huge improvements in healthcare today.
c a high level of immigration during that period.
d a steady population increase from 22 thousand to over 80 thousand.
e a large number of young people deciding to have children.

4 For each expression (1–4), use phrases from the table below to write cause and effect sentences. More than one answer may be possible.

effect		cause
People living longer	1 was the result of	improvements in medical care.
A population decrease	2 was brought about by	an increase in people over 65.
A population increase	3 can be traced back to	people moving out of the country.
The steady population	4 was due to	the high number of people over 65.

1 <u>People living longer was the result of improvements in medical care.</u>

2 _____

_____

3 _____

_____

4 _____

_____

PRONUNCIATION FOR SPEAKING

SKILLS

Contrastive stress in numbers and comparisons

A speaker comparing numbers usually stresses the numbers and the comparison words to emphasize the importance of the numbers.

By <u>2100</u>, the youth population will make up <u>12%</u> of the country's total population. This figure is <u>significantly higher</u> than the figure of <u>3%</u> predicted for <u>2050</u>.

5 🔊 8.4 Listen to the sentence pairs. Underline the stressed words and numbers. The first one is done for you.

1 <u>Today</u>, the over-65s make up <u>2.5%</u> of Country D's total population. This figure is <u>smaller</u> than the figure of <u>7%</u> for Country E.
2 The population of Country E will be 77 million in 2050. This number is much larger than the figure of 1.4 million for Country D in 2050.
3 By 2050, Country D's population will rise to 1.78 million people. The population for Country E also peaks in 2050 with 9.2 million people.

6 Work with a partner. Practise saying the sentences in Exercise 5 with the underlined words and numbers stressed.

SPEAKING TASK

▶ Give a presentation on how ageing has changed a country's population over time and the impact this is likely to have on its society in the future.

PREPARE

1 Look back at your notes about the country you chose (A, B or C) in Critical thinking. Add any new information.

2 Write notes on the following areas for your talk. Use language from Preparation for speaking to help you.

1 Presenting your data
2 Talking about the causes and effects of your data
3 Making predictions for the future of the country you chose

3 Refer to the Task checklist below as you prepare your presentation.

TASK CHECKLIST	✔
Reference data in your presentation.	
Make predictions based on data.	
Explain causes and effects.	
Use contrastive stress when making comparisons.	

PRACTISE

4 Practise your presentation in your group.

PRESENT

5 Form a new group with people who chose the other two countries. Give your presentation to your new group. Were your presentations similar? Why / Why not?

OBJECTIVES REVIEW

1 Check your learning objectives for this unit. Write *3*, *2* or *1* for each objective.

3 = very well   2 = well   1 = not so well

I can ...

watch and understand a video about a Japanese woman who designed a mobile app at the age of 82. _____

understand specific observations and generalizations. _____

analyze and use data from a line graph. _____

use verbs with infinitives or gerunds. _____

reference data in a presentation. _____

explain details and trends in a graph. _____

explain causes and effects. _____

give a presentation using graphical data. _____

2 Use the *Unlock* Digital Workbook for more practice with this unit's learning objectives.

UNLOCK ONLINE

WORDLIST

ancestor (n) ⊙	devote (v)	pension (n) ⊙
asset (n) ⊙	ensure (v) ⊙	permit (v) ⊙
assist (v) ⊙	generation (n) ⊙	property (n) ⊙
contribute (v) ⊙	indicate (v) ⊙	provider (n)
cooperate (v)	institution (n) ⊙	responsibility (n) ⊙
dependent (n) ⊙	participate (v) ⊙	retirement (n) ⊙

⊙ = high-frequency words in the Cambridge Academic Corpus

GLOSSARY

⊙ = high-frequency words in the Cambridge Academic Corpus

Vocabulary	Pronunciation	Part of speech	Definition
UNIT 1			
consumer ⊙	/kən'sjuːmə/	(n)	someone who buys or uses goods or services
discount ⊙	/'dɪskaʊnt/	(n)	a reduction in price
domestic ⊙	/də'mestɪk/	(adj)	related to a person's own country
goods ⊙	/gʊdz/	(n)	items for sale
greenhouse	/'griːnhaʊs/	(n)	a building used to grow plants that need constant warmth and protection
import ⊙	/ɪm'pɔːt/	(v)	to bring products in from another country to sell or use
investigate ⊙	/ɪn'vestɪgeɪt/	(v)	to carefully examine something, especially to discover the truth about it
labour ⊙	/'leɪbə/	(n)	work
multinational	/ˌmʌlti'næʃənəl/	(adj)	active in several countries
outsourcing	/'aʊtˌsɔːsɪŋ/	(n)	a situation in which a company employs another organization to do some of its work, rather than using its own employees to do it
overseas ⊙	/ˌəʊvə'siːz/	(adv)	in, from, or to other countries
produce ⊙	/'prɒdʒuːs/	(n)	food or any other substance or material that is grown or obtained through farming
produce ⊙	/prə'dʒuːs/	(v)	to create something or bring it into existence
production costs	/prə'dʌkʃən ˌkɒsts/	(n)	the money spent to make something

Vocabulary	Pronunciation	Part of speech	Definition
profit 👁	/'prɒfɪt/	(n)	financial gain
prosperity 👁	/prɒs'perəti/	(n)	the state of being successful and having a lot of money
purchase 👁	/'pɜːtʃəs/	(v)	to buy something
supply chain	/sə'plaɪ ˌtʃeɪn/	(n)	the system of people and things that are involved in getting a product from the place where it is made to the person who buys it
transport 👁	/'trænspɔːt/	(n)	the movement of people or goods from one place to another

UNIT 2

Vocabulary	Pronunciation	Part of speech	Definition
academic 👁	/ˌækə'demɪk/	(adj)	related to subjects that require thinking and studying
acquire 👁	/ə'kwaɪə/	(v)	to get or receive something, or to learn something
adviser	/əd'vaɪzə/	(n)	someone whose job is to give advice about a subject
complex 👁	/'kɒmpleks/	(adj)	involving a lot of different but related parts
internship	/'ɪntɜːnʃɪp/	(n)	a period of time during which someone works for a company or organization in order to get experience of a particular type of work
manual 👁	/'mænjuəl/	(adj)	involving the use of the hands
mechanical 👁	/mə'kænɪkəl/	(adj)	related to machines
medical 👁	/'medɪkəl/	(adj)	relating to the treatment of disease and injury
physical 👁	/'fɪzɪkəl/	(adj)	relating to the body
practical 👁	/'præktɪkəl/	(adj)	relating to experience, real situations or actions rather than to ideas or imagination

Vocabulary	Pronunciation	Part of speech	Definition
professional 𝗢	/prəˈfeʃənəl/	(adj)	relating to a job that needs special education or training
secure 𝗢	/sɪˈkjʊə/	(adj)	dependable; not likely to change
specialist 𝗢	/ˈspeʃəlɪst/	(n)	someone with a lot of skill or experience in a subject
technical 𝗢	/ˈteknɪkəl/	(adj)	relating to the knowledge, machines or methods used in science and industry
understanding 𝗢	/ˌʌndəˈstændɪŋ/	(n)	knowledge about a subject
vocational	/vəʊˈkeɪʃənəl/	(adj)	providing skills and education that prepares you for a specific trade or profession

UNIT 3

aid 𝗢	/eɪd/	(n)	help
antibiotic	/ˌæntibaɪˈɒtɪk/	(n)	a medicine that kills bacteria
clinical 𝗢	/ˈklɪnɪkəl/	(adj)	related to medical treatment and tests
contract 𝗢	/kənˈtrækt/	(v)	to catch or become ill with a disease
controlled 𝗢	/kənˈtrəʊld/	(adj)	limited
data 𝗢	/ˈdeɪtə/	(n)	information or facts about something
factor 𝗢	/ˈfæktə/	(n)	a fact or situation that influences the result of something
in favour of	/ɪn ˈfeɪvər əv/	(adj)	on the side of or in support of
infected 𝗢	/ɪnˈfektɪd/	(adj)	having a disease as a result of organisms such as bacteria or viruses entering the body
occur 𝗢	/əˈkɜː/	(v)	to happen
outbreak 𝗢	/ˈaʊtbreɪk/	(n)	a sudden appearance of something, especially of a disease or something else dangerous or unpleasant

Vocabulary	Pronunciation	Part of speech	Definition
precaution	/prɪˈkɔːʃən/	(n)	an action that is taken to stop something bad from happening
prevention ◉	/prɪˈvenʃən/	(n)	the act of stopping something from happening
prove ◉	/pruːv/	(v)	to show to be true
recover ◉	/rɪˈkʌvə/	(v)	to become completely well again after an illness or injury
researcher ◉	/rɪˈsɜːtʃə/	(n)	a person who studies a subject in detail to discover new information about it
treat ◉	/triːt/	(v)	give medical care to
treatment ◉	/ˈtriːtmənt/	(n)	something that you do to try to cure an illness or injury, especially something suggested by a doctor
trial ◉	/ˈtraɪəl/	(n)	a test to find out how effective or safe something is
urgent	/ˈɜːdʒənt/	(adj)	requiring immediate attention
virus ◉	/ˈvaɪərəs/	(n)	an organism that causes disease

UNIT 4

Vocabulary	Pronunciation	Part of speech	Definition
adapt ◉	/əˈdæpt/	(v)	to adjust to different conditions
affect ◉	/əˈfekt/	(v)	to have an influence on something
coastal ◉	/ˈkəʊstəl/	(adj)	on or related to land by the sea or ocean
conservation ◉	/ˌkɒnsəˈveɪʃən/	(n)	the act of being careful not to waste water, energy, etc.
copper ◉	/ˈkɒpə/	(n)	a reddish-brown metal, used in electrical equipment and for making wires and coins
decline ◉	/dɪˈklaɪn/	(v)	to gradually become less, worse or lower

Vocabulary	Pronunciation	Part of speech	Definition
diamond	/ˈdaɪəmənd/	(n)	a transparent, extremely hard precious stone that is used in jewellery, and in industry for cutting hard things
exploit ◉	/ɪkˈsplɔɪt/	(v)	to use something in a way that helps you (or unfairly for an advantage)
extract ◉	/ɪkˈstrækt/	(v)	to remove or take out something
habitat ◉	/ˈhæbɪtæt/	(n)	the natural surroundings where a plant or animal lives
harsh ◉	/hɑːʃ/	(adj)	severe and unpleasant
impact ◉	/ɪmˈpækt/	(v)	to have an influence on something
impact ◉	/ˈɪmpækt/	(n)	the strong effect something has on a situation or person
mineral ◉	/ˈmɪnərəl/	(n)	a valuable or useful chemical substance that is formed naturally in the ground
mining ◉	/ˈmaɪnɪŋ/	(n)	the industry or activity of removing valuable substances from the earth
modify ◉	/ˈmɒdɪfaɪ/	(v)	to change something, usually to improve it or make it more acceptable
natural gas	/ˈnætʃərəl ˌgæs/	(n)	fuel for heating or cooking that is found underground
occur ◉	/əˈkɜː/	(v)	to happen
survive ◉	/səˈvaɪv/	(v)	to continue to live or exist
waste ◉	/weɪst/	(n)	unwanted substances or material
wilderness	/ˈwɪldənəs/	(n)	a place that is in a completely natural state without houses, industry, roads, etc.

UNIT 5

Vocabulary	Pronunciation	Part of speech	Definition
abandon ◉	/əˈbændən/	(v)	to leave something forever
acquire ◉	/əˈkwaɪə/	(v)	to buy or get something

Vocabulary	Pronunciation	Part of speech	Definition
adequate ⊙	/ˈædəkwət/	(adj)	enough or satisfactory for a specific purpose
ambitious ⊙	/æmˈbɪʃəs/	(adj)	not easily done or achieved
anticipate	/ænˈtɪsɪpeɪt/	(v)	to expect that something will happen
appropriate ⊙	/əˈprəʊpriət/	(adj)	suitable or right for a specific situation or occasion
collapse ⊙	/kəˈlæps/	(v)	to fall down suddenly
concerned ⊙	/kənˈsɜːnd/	(adj)	worried or anxious
contemporary ⊙	/kənˈtempərəri/	(adj)	happening now; modern
contribute ⊙	/kənˈtrɪbjuːt/	(v)	to be one of the reasons why something happens
controversial ⊙	/ˌkɒntrəˈvɜːʃəl/	(adj)	causing a lot of disagreement or argument
convert ⊙	/kənˈvɜːt/	(v)	to change something from one thing to another
existing ⊙	/ɪgˈzɪstɪŋ/	(adj)	that exists or is being used at the present time
expand ⊙	/ɪkˈspænd/	(v)	to increase, or cause to increase, in size, number or importance
feature ⊙	/ˈfiːtʃə/	(n)	a noticeable or important characteristic or part
maintain ⊙	/meɪnˈteɪn/	(v)	to continue to have, or keep in existence
obtain ⊙	/əbˈteɪn/	(v)	to get something, especially by a planned effort
potential ⊙	/pəˈtenʃəl/	(adj)	possible when the necessary conditions exist
sympathetic ⊙	/ˌsɪmpəˈθetɪk/	(adj)	agreeing with or supporting
transform ⊙	/trænsˈfɔːm/	(v)	to completely change the appearance, form or character of something

Vocabulary	Pronunciation	Part of speech	Definition
UNIT 6			
capacity ⊙	/kəˈpæsəti/	(n)	the amount that something can produce or contain; the ability to do something in particular
challenge ⊙	/ˈtʃælɪndʒ/	(n)	something requiring great effort to do successfully
consistent ⊙	/kənˈsɪstənt/	(adj)	always acting in a similar way
consumption ⊙	/kənˈsʌmpʃən/	(n)	the act of using, eating or drinking something
cycle ⊙	/ˈsaɪkəl/	(n)	a set of events that repeat themselves regularly in the same order
decline ⊙	/dɪˈklaɪn/	(n)	a decrease in something
drawback	/ˈdrɔːbæk/	(n)	a disadvantage or negative part of a situation
efficient ⊙	/ɪˈfɪʃənt/	(adj)	producing good results without waste
element ⊙	/ˈelɪmənt/	(n)	one part of something
experimental ⊙	/ɪkˌsperɪˈmentəl/	(adj)	new and not tested
function ⊙	/ˈfʌŋkʃən/	(n)	a role or purpose
generate ⊙	/ˈdʒenəreɪt/	(v)	to produce
generation ⊙	/ˌdʒenəˈreɪʃən/	(n)	the production of energy in a particular form
limitation ⊙	/ˌlɪmɪˈteɪʃən/	(n)	a situation that restricts something
mainland ⊙	/ˈmeɪnlænd/	(n)	the biggest or primary part of a country, not including the islands around it
maintenance ⊙	/ˈmeɪntənəns/	(n)	the work needed to keep something in good condition
network ⊙	/ˈnetwɜːk/	(n)	a system of parts that work together
potential ⊙	/pəˈtenʃəl/	(n)	something's ability to develop, achieve or succeed

Vocabulary	Pronunciation	Part of speech	Definition
reservoir	/ˈrezəvwɑː/	(n)	a natural or artificial lake that stores and supplies water
source ⊙	/sɔːs/	(n)	the origin or place something comes from
volume ⊙	/ˈvɒljuːm/	(n)	the number or amount of something

UNIT 7

Vocabulary	Pronunciation	Part of speech	Definition
analyze ⊙	/ˈænəlaɪz/	(v)	to study something in a systematic and careful way
appreciate ⊙	/əˈpriːʃieɪt/	(v)	to recognize how good or useful something is
comment ⊙	/ˈkɒment/	(v)	to express an opinion
composition ⊙	/ˌkɒmpəˈzɪʃən/	(n)	the way that people or things are arranged in a painting or photograph
creativity ⊙	/ˌkrieɪˈtɪviti/	(n)	the ability to produce original and unusual ideas, or to make something new or imaginative
criticism ⊙	/ˈkrɪtɪsɪzəm/	(n)	the act of saying that something or someone is bad
display ⊙	/dɪˈspleɪ/	(v)	to show something in a public place
focus on	/ˈfəʊkəs ɒn/	(phr v)	to give a lot of attention to one particular person, subject or thing
identity ⊙	/aɪˈdentəti/	(n)	who someone is; the qualities that make a person different from others
interpret ⊙	/ɪnˈtɜːprɪt/	(v)	to describe the meaning of something, often after having examined it in order to do so
reject ⊙	/rɪˈdʒekt/	(v)	to refuse to accept or believe something
restore ⊙	/rɪˈstɔː/	(v)	to return something to an earlier condition

Vocabulary	Pronunciation	Part of speech	Definition
reveal 🔘	/rɪˈviːl/	(v)	to show something that was previously hidden or secret
right 🔘	/raɪt/	(n)	a person's opportunity to act and be treated in particular ways that the law promises to protect for the benefit of society
self-expression	/ˌselfɪkˈspreʃən/	(n)	how someone expresses their personality, emotions or ideas, especially through art, music or acting
vandalism	/ˈvændəlɪzəm/	(n)	the crime of intentionally damaging property belonging to other people

UNIT 8

Vocabulary	Pronunciation	Part of speech	Definition
ancestor 🔘	/ˈænsestə/	(n)	a person related to you who lived a long time ago
asset 🔘	/ˈæset/	(n)	something valuable that is owned by a person, a business or an organization
assist 🔘	/əˈsɪst/	(v)	to help
contribute 🔘	/kənˈtrɪbjuːt/	(v)	to help by providing money or support
cooperate	/kəʊˈɒpəreɪt/	(v)	to work together
dependent 🔘	/dɪˈpendənt/	(n)	a person who is financially supported by another person
devote	/dɪˈvəʊt/	(v)	to use time, energy, etc. for a particular purpose
ensure 🔘	/ɪnˈʃɔː/	(v)	to make something certain to happen
generation 🔘	/ˌdʒenəˈreɪʃən/	(n)	all of the people of about the same age within a society or within a particular family
indicate 🔘	/ˈɪndɪkeɪt/	(v)	to show, point or make clear in another way
institution 🔘	/ˌɪnstɪˈtʃuːʃən/	(n)	a place where an organization looks after people for a period of time

Vocabulary	Pronunciation	Part of speech	Definition
participate 💿	/pɑː'tɪsɪpeɪt/	(v)	become involved in an activity
pension 💿	/'penʃən/	(n)	a sum of money paid regularly to a person who has stopped working because of old age
permit 💿	/pə'mɪt/	(v)	to allow something; to make something possible
property 💿	/'prɒpəti/	(n)	land and buildings owned by someone
provider	/prə'vaɪdə/	(n)	someone who brings money and resources to a family
responsibility 💿	/rɪˌspɒnsɪ'bɪləti/	(n)	the duty to take care of someone or something
retirement 💿	/rɪ'taɪəmənt/	(n)	the point at which someone stops working, usually because of having reached a particular age

VIDEO AND AUDIO SCRIPTS

UNIT 1

▶ **NBA making a play for China**

Commentator: They're on a charm offensive in China. These US basketball stars are opening NBA-sponsored facilities in the southern city of Shenzhen. It's one way for the American league to promote itself as it tries to tap into the vast potential financial rewards on offer.

American interviewee: China is a huge market for the NBA, and I think it is very important to bring games here because when we bring games here it gives people a chance to experience the NBA sort of ... up close and personal, as we say.

Commentator: The Chinese market is worth nearly $150,000,000 in merchandising and broadcast deals, 5% of the NBA's income. Two pre-season matches between the Charlotte Hornets and the LA Clippers here and in Shanghai have caused a ripple amongst fans.

Fan 1:   I've never seen a match live in person. So when I heard they'd be coming to China, I came here because you don't often get a chance like this.

Commentator: Many eyes are on Jeremy Lin, the first Chinese American to play in the sport's top league and a superstar in China and beyond. The Hornets edge this game but in the end, it appears to be as much about building commercial links as preparing for the new season.

Basketball player 1:   An honour to play in the first game er ... ever in Shenzhen er ... we've had an incredible few days here.

Basketball player 2:   We had a terrific time here in Shenzhen, it was er ... just a fabulous city.

Basketball player 1:   It's a great city, and erm ... the passion of, er ... Chinese NBA fans is very, very evident.

Commentator: Basketball's popularity in China seems to be going from strength to strength, and if the fans have their way, the next step could be a regular season NBA game in Asia, rather than just a friendly.

 **1.1**

Host: Today on *The world close up – The 48,000-kilometre fruit salad*. With globalization, the world has become a smaller place. On last week's programme, we talked about how people around the world are watching foreign TV programmes, wearing clothes from other countries and working at companies with several international offices. On this week's programme, let's look at how globalization allows us to taste food from different cultures around the world, without leaving the country. We don't just mean speciality products, like Turkish sweets and Japanese desserts. Think about the regular food products customers are buying every day. Where do they come

from? How do they get to your supermarket? And what is the true <u>environmental cost</u> of your usual shopping list? Our reporter Darren Hayes has gone to a Freshmart in central London to **investigate** this issue and to see just what *countries* customers are putting in their baskets.

Reporter: Hello, I'm here at the Freshmart in central London. There are a lot of healthy **consumers** here, and David Green is one of them. David, can we take a look in your basket? What are you buying today?

David: Mostly fruit and vegetables. I've got <u>a bunch of grapes</u>, some bananas, some <u>kiwis</u>, a small packet of blueberries, tomatoes and a lettuce. I'm making a fruit salad for lunch as I'm trying to eat <u>healthily</u>.

Reporter: I notice on the label that the bananas are from Colombia.

David: Yeah ... so?

Reporter: Do you mind if I check the grapes? Hmmm ... they're from South Africa. The kiwi comes from ... New Zealand and the blueberries are from Argentina. David, did you realize that all of this fruit is **imported** from **overseas**?

David: Well, I guess as it's winter we can't grow these fruits in our country. They *have* to be imported. If they weren't, then how would we get fresh fruit in winter?

Reporter: Good point. The <u>global food industry</u> – and the <u>speed of shipping</u> fresh foods by aeroplane – allows people all over the world to eat a huge variety of fresh fruit and vegetables <u>all year round</u>.

David: It's just more convenient, isn't it? Most of the fruit and vegetables I like, like peppers, oranges, and bananas, grow in hotter climates. A lot of the fruit and veg that grow here in the UK is so boring.

Reporter: It *is* possible to grow fruit and vegetables from hot countries here, but they have to grow in **greenhouses**, which increases production costs. If you look at these tomatoes, which were grown on a local farm, they're almost twice the cost of the tomatoes you have here from Morocco, over 3,500 kilometres away.

David: I'd never pay that for a few tomatoes! Local food can be so expensive. It's not worth it.

Reporter: I know, but <u>cheap food comes at a price</u>. Let's look at the figures. The bananas from Colombia must have travelled more than 8,500 kilometres to reach Freshmart, the grapes from South Africa must have come more than 9,600 kilometres, and the Argentinian blueberries nearly 11,100 kilometres. The kiwi from New Zealand? That must have flown about 18,800 kilometres. So, that's about ... 48,000 kilometres of air travel in one bowl! That's an incredi<u>bly long food supply chain</u>. It's also a <u>huge carbon footprint</u>, which means a huge amount of pollution was **produced** to get this food to the shelves.

When food travels, a lot of carbon dioxide pollution is produced, and most people now believe that carbon dioxide in the air is causing climate change – causing the Earth to get generally warmer.

David: I've never really thought about it that much. What about this lettuce? It's local.

Reporter: Even something that looks like it's local can have a big impact on the environment. It's far cheaper for supermarkets to have several large factories than a lot of small ones all over the country, so food grown around the country is transported to large factories to be packaged and sold. This lettuce may be local, but the farm it came from could have transported it across the country and then put it into this plastic packaging. It's sometimes then transported back to the place it was grown in the first place.

David: So, before arriving at Freshmart, this local lettuce might have travelled …

Reporter: … maybe up to 500 kilometres? You can only really be sure how far something has travelled if you **purchase** it directly from a farm or if you grow it yourself.

David: Wow. I can't believe it. Maybe I should pay the extra money for local food …

Reporter: Thanks for your time, David. A 48,000-kilometre fruit salad that comes from four different countries isn't very expensive for the consumer. But the big question is, what's the true environmental cost of such a well-travelled salad? That's all for today. Thanks for listening to *The world close up.*

1.2

1 … cheap food comes at a price.
2 A 48,000-kilometre fruit salad …
3 … what's the true environmental cost of such a well-travelled salad?

1.3

1 These agricultural products are already going abroad.
2 We grow many kinds of tea on this plantation.
3 The police regularly find illegal imports.
4 The company produced more crops overseas last year.
5 The bananas are timed so that they ripen together
6 Flying the crops causes air pollution.
7 The products pass through customs easily.
8 I want to know why these routes cost more.

1.4

There hasn't been much support from the government over the issue of imported agricultural crops. There are three issues with this. Firstly, nearly a sixth of all imported fruit cannot grow in our climate. Secondly, the state should help our own farmers rather than foreign growers. Finally, we should not fall into the trap of not growing enough food. What would happen if it didn't rain and we were left with a food shortage?

1.5

For my presentation today, I'd like to talk about globalization and the film industry.

What is the first place that comes to mind when you think of films?

When people think about films, they most often think about Hollywood in the United States. Hollywood is in Los Angeles in California. Hollywood was originally an agricultural town founded in the 1850s. It was not until the early 1900s that filmmakers moved to Hollywood. Since then, Hollywood has become more and more famous for its big-budget films.

However, film production is not just an American business, as production companies making films for their **domestic** markets exist all over the world. For example, one of the more famous film industries is Bollywood in India. There are other 'Ollywoods' that make films for their countries, such as Nollywood in Nigeria, Zollywood in Zimbabwe and Ghollywood in Ghana. Pakistan has two: Lollywood is based in Lahore and Kariwood is based in Karachi.

But even Hollywood itself has become more **multinational**. More than 50% of American films had parts that were filmed overseas. More than 25% were completely filmed outside of the United States, making the film industry more and more global.

Next time you watch a film with New York City as the location, you may not be seeing New York at all. Many films that are set in New York are actually not filmed in New York; instead, they are often filmed in Toronto, Canada. The number is so high that Canada is sometimes called 'Hollywood North'. The film industry added nearly two million dollars to that country's economy between April 2014 and March 2015. So, why are so many American films made in Canada? I can give one simple reason: money. Film directors get a big **discount** on **labour**. It is cheaper to pay for labour costs in Canadian dollars than it is to pay for them in the United States. Canada also gives the United States tax credits, making it a great deal for both countries. Look at these statistics. Producers still have to pay for labour costs, which in the past was as much as 35% of the budget. But nowadays producers can get a 16% tax credit, which makes the costs much lower than in the United States. British Columbia offers an extra 18% if producers choose their province for filming. And there's more! Companies can get a 15-to-20% tax break if they create their digital effects in Canada. In order to get this tax credit, one of the two highest-paid actors in the film must be Canadian. Because of this, **profits** increase for both countries!

Are you familiar with the Hollywood film *Titanic*? For that film, a large production set was actually built in Mexico! Since films made in Mexico are considered exports, they are free from some taxes, making Mexico an appealing location for film-makers. And of course, it brings jobs and money to Mexico. Consequently, it is a win-win for both sides!

Another popular area for filming is the Middle East: for example, Hollywood has made films in the United Arab Emirates and Jordan. The reason for the popularity of these countries is similar: tax incentives. In addition to great locations with sun, deserts, water and cities, the United Arab Emirates offers a 30% rebate on **production costs,** and even helps Hollywood organize permits, visas, customs clearance and script approval. Jordan helps producers avoid taxes, such as the VAT or 'Value Added Tax' that is added to **goods** and services that are bought. Therefore, more and more films are being filmed there.

In conclusion, the Hollywood film industry has become more and more globalized. Not only does it bring its films to viewers around the world, it is also bringing jobs and money into countries outside the United States.

🔊 **1.6**

I'd like to talk about where your money goes when you buy a cup of coffee. There has been a lot of discussion in the media recently about fair prices for the people in countries that grow crops like coffee. Many people believe that it's not right that a cup of coffee can cost £3 or more, of which the farmers only get a few pennies. However, others have pointed out that the coffee beans are only one part of the cost of supplying a cup of coffee. They say that the other ingredients, such as milk and sugar, are also a big part of the cost of a cup of coffee. However, I would like to show that in a typical coffee shop the ingredients are only a small part of the overall cost. Let's look at some data. If you consider the information in this chart ...

🔊 **1.7**

This pie chart shows where your money goes when you buy a cup of coffee. Firstly, as you can see, the largest part of the cost is administration, at 26%. That's more than a quarter of the cost per cup. Secondly is labour, which you'll notice accounts for 20% of the cost. Next, tax, profit and rent each make up about 14% of the cost, or a total of 42% of the price of your cup of coffee. Finally, I'd like to draw your attention to the three parts that are related to the product you take away – milk at 6%, the cup, sugar and lid at 4%, and the coffee itself at 2%. Together, they make up 12% of the price you pay.

UNIT 2

▶️ Langton School science programme

Narrator: In the southeast corner of England, near the famous city of Canterbury, is the Simon Langton School. It is certainly no ordinary school. The research conducted by science students at the school ranks up there with work done by scientists at NASA and at CERN, the international atomic physics research facility in Switzerland.

For more than ten years now, the school has ignored the official government science curriculum and engaged students in real research projects that have drawn the attention of the scientific world. Fifty percent of the school's students go on to STEM subjects—that's Science, Technology, Engineering and Maths—at university. Probably their most well-known effort is a physics and astronomy project. Following a visit to CERN in 2007, Langton students designed a device that could detect radiation in space. One of the students describes the project.

Tom Stephenson: Our data is very relevant to NASA because cosmic rays' effects on electronics and technology can cause corruption of data and things in satellites, but also there's aspects to do with astronaut safety.

Narrator: Dr Becky Parker, Head of Physics at Langton, thinks that the study of space can inspire young students and get them excited about a wide range of scientific research. She told us that the students are doing fundamental research while they're at school. Instead of students just learning to pass the exam, she believes that they should be contributing to science, doing science and living science. This is a new approach to science education. And Langton science students are not just studying physics. They are also doing ground-breaking research in the health sciences, with one project looking at the structure of a protein that plays a role in the degenerative nerve disease, MS. They may be the only school with a licence to modify the human genome, the complete set of human DNA. The students are aware of how unusual this experience is.

Christopher Cundy: You look at new drugs and they're always manufactured by pharmaceutical companies and you look at new products and they're always done by big corporations, but this is just, you know, a school.

Narrator: Tom Ziessen of the Wellcome Trust, which helps fund some of these projects, describes the Langton science curriculum in this way.

Tom Ziessen: I think that Langton is inspiring for what they're doing. It's absolutely phenomenal. I mean, they're doing not just real experiments, but they're doing real experiments into things that nobody knows the answer to and that's sort of ... fairly unheard of in schools. I've never heard of another school doing something like that.

2.1

Laura: Hello, I'm Laura. Are you my **adviser**?

Adviser: Yes, Laura. Welcome to the careers office. Good to see you.

Laura: Hello.

Adviser: Now, I saw from your file that you're looking for advice on what to do after you graduate. You're considering going to college, aren't you?

Laura: Yes, that's right. But I'm not really sure which course to apply for.

Adviser: Well, what are you considering?

Laura: I like Maths and Physics, and I'm doing well in those classes.

Adviser: Looking at your file, I couldn't agree more! You should make use of your Maths and Physics abilities. Any ideas about an area of study?

Laura: Well, I'm considering studying Engineering.

Adviser: Ah, Engineering. That's a big field. Well, Engineering jobs are definitely popular. The world will always need engineers! What kind of Engineering are you interested in? Electrical? Civil? Computer?

Laura: I'm not sure. I've always been interested in the way things work, like cars and other machines. I'd like to study something technical, that's for sure. You know, I'm actually really interested in space flight. I'd love to build rockets and spacecraft!

Adviser: Maybe you should consider **Mechanical** Engineering, then. That would be a start anyway. That's a good, basic Engineering degree – it covers the basic subjects. Mechanical engineers often go on to become **specialists** in lots of different areas – Aerospace Engineering is just one of them. It would definitely be a way to use your Maths and Physics skills. You'd also **acquire** some really useful new skills and an in-depth **understanding** of the field.

Laura: Okay, but I'm not sure if that would be for me. An Engineering degree would be very **academic**. I wonder if I should try something more **vocational**. I actually like manual work better. I'd rather make something than write about it! Is it possible to do both? Maybe I could do an **internship** at an Engineering firm. Then maybe I could study later, after I see how the internship goes.

Adviser: Of course, you should consider an internship, but it would be helpful to think about Engineering courses too. Have you done much research on different courses that are available?

Laura: Not yet.

Adviser: I suggest that you try to find out more about Engineering courses. I could give you the names of some universities and colleges that teach Engineering. You could visit them and discuss their courses in detail.

Laura: Yes, that's a good idea. I think I could do that. I'd like to know more about what engineers actually do, and I'd rather talk to someone than just read the information on websites. Thanks.

Adviser: In that case, have you considered talking to some engineers about their work?

Laura: I don't know any engineers.

Adviser: Well, there are several engineering firms that will be attending the careers fair next week. You should definitely attend that. Also, I know that some Engineering graduates will be attending the careers fair as well. I'm sure we could arrange for you to talk with them. You could ask them what their jobs are like.

Laura: That would be great. I really want to know how hands-on Engineering work is. I wouldn't mind the academic side of Engineering, the Maths and the Physics, but I think I'd really enjoy the actual work of Engineering – you know, designing and making things. Computer Engineering could be really interesting.

Adviser: You might want to try contacting a Computer Engineering firm here in the city, then. In fact, I could help you with that. We could probably arrange a visit for you.

Laura: That would be fantastic. Thank you.

 2.2

See script on page 42.

2.3

1 You're considering going to college, aren't you?
2 I like Biology, so I really want to be a doctor.
3 You should consider the subjects you like and the subjects you do well in when choosing a degree course.
4 I'm considering studying Art History.
5 I've always been interested in the way things work.
6 I think I could do that.
7 I wouldn't mind the academic side of Biology …
8 … but I might enjoy the practical side of Linguistics.

2.4

Medical student: Hey, Adam. Come in. Sit down. Want something to drink?

Adam: No, thanks, I'm OK.

Medical student: Have you thought about the **medical** courses I suggested?

Adam: A little. I've done a little research, but I'm having a hard time deciding what I want to do.

Medical student: That's understandable. There's a lot to think about. Is studying medicine the most important consideration for you?

Adam: Yes and no. The most important thing is probably that I do a medical course of some kind, but not necessarily one that involves a lot of study.

Medical student: OK.

Adam: I definitely want a **secure** job after I finish my course; that is important to me. And I really want to help people.

Medical student: What about location? Do you care about where you study?

Adam: Not really. That's probably the least important factor.

Medical student: OK, good. Well, I think we're getting somewhere. You're getting really good marks; maybe you should consider studying to become a doctor.

Adam: I'm not sure about that.

Medical student: Really? Why not?

Adam: Well, I guess another one of my criteria is that the job is very **practical**.

Medical student: Sorry, but I have to disagree. I think being a doctor is a very practical job!

Adam: Yes, but if I choose that option, I'll be studying for so many years and I'd rather not!

Medical student: Maybe you should consider becoming an A & E nurse, working in the Accident and Emergency department.

Adam: I've looked into that. It's a degree course.

Medical student: You don't sound too keen. If you're not too interested in that, what else are you considering?

Adam: It depends. I'm not sure what I can apply to study. There are a few programmes where you can study to become an emergency medical technician – an EMT. They're the people who work on ambulances, assessing patients' conditions, performing emergency procedures, like applying **manual** pressure on someone's wounds after an accident. It also requires some **technical** knowledge of ambulance equipment. It's **professional** and practical.

Medical student: That's a tough job. Exciting, but tough, and very **physical**.

Adam: Yes, but it seems like a great way to really help people when they need it.

Medical student: So, what's the difference between the two courses?

Adam: The EMT course is very practical. When you work in an ambulance, you need a lot of practical skills to help people. You have to be very independent and confident to make decisions on your own, and of course there's the driver training, too!

Medical student: OK, I see your point.

Adam: The A & E nursing course is also practical, but it includes more theoretical work. Especially when you study the core subjects – learning about the human body and about medicine, and so on. It would involve a lot more **complex** study. You have to work closely with hospital staff. It's a degree course.

Medical student: And the EMT course?

Adam: It's a diploma course. So, it would take a lot less time, and I'd be able to start work quickly. It would be great to actually work after so much study. I've been studying my whole life. I'm ready to *do* something, have some adventures, so I'm not too sure about nursing.

Medical student: Yes, I can see that. Continuing with more studying like me isn't for everyone. It may not be the ideal course for you.

Adam: EMTs need in-depth understanding of how to deal with emergencies, and they need the ability to make quick decisions.

Medical student: I think you'd be good at it.

Adam: And if I wanted to continue my training, after working as a basic EMT, I could study to become an EMT specialist. That's another diploma course.

Medical student: But wouldn't you rather study to be a nurse? I imagine the pay would be better.

Adam: You're probably right, but it's not for me. I definitely won't be studying Nursing.

Medical student: Why don't you get some more information about EMT courses, then, and find out which colleges offer that diploma.

Adam: That's a great idea. I am going to make a list of colleges this weekend.

Medical student: I guess you've made a decision, then. You're not going to follow in my footsteps and this time next year you'll probably be working as an EMT – that's pretty exciting!

Adam: I think that's really what I want to do.

🔊 **2.5**

A: I think the most important factor is probably financial need.

B: I'm not sure about that. What if we say that financial need is number two?

C: So, what's number one?

B: I feel it's important to really focus on the applicants' potential contribution to society.

C: I think that's right. Why don't we rank the proposed courses of study according to their contribution to society?

A: OK, I can see your point, but why don't we just say that the interview is number one and financial need is number two?

C/D OK.

B: Wait a minute. I don't agree with that at all. Academic ability is much more important. What if we say that academic score is the most important factor?

A: I think the rest of us are in agreement about the most important factors.

D: Well, I think the least important thing is the student's written application.

C: Sorry, I don't think I agree. They need to be able to write well.

B: Wait! Have you considered looking at the applicants' family situation?

🔊 2.6

1 **A:** Students need to be good at both writing and speaking.
  B: I see. That's understandable.
2 **A:** Hotel workers are important, but doctors save lives.
  B: OK, I see your point.
3 **A:** The Chinese language is becoming more important all the time.
  B: You might be right about that.
4 **A:** Why don't we say doctors have the most important job?
  B: OK, I think we can all agree with that.
5 **A:** Do we all agree that financial need is the most important factor?
  B: Yes. We've made a decision.
6 **A:** Can we agree that academic score is the most important factor?
  B: I think we've come to an agreement.

UNIT 3

▶ **New 'health tablet' gives instant test results**

Commentator: A government-run clinic unlike any other. Set up in a slum on the outskirts of the national capital, it uses technology to bring quality change to the poorest. A hand-held device called a Swasthya, or Health Tablet, is making all the difference. It provides instant results of 33 diagnostic tests including pre-natal screening, diabetes, malaria, hepatitis, typhoid and even HIV. 54-year-old Kussum has a blood sugar test. With results instantly displayed, the doctor prescribes her medicines. What could have taken her a few trips and a couple of days, she walks out within minutes. The device also stores medical records in the cloud for future reference. Three hundred patients are attended to every day. They are mainly the underprivileged, who otherwise would struggle to get basic medical care.

Patient 1: It used to take us up to three days to get tests and results after a number of trips to hospitals and clinics. Here it's all immediately done whilst seeing the doctor. We're very happy and satisfied with the clinic.

Commentator: The government plans to open 1,000 such community clinics, using the same technology. This 400-pound device is the brainchild of Dr Kanov Kahol. A professor at the Arizona State University, he quit and returned to India to create affordable health technologies. With a small team, he is now working on improving and creating other devices that can potentially revolutionize medical care for the masses.

Dr Kanov Kahol: Most innovations are made for the top one percent of the world, right? And then they somehow trickle down to the bottom billion, and I was very interested in reversing that pyramid. I said, why don't we actually start making innovations for the bottom billion? Because they will have to work in conditions and environments that are not necessarily very friendly, but once you get it to work there, it can always go ahead and work for across the world.

Commentator: India spends less than 1.5% of its GDP on public health, one of the lowest in the world. Every year millions of Indians are pushed into poverty due to medical cost. In an overburdened and creaking health system, new technologies may just be the cure.

🔊 3.1

Teacher: Throughout history, there have been many pandemics around the world: measles, malaria, cholera, the flu. So how does a common disease turn from an **outbreak** into a pandemic? Any ideas?

Student 1: People's general health and how close they live to each other can be major **factors** in the spread of disease, can't they?

Student 2: Yes, so governments need to make sure people are in good health and have good living conditions to stop diseases from spreading.

Teacher: Well, that's a good idea, but there's a limit to what governments can do, especially in times of economic difficulty.

Student 2: And governments don't always have the power to say exactly how everyone should live.

Teacher: So what factors do you think would make a country at a high risk for a pandemic?

Student 3: Well, countries with large populations are probably at risk, especially where large numbers of people live close together.

Student 1: And countries which a lot of international travellers pass through, like the UK and other countries in dark and medium blue on the map.

Teacher: That's right. The countries most at risk of a pandemic these days are wealthier countries like the UK, South Korea, the Netherlands and Germany. What do those countries have in common?

Student 2: They're not all large countries, but they do all have large cities with big populations.

Student 1: And they're all places where a lot of international travellers might go. They have a lot of busy airports and potentially thousands of people coming in every day, from all over the world.

Teacher: Correct. If you look at those countries in light blue, they're at a medium or low risk for a pandemic because they have less dense populations, less international travel, fewer borders, etc. OK, so imagine you're an adviser to your government. You want to protect your country from a pandemic. What should you do?

Student 1: You should give everyone a vaccine.

Teacher: A vaccine. OK, good idea. Can anyone explain what that is?

Student 2: It's a kind of medicine, isn't it?

Teacher: Yes, sort of. Most medicines are given to patients after they develop an illness, to help them **recover**, but a vaccine is different. A vaccine provides disease **prevention**. If people have the flu vaccine, they often don't become **infected**. So if we wanted to avoid pandemics, then governments would need to implement vaccination programmes for common diseases, wouldn't they?

Student 3: The government should force everyone to have vaccines. They should give a vaccine to people as soon as an outbreak **occurs**, because prevention is generally much easier than **treatment**. When governments focus on the prevention of disease, pandemics become very rare.

Student 2: I'm not sure I agree. The trouble is, organisms that cause disease, like bacteria or viruses, change every year. So a vaccine that worked really well last year may not be effective this year.

Student 1: There's another thing to consider too; a lot of people don't want to have a vaccine that might not work. The government can't force people to have a vaccine, can it?

Teacher: Well, I don't think any governments do, but in the event of a pandemic, they definitely encourage people to have it, and a lot of people do. People don't want to **contract** a disease, do they? So, other than vaccination, what other ways are there of stopping the spread of disease?

Student 1: International travel is a big risk to a disease spreading quickly. We shouldn't allow people with diseases into the country.

Student 3: I'm not sure I agree. The trouble is most people spread diseases before they even know they have them.

Student 2: And there's another problem. How could people prove whether or not they have diseases? It would be impossible to set up a system for checking it.

Student 1: During a pandemic, we should stop all flights from countries that are affected, shouldn't we? If we don't let people into the country, then the disease won't get here.

Student 2: But there's another side to that argument. People travel all the time for business. It would have a terrible effect on the economy, wouldn't it?

Student 3: But also, in most countries, people who live near a border travel back and forth across it, sometimes every day. If countries stopped people from travelling, a lot of people could lose their jobs. It could also separate families.

Teacher: Well, those are some really interesting views from all of you. Can anyone think of some simpler suggestions for decreasing the risk of pandemics, then? Perhaps not as large scale as closing down country borders?

Student 1: Well, people who have the flu should stay at home from school or from work, shouldn't they?

🔊 **3.2**

1 So this is a very serious disease, isn't it?
2 So this is a very serious disease, isn't it?
3 It's a kind of medicine, isn't it?
4 Governments would need to implement vaccination programmes for common diseases, wouldn't they?
5 The government can't force people to have a vaccine, can it?
6 People don't want to contract a disease, do they?
7 During a pandemic, we should stop all flights from countries that are affected, shouldn't we?
8 People who have the flu should stay at home from school or from work, shouldn't they?

🔊 **3.3**

1 A lot of people don't want to have a vaccine that might not work. The government can't force people to have a vaccine, can it?
2 During a pandemic, we should stop all flights from countries that are affected, shouldn't we?
3 People travel all the time for business. It would have a terrible effect on the economy, wouldn't it?

🔊 **3.4**

Host: Flu season is here, but experts and the public are divided on the subject of vaccination. Those **in favour of** the flu vaccine say that it may help you avoid getting ill and may also help stop the spread of the disease. They point out that this may save lives. Those experts against the flu vaccine argue that there is no proof that it works. Some go so far as to say that it may be unsafe because it is produced very quickly, though there is no evidence to support this claim. The fact is that there is no research or **clinical** evidence to show that either side is correct. As the debate continues, statistics show that only about 30% of us choose to have the flu vaccine each year.

🔊 **3.5**

Host: Since the news that this year's flu vaccine is ready, the government has advised that the old, the young and people with medical problems be vaccinated. However, not everyone thinks vaccination is a good idea. According to NHS England, less than 50% of those eligible to have the flu vaccine – most people except for the very young and very old – got the flu vaccine as a **precaution** last year. That means over 50% did not get vaccinated. Of that 50%, some are actively against the flu vaccine.

In today's debate, we'll begin with flu expert Dr Sandra Smith, who is in favour of flu vaccination. After that, we'll hear from alternative medicine practitioner Mark Li, who is against flu vaccination.

Dr Smith will now begin. Dr Smith?

Dr Smith: Thank you. Well, influenza, or the flu, is a respiratory disease that can make you feel extremely ill. Most people who get the flu recover after several days. While they may feel terrible, there are usually no long-lasting problems. However, the flu can cause severe illness or worse for a small percentage of the people who get it. It may not sound like a lot, but actually this is hundreds of thousands of people around the world each year. It can be especially serious for the very old and the very young. Obviously, we want to do everything in our power to stop the infection from spreading. This brings us to vaccination. When people get vaccinated, less flu can spread through the population.

Vaccines have saved millions of lives. They're a proven method of disease prevention. Scientists have been developing flu vaccines from the 1930s up to today, so we have a lot of experience with them. **Researchers** make new flu vaccines every year, based on the previous year's flu virus. The World Health Organization recommends that children between the ages of six months and five years, people over 65, pregnant women and anyone who already has a serious illness should have the flu vaccine. They also recommend vaccinations for healthcare workers.

To finish up, let me say this: I'm a flu specialist. I research the virus and work closely with flu patients all the time, so I'm constantly around the virus. I've had the vaccine. All of my colleagues have had the vaccine. None of us have caught the flu. If we hadn't had the vaccine, we could have caught the flu each year. There's no guarantee that vaccination will prevent you from getting the flu, but it won't hurt you, and there's a chance it could save your life. How would you feel if someone in your family did not have the vaccine and then became really ill?

Host: We'll now have the statement against vaccination from Mark Li.

Mark Li: Thank you, and thank you, Dr Smith. Let me start by saying that I'm not against all vaccines. Dr Smith is absolutely right that many vaccines work very well and that millions of lives have been saved by vaccination. There's plenty of good scientific **data** that **proves** that. If scientists hadn't developed the polio vaccine, the world would be very different today. But let me ask you this: has the flu vaccine been properly tested? Have there been proper clinical **trials** to prove

that it works, that it stops infection? Does it really provide prevention of the disease?

For most medicines, the government makes sure that proper tests are carried out, but this isn't the case with the flu vaccine. There isn't one single scientific study that proves that this year's flu vaccine works. The packaging on this flu vaccine clearly states that 'No **controlled** trials have been performed that demonstrate that this vaccine causes a reduction in influenza'. It's here in black and white.

If it says on the package that there's no proof that it's an effective prevention, why are we using it? Yes, vaccination can be good, but flu vaccination is just a big experiment, and it may actually be doing more harm than good. If it were proven, then I would consider it.

Host: Thank you, Mr Li. Dr Smith, do you have anything to add?

Dr Smith: Thank you. You make some interesting points, Mr Li. It's true that when the flu emerges every year, it's a bit different than the year before. When making a vaccine, researchers have to try to figure out how the flu is going to change and adjust it to the new virus. If we waited until the new virus emerges, it would be too late.

So while Mr Li is right – we don't do clinical trials of the flu vaccine in the way that we do trials for other medicines – that doesn't mean we aren't scientific in our methods. I'd definitely like to challenge the idea that there's no scientific basis for our work. I disagree with Mr Li on that point. Let me tell you more about my work in that area.

We can prove in the laboratory that vaccines can reduce the risk of getting a disease, generally. What we don't know is exactly how this year's flu virus will change, but we can use our experience to make a prediction. As for the question of the vaccine being dangerous: it doesn't contain a live virus, so you definitely can't get the flu from the vaccine. If people are vaccinated and then happen to become ill, that doesn't logically mean the vaccine caused the illness. They were most likely in contact with the virus before they were vaccinated.

Mark Li: Well, I'm sure Dr Smith is a very good doctor, but I think the flu vaccine package I mentioned earlier is clear. It's obvious that the vaccine hasn't been properly tested.

The other big concern, of course, is safety. A lot of us believe that the vaccine actually causes people to become ill rather than making them well – so she and I disagree on that point. I'm talking about side effects. Some people have become really ill after being vaccinated. This can be anything from headaches to stomach problems. Do you really want to use a medicine that might make you ill? Supposing you gave your children the vaccine and it made them worse rather than better? Some people also believe that the vaccine may give you the flu, rather than stopping you from catching it. I've had patients who were healthy, then had the flu vaccine and became ill. Medicines shouldn't make us ill. That's why I'm against the flu vaccine, and that's why I don't think anyone at all should have it.

Host: Thank you both.

UNIT 4

▶ **Cloning endangered species**

Reporter: They are called bantengs, and although one of the week-old calves just died, the fact that they were born at all could put scientists one step closer to saving some endangered species. The animals were cloned from the frozen skin cells of a banteng which died 23 years ago.

Man: I'm rather still astounded by the fact that you can take the nucleus of a cell and produce a living animal.

Reporter: It's called *nuclear cell transfer*, injecting the banteng's genetic material into the egg of a living cow. It's been done before with an endangered animal called a gaur. It died in just two days. The banteng was euthanized after developing complications from the cloning. While the news of the birth is astonishing, it also worries some conservationists.

Conservationist: If you don't deal with protecting habitat and dealing with all the root causes of endangerment, it doesn't matter how many animals you are able to produce in the lab and try to sort of fling back into the wild, they're going to face the same fate as their wild counterparts.

Reporter: The scientists at Advanced Cell Technology in Massachusetts, where both the banteng and gaur were cloned, agree to some extent.

Scientist: However, it doesn't make much sense to preserve the habitat if you don't have any animals to preserve.

Reporter: If you're wondering, 'Can this technology be used to clone extinct animals like the mammoth?', hold on. Since cloning needs preserved animal tissue, bringing back the dinosaurs remains the stuff of science fiction, for now.

🔊 **4.1**

Planet Earth is dynamic and always changing. Just 10,000 years ago, about half of the planet was covered in ice. Today this is around 10%, as the Earth has been warming since that time. Part of this environmental change is due to natural, rather than human, causes.

Sometimes, natural forces can destroy the environment. In 1991, a volcano in the Philippines erupted and killed many people and animals. It destroyed around 800 square kilometres of farmland and a huge area of forest. It also caused severe floods when rivers were blocked with volcanic ash.

However, humans are also responsible for a lot of habitat destruction. There were originally more than 16 million square kilometres of rainforest worldwide. Only nine million remain today, and deforestation is occurring at a rate of approximately 160,000 square metres per year. In Europe, only about 15% of land hasn't been **modified** by humans.

In some places, **habitats** haven't been destroyed, but they have been broken into parts, for example, separated by roads. This is called fragmentation. If animals are used to moving around throughout the year and a road is built through the middle of their habitat, fragmentation can cause serious problems.

Humans haven't only affected the land and its animals; they have also affected the sea. Pollution from **coastal** cities has damaged the ocean environment and destroyed the habitat of fish and other sea life.

Habitat destruction hasn't been bad news for all animals. In fact, some species have **adapted** extremely well to living closely with people and benefit from living near them.

In Africa and Asia, monkeys live in cities alongside people and **exploit** the human environment by stealing food or eating things that humans have thrown away. In Singapore, the 1,500 wild monkeys that live in and around the city have become a tourist attraction.

In Australia, Europe, Japan and North America, foxes live in urban areas, even big cities such as London. They have different diets, depending on their environment; they survive in the city by eating a wide variety of things, from rubbish out of bins to insects and wild birds. Not everyone welcomes the foxes; they sometimes enter people's homes to steal food and they occasionally bite people. Likewise, police in India recently spotted several young leopards in the streets of Mumbai. The leopards had moved into the city from the nearby forests. One expert said that the surprising thing was that leopards had been in the city for a long time, but people rarely saw them. Leopards are very secretive, and they prefer not to be seen.

One other animal that is as at home in the city as in the countryside is the raccoon. In fact, raccoons are so at home in the city that the number of city raccoons has increased. Raccoons have different diets depending on their environment. Common foods include fruit, plants, nuts and rodents. Much like the foxes of London, raccoons living in the city are known to eat rubbish out of bins, steal food from people's homes and occasionally bite people.

We tend to think of human activity as always having a negative **impact** on the environment. However, some people feel that we can have a positive impact, too.

Conservation means trying to save habitats. Ecotourism is an approach to travel and holidays where people visit natural areas such as rainforests, except rather than destroy the environment, they help preserve it. Visitors to the La Selva Amazon Eco Lodge in Ecuador watch and learn about local wildlife, visit tribes who live in the forest, and stay in an environmentally friendly hotel. Their presence doesn't damage the local environment, and most guests leave the hotel as conservationists. When they experience the beauty of nature firsthand, they feel strongly that they want to protect and preserve it.

Not everyone feels that ecotourism is actually helping the environment. Tourists who travel long distances by aeroplane create pollution, as do resorts, which use local resources such as fresh water and produce **waste** that creates pollution in the local environment.

🔊 4.2

See script on page 88.

🔊 4.3

See script on page 88.

🔊 4.4

Before she wrote her influential book *Silent Spring* in 1962, Rachel Carson had spent years working for the US government at environmental agencies like the US Bureau of Fisheries and the US Fish and Wildlife Service. During her time there, she did her own personal research and writing. By 1955, Carson had already published several books on environmental research when she began to do research full-time. One subject that she was particularly interested in was the effects of pesticides on the environment and on human health. During World War II, the government used the pesticide DDT to protect people against diseases caused by pests. After the war, farmers sprayed large amounts of DDT into the air to protect their crops. Carson had heard that the chemical was making people ill with cancer and was causing animals to die, so she decided to do scientific research on the subject and publish it as a book, to warn people about the risks. After Carson had released *Silent Spring*, the pesticide industry attacked her for her research. However, the US government responded by banning the use of DDT in the United States. Soon her book was translated into several languages and was published around the world.

🔊 4.5

The topic of my talk is the decline and destruction of the world's deserts. First, I'm going to talk about the desert environment and wildlife. Then we'll look at the threats to this environment. Finally, we'll talk about what is being done to save the world's deserts.

Let's begin by looking at some background information from the United Nations Environment Programme. The United Nations reports in *Global Deserts Outlook* that the Earth's deserts cover about 33.7 million square kilometres, or about 25% of the Earth's surface. Deserts are home to 500 million people, or about 8% of the world's population but, as I'll explain, people all over the world rely on things that come from this environment.

Humans have learned to exploit the resources of the desert for survival and profit by adapting their behaviour, culture and technology to its **harsh** environment. To give you an example, tribes such as the Topnaar in southwest Africa are known for their ability to survive in deserts due to their use of local plants and animals for food, medicine and clothing. They have an understanding of the natural world. The Bedouins, who live from North Africa to the Syrian deserts, are skilled at using animals to provide transport, food and clothing and also at growing basic foods around desert rivers. The Topnaar and the Bedouins are just two examples of people who live in and rely on the desert environment for the things they need. However, city dwellers benefit from the desert, too.

Certain **minerals** are commonly found in deserts, which provide a large portion of the world's **diamonds**, together with **copper**, gold and other metals. They are a major source of oil and **natural gas**, too. These desert products are used by industries and people all over the world every day. So what I'm saying is that even though most people may not live in a desert, we are affected by changes to this desert environment.

Agricultural products are also grown in deserts and exported around the world. Because the climate is warm and land tends to be inexpensive, desert countries are able to grow and sell food all year. A good example of this is Egyptian cotton, famous all over the world. New methods of irrigation are being developed so that desert agricultural systems can use water more efficiently. So we can see that deserts are important, not only for the people who live in them, but for everyone who uses products that come from a desert environment. That's all I have to say on that point.

Moving on now to the typical desert environment. In summer, the ground surface temperature in most deserts reaches 80 degrees Celsius, and there is very little rain. Despite these harsh conditions, a wide variety of plants and animals live in and are supported by this environment. For example, there are reportedly over 2,200 different plant species in the desert regions of Saudi Arabia, based on research from King Saud University.

Small plants are especially important in a desert environment because they hold the soil in place, which allows larger plants to grow. Acacia trees can grow well in extremely hot, dry conditions, but the seeds need stable soil to begin growing. Smaller plants, therefore, help the larger ones and in this way, all desert plants help hold the dry soil in place, which helps to reduce dust storms.

Deserts are also an important animal habitat. One of the best known desert animals in the Arabian Peninsula is the Arabian oryx, which weighs about 70 kilograms and is about one metre tall. It rests during the heat of the day and searches for food and water when temperatures are cooler. Experts say that the oryx can sense rain and move towards it.

These examples show that the desert is an ecosystem that supports a variety of important plant and animal life. The problem is that human activity is affecting modern deserts all over the world. According to the United Nations, traditional ways of life are changing as human activities such as cattle ranching, farming and large-scale tourism grow. The process of bringing water into the desert to grow plants is making the soil too salty. The construction of dams for power generation and water supply and an increase in **mining** have also begun to have a greater impact on the desert. Owing to the destruction of desert plants, dust storms are more likely and desert animals, therefore, have less food to eat. Data from the United Nations shows that every year nearly 2% of healthy desert disappears. Today, more than 50% of the world's desert habitats are untouched **wilderness**, but by 2050, it may be as low as 31%.

If we lose the world's deserts, we lose everything I spoke about in the first part of my talk. The Topnaar and Bedouin way of life will certainly disappear, but what does this mean for the rest of the world? Well, everyone on Earth will experience an increase of dust and dirt in the air as desert plants die. If desert soil becomes too salty to grow plants, we'll also lose a valuable source of food, and I'm talking about foods that we all eat. If we allow deserts to be destroyed, life all over the Earth will change. To put it another way, we will all be affected. Now, the big question is, what is being done about the destruction of deserts?

The United Nations Environment Programme offers two main solutions. First, we can begin to manage desert resources carefully, instead of abusing them. This means using the desert for things we need, as well as not damaging it further. It might mean not allowing activities such as raising cattle in certain areas. It would mean carefully controlling the way we use water. Secondly, we can apply technological solutions. The UN gives the example of using the latest computer technology to help forecast how climate change will affect deserts, and using that information to prepare for these changes.

We can also make better use of two resources freely available in the desert: the wind and the sun. These can be used to provide clean energy on a fairly small scale within existing desert cities. According to a blog called *A Smarter Planet*, scientists in Saudi Arabia are already using solar energy to produce fresh water in the desert for agricultural use.

To summarize, deserts are not only important to the people who live in them, but to plants, animals and people everywhere, from the Bedouin tribes to city dwellers. Human activity is causing the destruction of desert habitats, but there are ways in which we can help to stop this.

UNIT 5

▶ **The skyscraper**

New York City may have made them famous, but skyscrapers were born in Chicago, Illinois. A terrible fire in 1871 made it possible for architects to experiment with new building techniques that would allow them to make buildings taller than ever before. These stately brown-stone buildings are some of the world's first skyscrapers.

Louis Sullivan, known as the father of the skyscraper, lived and worked in Chicago. This is his Auditorium Building on Michigan Avenue, completed in 1889. Sullivan believed that the new social and economic strength of the United States required a new architecture. And his idea that tall buildings represent power is still popular 125 years later.

Sullivan described the skyscraper as the perfect symbol of the proud spirit of the American man. But it was really the symbol of the proud American businessman. By 1920, there were over 300,000 corporations in the United States, serving 100 million consumers in an enormous single market – it was the biggest, most powerful economy the world had ever seen.

Above all, skyscrapers represented American corporate success. They changed the appearance of American cities. The skylines of New York and Chicago looked like bar charts or graphs, with the tallest buildings representing the richest, most powerful companies. And the same is still true in cities around the world today – from Dubai to Shanghai, from Seoul to Kuala Lumpur.

🔊 **5.1**

Alan: Khalid, we need to talk about that warehouse the company plans to **obtain** in Westside.

Khalid: OK. I've just seen the pictures; I think there's a lot of **potential** there.

Alan: Really? I'm afraid we might be biting off more than we can chew.

Khalid: Do you think so? Why?

Alan: First, the problem is the Westside area itself. Thirty years ago, it was a thriving industrial neighbourhood with a lot of businesses. Now, it's a half-empty waste ground. It's ugly. There are lots of abandoned buildings, and the area isn't really used for anything. No one wants to go there. Second, the warehouse we're looking at is in a terrible condition. It was abandoned about 20 years ago. It's beginning to sink into the ground, and it's falling apart – we would need to do some serious work to bring the building back to good condition. Acquiring such an old building could be a huge mistake.

Khalid: Really? I think the project is going to be a great success. In fact, I think it's a potential goldmine.

Alan: Um, OK. Could you expand on that?

Khalid: There's been a lot of activity in Westside recently. There is development and renovation going on nearby, and I think it's really going to **transform** the area. Westside is becoming popular with people who work in the financial district, which is close by. Rents are still low there, and a new restaurant opens almost every week. I **anticipate** the neighbourhood becoming really trendy. No one has spent much money there in the past 20 years, but investment in the area has increased in the past year. We're going to see a lot more improvement as well.

Alan: That may be true, but that building is more like a prison than a potential shopping centre. People would never want to go shopping there. I think the first thing we'd need to do would be to knock it down, and that would cost us a lot of money.

Khalid: Have you considered renovating the building instead of knocking it down? It has some beautiful original **features**.

Alan: It looks as though it's about to **collapse**!

Khalid: I'm not sure it's that bad. I think the original building has a lot of potential.

Alan: I think we really want to transform the area with something modern. Why not just start again with a new building?

Khalid: If we designed it properly, we could maintain the old architectural features, such as the red bricks and the stone. Those construction materials would better match the style of some of the other buildings around it. It would reflect the character of the area. We could give the old building a new lease of life.

Alan: Maybe, but I think it would be better to transform the area with an architectural landmark, something new and **contemporary**. It would be more of a transformation if we built a modern building made of materials like steel and glass.

Khalid: Couldn't we do both? We'll maintain more of a connection to the past if we include the old building as part of the new one. We could rebuild the warehouse using red brick similar to the original structure, and construct a new glass and steel extension – adding on rather than constructing a whole new building. It would also create more floor space that could be used for retail space. We'd have enough room for at least two or three more shops there.

Alan: I hadn't thought of doing it that way.

Khalid: Another option to consider would be putting shops on the ground floor and flats or offices above. If we added a floor or two to the top of the building, we could definitely use glass and steel for that.

Alan: Would they be luxury flats?

Khalid: Maybe. We could have a modern, urban design, but still using the old architectural materials and features.

Alan: Such as?

Khalid: We could keep some of the original features as they are, such as the long, wooden beams used to support the ceilings and the exposed red brick walls that help support the roof. They would then become a decorative feature.

Alan: So not traditional flats at all, then?

Khalid: No, not at all. Very modern.

Alan: It's an expensive plan, and not everyone will like it.

Khalid: We wouldn't be the first to do this sort of thing, though. We can look at some other examples around the city where the same thing has been done successfully, if you're interested in the idea.

Alan: If we make that the first phase of our planning process, we can make a better decision about how to balance the traditional and modern features of the project, before we go on to the design and building phases.

Khalid: There's probably a Westside neighbourhood association or business association. We could meet with them and get their views.

Alan: You're right. We really should speak to some businesspeople in the area and arrange to take a better look at the building.

Khalid: Let's do it.

🔊 5.2

See script on page 109.

🔊 5.3

Jamal: Maria, John. Thanks for taking the time to meet with us.

Maria and John: No problem. / My pleasure.

Jamal: We have the first set of plans, and we think you'll be really pleased with what we've put together. After discussing a lot of options, we now anticipate building a single eight-storey block of flats.

Tom: You can see from the pictures here that we are planning on fitting this into the area by using part of the waste ground behind the current housing area.

Jamal: One of the biggest benefits of this plan is that it will create housing for as many as 200 people.

Maria: I can't quite tell from the drawing ... what materials are you going to use?

Tom: The outside is made of glass and steel.

John: And what's the cost of this plan?

Jamal: Around eight million pounds.

Maria: Eight million? Well, the plan is definitely **ambitious**!

Jamal: Yes, we're aware that it's over the construction budget of 7.5 million, but we are going to review the budget in light of some of our suggestions.

Maria: Well, I have to say, we weren't expecting the building to be so tall.

John: Exactly. The **existing** buildings in the neighbourhood are no higher than two storeys, and you've placed the new building very close to them. I'm **concerned** about the other buildings on the site. The plan would block daylight for existing homes. We're probably going to get a lot of complaints from the current residents.

Jamal: We could consider using reflective glass instead, then. You know, like a mirror. It's used in big cities to give a feeling of open sky.

Maria: That's a great idea, but I'm not sure it addresses the main problem. The real issue here is the height of the building. I strongly recommend that you reconsider this. After all, we originally suggested housing for about 100 people.

Tom: Yes, we've doubled that.

Maria: OK. Would you mind telling us a bit more about why you decided that?

Jamal: Well, our thinking was that this would increase your company's income from the building because you could sell or rent out more flats.

John: We thought that might be an option at first, too, but now we realize it won't work. We have to think about the houses that are already in the area. We really need to consider how the new building will contribute to the look of the area – that is, how it will fit in with the other buildings.

Tom: When you say 'fit in', do you mean we should copy the style of existing buildings?

John: No. We don't expect you to copy, but we also don't want to completely transform the feeling of the area either. So by 'fit in', I mean that it should look as though it belongs there. Our original suggestion was that the building should reflect the size and materials of the other buildings in the area.

Tom: OK, I see what you mean.

John: I have one other concern. You described the natural area you'd like to build on as waste ground, but actually, that's a woodland. The children who already live in the area play there, and we want to maintain

that open, natural area with all the trees. The residents really value having access to nature nearby.

Maria: Exactly.

John: As it stands, this plan with the tall, single building and the loss of the woodland would be very **controversial**. Wouldn't it be better if we used this first design you have supplied to identify a few priorities?

Jamal: Yes, that's a good idea.

Maria: OK ... first, we need to think about what will be **appropriate** with the existing houses. What about more, smaller, lower buildings? We could have four two-storey buildings and, following our original plan, try to house 100 rather than 200 people. That might be better.

John: And while we like the idea of contemporary design, I'm not sure glass and steel is appropriate. Lots of glass is a great idea but, in my view, the only viable option is to use brick, like the existing buildings.

Tom: OK. So we're talking about four two-storey brick buildings that can house about 25 people each?

John: Right.

Tom: That seems like an obvious solution, but it doesn't address the issue of cost.

John: What do you mean?

Tom: Well, four smaller buildings will cost more than one larger one.

John: Well, I guess we'll have to see the actual costs to discuss that. Are we going to perhaps consider only three buildings?

Tom: Yes, that's a possibility.

Jamal: And you mentioned having **adequate** green space. We didn't realize children play in those woods. We need to be **sympathetic** to their needs, so we need to find a different solution. How about we position the new buildings near the edge of the woods?

Maria: Yes, that's possible. We can't acquire the land next to our site because it's public property, but we can benefit from being near that open space. The residents would definitely be able to enjoy the views then.

Tom: I like your thinking. I completely agree.

Jamal: OK, so I think we need to go back and start over again.

John: Yes, I think you're right. I'm sorry, I hope we didn't waste your time.

Jamal: Not at all. I think we understand the site a lot better now, and I feel confident we can come up with a good plan over the next two weeks.

 5.4

See script on page 115.

5.5

See script on page 118.

UNIT 6

▶ **Jeju Island goes carbon-free**

Narrator: Most countries in the world are trying to reduce their carbon emissions, in accordance with the Paris Climate Agreement, the international agreement to reduce greenhouse gases. Some countries and communities are aiming for carbon neutrality, that is, their goal is to balance their carbon emissions with other actions that will reduce carbon in the atmosphere, for example, by planting trees.

Some communities are going even further, however. Their aim is not just neutrality; it's zero emissions. They want to be carbon-free. One such community is the South Korean island of Jeju. A United Nations Natural Heritage site, it's often called the Hawaii of South Korea.

Jeju is located at the southern tip of the country, has 600,000 residents and is known for its stunning natural beauty. Fifteen million visitors come every year, mostly from the Korean mainland, to enjoy the island's lovely beaches, sparkling waterfalls and lush forests.

Both the island's residents and the South Korean government would like to preserve Jeju's beauty, so they've created a plan to make the island carbon-free by 2030. Residents and visitors will use only renewable energy sources—wind and solar power. And only electric vehicles will be permitted on the island.

There's been progress towards these goals, but there's still some way to go. In 2015, there were just 3,319 electric vehicles on Jeju; in 2017 that number had doubled. By 2030, there will be 300,000, if all goes according to plan. To encourage people to use renewable energy and electric vehicles, the government is helping residents pay for solar panels on their homes and for electric vehicles. Jeju is the ideal size for electric vehicles because you can drive all the way around the island on just one charge. But that won't be necessary. There are already 8,000 charging stations on Jeju and that number is increasing every year.

South Korea hopes that Jeju will be a model that other cities and even countries can learn from. The government also hopes that 'The Island without Carbon' will attract not just visitors from the Korean mainland, but also international eco-tourists to enjoy the island's natural beauty.

🔊 **6.1**

Reporter: This is Andrew Thompson, reporting from the Spanish island of El Hierro, about 400 kilometres off the coast of Africa. It's pretty far from Madrid, which is about 2,000 kilometres away. Today, we're going to talk to two of the 11,000 people who live here, to find out what's so special about the island. First, this is Pedro Rodriguez, who owns a seafood restaurant on the island. Hello, Pedro.

Pedro: Hello, Andrew.

Reporter: So, how long have you lived on El Hierro?

Pedro: I haven't lived here for very long. I came from Madrid about five years ago.

Reporter: You don't like it here, then?

Pedro: I love it here! I wish I had come a lot sooner than I did. I spent a lot of my life in Madrid.

Reporter: City life can be tough. I suppose island life is rather more relaxing?

Pedro: Exactly. El Hierro is my home now.

Reporter: So, what's so great about El Hierro?

Pedro: In the city, everyone hurries everywhere. You are surrounded by traffic, and you never feel like you can really relax. What's more, my career was in banking, which is a particularly stressful job.

I love the sound of the sea. I love the peace and quiet, and I feel free here. City life was never like that. When I was living in the city, I worked in banking, as I said. It paid well and I was able to buy my restaurant, but I should have left the city when I was a much younger man.

Reporter: So you love the quiet life on El Hierro, but is there anything else that makes El Hierro special?

Pedro: Well, another thing is, El Hierro is completely energy independent!

Reporter: Energy independent?

Pedro: Yes. In the past, the power on the island was produced by oil. A lot of money was paid to ship 40,000 barrels of oil over from the **mainland** every year. It cost the island over 1.7 million euros a year. Now, all our energy is created right here on the island.

Reporter: And for more about that, we'll now talk to engineer Sofia Martinez.

Sofia: Hello, Andrew.

Reporter: I wonder if you could tell us about the way you **generate** energy here on El Hierro.

Sofia: Well, if you've spent a day or two here, you may have noticed we have a lot of wind.

Reporter: Yes. In fact, it's blowing pretty hard outside right now.

Sofia: Well, for about 3,000 hours, or for about 35% of the year, the wind here blows hard enough to turn wind turbines, which can provide electricity.

Reporter: Does El Hierro rely completely on wind to power the island?

Sofia: No. The island's wind turbines have a **capacity** of about 11 megawatts, about enough to power 3,500 homes, but it's only one **element**. The bigger problem is that the wind doesn't blow all the time, so the power source isn't **consistent**.

Reporter: So you need another energy source on windless days?

Sofia: That was the challenge: to create an energy generation system, or a **network** of systems, that could supply enough energy for the island all the time. And the solution was hydroelectric power.

Reporter: What is hydroelectric power exactly?

Sofia: Hydroelectric power is when energy is converted into another form, such as electricity. The initial source of this energy is from water.

Reporter: But doesn't hydroelectric power require a river and a dam? Isn't El Hierro too small for a river?

Sofia: A river with a dam is the usual way of producing hydroelectric power, but really, all you need is water that can move from a high place to a lower place to get energy from the water.

Reporter: OK …

Sofia: At the centre of El Hierro is a dormant volcano – a volcano that is no longer active. In the middle of the volcano, we built a **reservoir** that holds over 500,000 cubic metres of water, at a height of 700 metres above sea level. So that's our water in a high place.

Reporter: But you don't get much rain here. What happens when all of the water runs out of the reservoir?

Sofia: Well, I mentioned the wind turbines. The wind power and the hydroelectric power are in a network together. When the wind is blowing, energy from the wind turbines pumps water up into the reservoir.

Reporter: So the wind turbines power the pumping station?

Sofia: Right. We also use the wind power for all of our electrical needs, when it blows. Then when the wind stops, we let water run out of the reservoir and through some turbines. The turbines turn generators and we have hydroelectric power we can access.

Reporter: So the water flows in a **cycle** – it's pumped up the hill by the wind power, then it's released when it's needed.

Sofia: Yes, that's right. What's more, the system also provides our drinking water and water for use in agriculture.

Reporter: But where does the water come from?

Sofia: We use seawater.

Reporter: But you can't drink saltwater …

Sofia: We have a desalination plant to take the salt out of the seawater so it can be used in agriculture and as drinking water. We're constantly adding new water and taking stored water out of the cycle as we need to use it. In fact, I've just come from the desalination plant, where we're having some problems today. Something isn't working properly and the replacement parts haven't arrived yet. We're a long way from the mainland, so delivery of anything takes at least a few days. If they don't come soon, we may have to ask people to use less water for a few days.

Reporter: You're a long way from everything out here, aren't you? It must be difficult sometimes.

Sofia: Yes, it's a real challenge living here. On the other hand, we all love it. It can be a hard life, but I wouldn't live anywhere else.

 6.2

Reporter: This is Andrew Thompson, reporting from the Spanish island of El Hierro, about 400 kilometres off the coast of Africa. It's pretty far from Madrid, which is about 2,000 kilometres away. Today, we're going to talk to two of the 11,000 people who live here, to find out what's so special about the island. First, this is Pedro Rodriguez, who owns a seafood restaurant on the island. Hello, Pedro.

Pedro: Hello, Andrew.

Reporter: So, how long have you lived on El Hierro?

Pedro: I haven't lived here for very long. I came from Madrid about five years ago.

Reporter: You don't like it here, then?

Pedro: I love it here! I wish I had come a lot sooner than I did. I spent a lot of my life in Madrid.

Reporter: City life can be tough. I suppose island life is rather more relaxing?

Pedro: Exactly. El Hierro is my home now.

Reporter: So, what's so great about El Hierro?

Pedro: In the city, everyone hurries everywhere. You are surrounded by traffic, and you never feel like you can really relax. What's more, my career was in banking, which is a particularly stressful job.

I love the sound of the sea. I love the peace and quiet, and I feel free here. City life was never like that. When I was living in the city, I worked in banking, as I said. It paid well and I was able to buy my restaurant, but I should have left the city when I was a much younger man.

Reporter: So you love the quiet life on El Hierro, but is there anything else that makes El Hierro special?

Pedro: Well, another thing is, El Hierro is completely energy independent!

Reporter: Energy independent?

Pedro: Yes. In the past, the power on the island was produced by oil. A lot of money was paid to ship 40,000 barrels of oil over from the mainland every year. It cost the island over 1.7 million euros a year. Now, all our energy is created right here on the island.

 6.3

Reporter: And for more about that, we'll now talk to engineer Sofia Martinez.

Sofia: Hello, Andrew.

Reporter: I wonder if you could tell us about the way you generate energy here on El Hierro.

Sofia: Well, if you've spent a day or two here, you may have noticed we have a lot of wind.

Reporter: Yes. In fact, it's blowing pretty hard outside right now.

Sofia: Well, for about 3,000 hours, or for about 35% of the year, the wind here blows hard enough to turn wind turbines, which can provide electricity.

Reporter: Does El Hierro rely completely on wind to power the island?

Sofia: No. The island's wind turbines have a capacity of about 11 megawatts, about enough to power 3,500 homes, but it's only one element. The bigger problem is that the wind doesn't blow all the time, so the power source isn't consistent.

Reporter: So you need another energy source on windless days?

Sofia: That was the challenge: to create an energy generation system, or a network of systems, that could supply enough energy for the island all the time. And the solution was hydroelectric power.

Reporter: What is hydroelectric power exactly?

Sofia: Hydroelectric power is when energy is converted into another form, such as electricity. The initial source of this energy is from water.

Reporter: But doesn't hydroelectric power require a river and a dam? Isn't El Hierro too small for a river?

Sofia: A river with a dam is the usual way of producing hydroelectric power, but really, all you need is water that can move from a high place to a lower place to get energy from the water.

Reporter: OK …

Sofia: At the centre of El Hierro is a dormant volcano – a volcano that is no longer active. In the middle of the volcano, we built a reservoir that holds over 500,000 cubic metres of water, at a height of 700 metres above sea level. So that's our water in a high place.

Reporter: But you don't get much rain here. What happens when all of the water runs out of the reservoir?

Sofia: Well, I mentioned the wind turbines. The wind power and the hydroelectric power are in a network together. When the wind is blowing, energy from the wind turbines pumps water up into the reservoir.

Reporter: So the wind turbines power the pumping station?

Sofia: Right. We also use the wind power for all of our electrical needs, when it blows. Then when the wind stops, we let water run out of the reservoir and through some turbines. The turbines turn generators and we have hydroelectric power we can access.

Reporter: So the water flows in a cycle – it's pumped up the hill by the wind power, then it's released when it's needed.

Sofia: Yes, that's right. What's more, the system also provides our drinking water and water for use in agriculture.

Reporter: But where does the water come from?

Sofia: We use seawater.

Reporter: But you can't drink saltwater …

Sofia: We have a desalination plant to take the salt out of the seawater so it can be used in agriculture and as drinking water. We're constantly adding new water and taking stored water out of the cycle as we need to use it. In fact, I've just come from the desalination plant, where we're having some problems today. Something isn't working properly and the replacement parts haven't arrived yet. We're a long way from the mainland, so delivery of anything takes at least a few days. If they don't come soon, we may have to ask people to use less water for a few days.

Reporter: You're a long way from everything out here, aren't you? It must be difficult sometimes.

Sofia: Yes, it's a real challenge living here. On the other hand, we all love it. It can be a hard life, but I wouldn't live anywhere else.

🔊 **6.4**

See script on page 132.

🔊 **6.5**

See script on page 132.

🔊 **6.6**

1 In certain countries fracking is banned, due to its dangerous effects on the environment.

2 Humans, animals and the environment could all be threatened by the use of nuclear energy.

3 The community refuses to allow the power company to build a new plant by the river.

4 Salt is removed from the water at the desalination plant.

5 We are a completely energy-independent country.

6 I don't think we should use fossil fuels at all anymore.

🔊 **6.7**

Jane: As you all know, there's been a proposal that we should try to reduce our energy **consumption** here in the office, both to save money for the business and to help the environment. The **function** of this meeting today is to get your ideas on how to do this and hopefully to come up with a plan to take forward. Would anyone like to start? What are your views? Yes, Zara.

Zara: Well, if we really want to do something to save on electricity costs long-term, why don't we consider an alternative energy source?

We could install some solar panels on the roof. That would generate plenty of environmentally friendly electricity.

Jane: That's not a bad idea. Would anyone like to add to Zara's comments? Allen?

Allen: It's true that we could go for a big solution like solar power generation. Even so, I think we could consider some rather simpler, smaller-scale ideas too, like changing to low-energy lightbulbs. There's a lot of potential to save energy there.

Jane: I think that's a great point, Allen. Abdul, would you like to expand on that?

Abdul: Yes. Allen's lightbulb idea is a really good one. Energy-efficient bulbs aren't hugely expensive to install. In addition, they pay for themselves quickly.

Jane: Pay for themselves?

Abdul: They don't use much energy, so they're cheap to run. It means they will soon save us more money than the cost of the new bulbs. Although these energy-efficient bulbs are expensive, we would save enough money in one year to pay for them.

Jane: I see. Do you have any other ideas?

Abdul: Yes. Some of the ideas are very simple: cleaning our dirty windows, for example. As a result of that, we'll allow more natural light in. Furthermore, we can turn off our computer screens when we get up from our desks.

Jane: Yes, Zara.

Zara: We could also consider turning off the air conditioning when it isn't too hot, so we can use less energy.

Jane: Great idea.

Zara: We could get rid of one of our photocopiers, as we don't really need two. The current machines use energy even when they're on standby.

Jane: Also a good plan. Now, I'd like to go back to Abdul. Abdul, you said we should consider smaller-scale solutions to our energy consumption here. Are you saying you're against installing a solar energy system?

Abdul: No, I really like that idea because once it's installed, the system will have a low operating cost, and it's an environmentally friendly way to generate electricity, which are two big positive points; but there are other considerations. For example, we'd have to look at the generating capacity of the system. It's very expensive to buy and install, and if it doesn't produce a lot of power, it'll end up costing rather than saving us money, at least for the first few years. The challenge is to choose ways of saving energy that also save money right now.

Allen: Yes, I agree with that. The other real environmental problem we have here in the office is rubbish. Most of us buy our lunch in plastic containers that have to be thrown away. It's a disgrace. We really should try to reduce the **volume** of rubbish we create here in the office.

Jane: Sorry, but that's not really what we're discussing right now. We can deal with waste and recycling later. Right now we're talking specifically about energy use.

Allen: Okay, fine. Sorry about that.

Zara: So, we were talking about turning off computer screens and turning off the air conditioning, but I don't think we should forget about installing solar panels, or a solar water-heating system.

Jane: But there are some **drawbacks** to that, such as installation cost, which Abdul mentioned.

Abdul: Right, and there's also the problem of—

Simon: Can I just say, by the way—

Jane: Sorry, but could you hold that thought until Abdul has finished, please?

Simon: Sure. Sorry.

Abdul: The fact is, both systems Zara mentioned are technically complex and expensive to install. There's also the problem of **maintenance**; we'd need to pay an engineer to come to do repairs if anything went wrong and for expensive parts that needed to be replaced. There could be a real decline in the amount of money we save if we ran into operational problems.

Jane: Can I just clarify something here? Abdul, is this **experimental** technology, or have alternative-energy generation systems been successful in other office environments?

Abdul: Well, every small-scale system is different because every building is different. The technology would have to be specially designed for our building in order to be **efficient**.

Allen: I can't help but feel that a solar energy project would be too ambitious. There would probably be technical **limitations** about the sort of system we could install on the office roof. I'm not sure it's even possible, or if the local government would let us.

Jane: I can assure you that the company wouldn't do anything unsafe or illegal.

Zara: It could be good publicity, though. We could market ourselves as a complete green business.

Simon: Maybe we should have some of our marketing people look at that. I think—

Jane: We're getting sidetracked. Can we stick to the main points of the meeting? We should probably move on to the next part of the agenda, so I'd just like to summarize the key points so far. First of all, we want to immediately start making the simple energy-saving changes mentioned, such as cleaning the windows, turning off computer screens and installing energy-saving lightbulbs. Second, we want to look into possible larger-scale alternative-energy systems such as solar panels or a solar water-heating system. However, we need to do a lot of research in that area to see if we could get permission to install a system on the roof. A positive to installing a larger-scale project would be that it could generate good publicity for the company. Have I missed anything?

Abdul: You didn't mention ...

🔊 **6.8**

A: So, to summarize the key points so far: we agree that we want to reduce energy consumption and we want to consider an alternative energy source. Does anyone have anything to say about a solar energy system?

B: I'm more concerned about our water usage.

A: Sorry, but that's not really what we're discussing right now.

🔊 **6.9**

See script on page 143.

UNIT 7

▶ Contemporary African art sale

Narrator: The African art market is heating up, as more and more art lovers have begun to collect African art. In 2017, the auction house Sotheby's held a modern and contemporary African art sale for the first time, with 80 works from 60 artists from 14 countries. Probably the most well-known of these artists is El Anatsui. He was born in Ghana but works primarily in Nigeria, where he creates stunning textiles from bottle caps and old aluminium cans. This work sold for £416,750 at the Sotheby's sale.

The work of South African artist, Irma Stein, whose paintings have lately sold for millions of dollars, was also represented. Her 1942 painting, *Sunflowers*, went for £728,750.

Yinka Shonabare was born in Britain but grew up in Nigeria. His work explores issues of race and class across a wide range of media, including textiles, sculpture, painting and photography. This sculpture, *Crash Willy*, fetched £224,750 at the Sotheby's auction. Heather O'Leary, head of Modern and Contemporary Art at Sotheby's, explains the motivation behind the sale.

Heather O'Leary: Sotheby's has really been watching this market grow over the last few years. It's still quite a young market, but in the last five to ten years we've seen phenomenal growth and that's really a combination of erm ... African buyers erm ... collecting art, also museums collecting art from Africa and there have been auction houses erm ... both here in Europe and in Africa who have been ... who have started new sales where they offer art from Africa.

In this auction, for example, I think we have three artists who sell in our contemporary art auctions, but we have over sixty, we have sixty artists here that don't, so erm ... there was a real need for ... for an auction in which to place them and ... and we know that there's a demand from the market as well.

The lowest erm ... estimate in the sales start at £1000 and the ... even the most expensive piece in the same is valued at less than £1,000,000 and so I do think there are great opportunities while the market is young to ... to really start collecting in this field in a serious way.

Narrator: O'Leary describes the work of El Anatsui:

Heather O'Leary: The initial inspiration for these pieces was the traditional *kante* cloth from Ghana. His father was a ... a master weaver of *kante* cloth and so you can see here that, erm ... he's used the colours of Ghana, the yellow and the red of ... that appear in the Ghanaian flag and the black erm ... and ... and then also the silver of the aluminium which looks like ... like silver from a distance as ... as he also uses gold in the same way so he's taking these discarded objects and creating shimmering, precious metal, sheets of precious metals out of them.

🔊 **7.1**

Reporter: Hello from the city centre. Overnight, the area's mystery graffiti artist has struck again. Although the **identity** of the painter remains unknown, their work is making an impact on the community. This large image has been painted on the side of an office building. A lot of people in the street on their way to work are stopping to look at it. Let's talk to a few of them and find out what they think of this latest spray-painted image.
Hello, excuse me?

Alex: Yes?

Reporter: I'm reporting on the recent increase in street art in the city centre. Can I ask you a few questions?

Alex: Sure.

Reporter: What's your name?

Alex: It's Alex.

Reporter: So, Alex, what do you think of this new artistic addition to the neighbourhood?

Alex: This street art? I think it's great. It's something interesting to look at, and it looks good, doesn't it? I live around the corner, so this is on my doorstep.

Reporter: What do you like about it?

Alex: I just think it's cool – it has a distinctive style. At first glance, it looks like the painting was done in a few minutes. But in fact, it's not just spray painting; it's the work of a talented artist. It really decorates the area, and I think the **creativity** makes a very ugly neighbourhood a lot better looking.

Reporter: Does everyone in the area like it?

Alex: Most of my neighbours do. We think this kind of thing could become a special feature of the area. It's a real shame that it's going to be covered up before many people have had a chance to see it.

Reporter: Covered up?

Alex: The police are going to paint over it soon because street art is illegal.

Reporter: Oh, right. Yes, we'll come back to that in a minute. Thanks for talking to us.

Alex: No problem.

Reporter: Clearly some people really like the painting. However, there's also already been some **criticism** of the piece. Let's see what more we can find out about this side of the story.

Hello, excuse me?

Office worker: Yes?

Reporter: I'm finding out what people think of street art in this area. Can I ask you a few questions?

Office worker: I'm just on my way into the office, so you'll have to be quick.

Reporter: What do you think of this painting?

Office worker: I don't really like it. It's just graffiti, isn't it?

Reporter: What do you mean?

Office worker: The people who own this building didn't ask for this, did they? I mean, what **right** does this person have to spray paint their message here? If somebody wants to express themselves in this way, they should get permission. I'd be really angry if someone did this in my neighbourhood.

Reporter: Do you think it's a work of art?

Office worker: No, not at all. Art is an exhibition in an art gallery. This is just somebody spraying paint onto a wall in the middle of the night. Like I said, it's just **self-expression**.

Reporter: Yes, I see what you mean. Thanks for taking a minute to talk.

Office worker: You're welcome.

Reporter: I think it would be a good idea to get a professional view on this now. I have a local police officer with me.

Hello, and thanks for talking to me today.

Police officer: Hello.

Reporter: What's your view on the latest work of the mystery painter?

Police officer: Well, to be honest, as a piece of art, I actually really like it, despite the fact that it's illegal. However, I also completely agree with the person you just spoke with. We can't have this sort of thing. It *is* vandalism, and it *is* against the law.

Reporter: It's against the law?

Police officer: Yes. **Vandalism** is a crime, because it is intentionally damaging property that belongs to the city or to other people.

Reporter: I'm very interested to hear you call this piece of vandalism a work of *art*.

Police officer: It is artistic, though, isn't it? I couldn't paint that. The person who did this, especially very quickly and at night, is very creative. This painting is really expressive, but I have to stress that it's illegal, and therefore we're going to paint over it later today. We remove all graffiti because it's the law.

Reporter: What would you recommend for people who want to express themselves through street art?

Police officer: My recommendation? Well, if this artist wants to paint where everyone can see the artwork, he or she should get permission. We can work with street artists to create art that people have chosen to have in their community.

Reporter: So you mean you can give someone permission to paint graffiti?

Police officer: Yes, well, sort of. However, they have to apply for a permit and get approval and so on. This makes it a legal activity rather than vandalism.

Reporter: Thanks a lot for talking with us.

Police officer: My pleasure.

Reporter: Next, I have an art critic here who agrees with some people about the quality of the latest street painting. This is Simone James, an art gallery owner and art critic. Hello, Simone.

Simone: Hello.

Reporter: Simone, could you **comment** on the latest creation of our illegal painter?

Simone: Many people think that the painting is just rough spray painting. However, the fact of the matter is the artist has created a very expressive piece of artwork using very basic tools and materials. The colour scheme and the **composition** work very well together. It's a strong piece. If this artist were to exhibit and sell their work, I think he or she could make a lot of money.

Reporter: Do you have any idea who the artist might be?

Simone: I have no idea at all, but technically, the work really is very good, so I'd like to find out!

Reporter: Thank you very much. Finally, there's one more person I'd like to speak with. This is Joseph, who's 15. Joseph, what do you think of the mystery artist's latest painting?

Joseph: I wish I'd done it! I think it's really good.

Reporter: What do you like about it?

Joseph: I think this type of art is a really good way of expressing your ideas. I don't know who did it, but I guess it's a young person like me and by doing this kind of art in this way, on the streets, the artist is communicating a message about how young people feel.

Reporter: OK, thanks, Joseph. So we've had a full range of responses to the latest street art in the city centre. However, the true identity of the graffiti painter remains a mystery.

 7.2

See script on page 153.

Robert: ... Okay everyone, are we ready to get back to business? The next item to look at today is the proposed budget to continue paying for public art in City Park. We've recently had to spend a lot of money repairing and restoring the sculpture we commissioned last year because vandals have broken parts of it. We've also spent a lot of time and money removing graffiti from it. The council finance office has confirmed that the total bill for cleaning and repairs has come to more than £7,000 so far this year. There's been a proposal that we sell the sculpture, stop paying for new public art and use the money to pay for a new leisure centre. Would anyone like to comment on this?

Bilal: Yes, Robert, I'd like to say something.

Robert: OK, Bilal. Go ahead.

Bilal: Personally, I'm not really sure that paying for art is an appropriate way to spend public money.

We assume that we should invest in art since so many other parks have art but, in reality, it's costing us a lot of money, and the art doesn't really benefit the city's population. A lot of people simply don't **appreciate** or like to **interpret** art. The truth of the matter is, more people would use and benefit from a leisure centre.

Robert: If I understand you correctly, Bilal, you're saying that we shouldn't spend more money commissioning art?

Bilal: Well, yes. I think public art is a waste of money.

Robert: I see. Yes, Ahmad, would you like to add something?

Ahmad: Yes, thank you, Robert. I see what you mean, Bilal, and I'm not an expert, but it's been said that art, and appreciating art, is an important part of any culture. OK, it's true that some people say we're wasting money by commissioning public art, but the fact of the matter is that art is an important part of any culture. Art can help make us proud of our city, and a lot of people really enjoy looking at it. We had 400,000 visitors to our city art gallery and museum last year, so people are interested in it.

Azra: That's true, Ahmad. Research has demonstrated over and over again that art can have a very positive effect on people.

Robert: Thank you, Ahmad and Azra. Yes, Sandra, you wanted to say something?

Sandra: Ahmad and Azra have good points, but one other thing to remember is that, although many people think that art is worth a lot of money because it's by famous artists or because the city invested in it, we don't actually know that the art is worth anything. Look at the sculpture there now, for example. Since it's been damaged and repaired so much, we don't know if we can sell the sculpture, even to a private collector. Do we really want to invest in more art?

Robert: OK, thank you all for your comments. I think we need to find out how much new art would cost us. We'll have to get an art expert to **analyze** the pieces we already have and like, and maybe we can **restore** them rather than buy new ones.

Would anyone else like to make a comment? Yes, Azra?

Azra: If we decide against commissioning further public art, we'll need to put something in its place.

Bilal: Like building the leisure centre instead.

Sandra: You say that, Bilal, but I'm not sure that would be popular enough. We'd need to talk to a lot of people to gather data and opinions about whether they like the art or if they want a new building, and this might **reveal** some really good ideas we haven't thought of.

Robert: Yes, I think you're right, Sandra. Let's put together a survey. It can ask about commissioning more art or building a leisure centre. We can also include three or four other ideas on spending public money. Then we can ask people to respond to it. Would anyone like to say anything else? Yes, Claudia?

Claudia: For me, there's a public safety issue here. The police reports have shown that kids climb on the public art we have there now. This happens almost every night, and they're breaking it and writing graffiti on it. This artwork really is causing more problems than it's worth.

Ahmad: You may be right, Claudia, but I wonder if it's the location of the artwork rather than the artwork itself that's the problem.

Bilal: In other words, you think we should move it?

Ahmad: I think moving it might solve the vandalism problem. It seems as if the art is just costing us money for cleaning and repairs. If we were to **display** it in a different spot, we probably wouldn't have these problems. Plus, we'd still contribute to the culture of the city by having the art available.

Sandra: I agree with Ahmad. I think we could consider moving the sculpture to the front of the council building, or next to the hospital, or possibly even inside the main shopping centre. In fact, the shopping centre has already expressed interest in this because they believe public artwork could be a tourist attraction. If we planned it properly, we could get people to see the artwork and do some shopping at the same time!

Bilal: So, Sandra, what you're saying is that you'd definitely rather move the current sculpture we have to another location?

Sandra: Yes, that's right.

Robert: OK, yes, those ideas make sense. I think we need to do more research here. First, we need to **focus on** identifying some places where future public art could be displayed. We need to **reject** any places where we feel vandals would be likely to damage it. Second, we need to consider the cost of our current piece of art, the sculpture that is already there in the park.

Sandra: There's one other point I'd like to raise.

Robert: OK. Go ahead, Sandra.

Sandra: What would we do with the money if we didn't commission any new art or build the leisure centre?

Robert: That's a good question. The money would be put back into the budget, and we'd have to determine a project that reflects what people really want.

Ahmad: Well, a leisure centre, or any other centre, is a good thing, but it isn't art. I think our children need to see art in public places, especially the work of a famous artist, right here in our city. We need to have a balance of investment in leisure activities and public art in the lives of our children.

Robert: OK, I think we need to look into this. We need to explore our options in more detail. Are there any other comments on this topic? No? OK. We'll move on, then …

🔊 7.4

See script on page 165.

UNIT 8

▶ Never too old to code

Narrator: Masako Wakamiya has always been a woman of action, ready to take on challenges. She was a banker before it was common for women in Japan to have such jobs, and when she retired at 60, she began a new chapter in her life, with new challenges. She had never used a computer before, but she read that using a computer could help her connect with other people while she stayed at home to look after her elderly mother. So, she bought one. Over the next 20 years, she taught herself about computers and the internet. She got a smartphone and started using apps, but she found that everything was designed for young people. She knew that older people could learn to use technology, and even have fun doing it, if someone designed with them in mind.

She contacted app designers and asked them to develop games for older users, but no one was interested. So, she did what she had always done: she did it herself. She learned Apple's coding language so she could develop an app for the iPhone. She used content that is familiar to older Japanese users: figures from the Japanese festival Hinamatsuri, or Doll's Day. On this day, dolls are placed on a platform in a specific order. In Wakamiya's game, the goal is to place all the figures in the correct order. The game is harder than it sounds; the arrangements are complex.

Tim Cook, the head of Apple, heard about Wakamiya and her app. Calling her work 'inspiring,' he invited her to an app developers' conference. At 82, she was the oldest participant.

Describing her experience developing the app, Wakamiya recalls:

Wakamiya: Elderly people don't play games on their phones much because games aren't interesting for them. I've heard a lot of people say that. So, I thought it would be nice if there were some apps which elderly people could enjoy. This game is based on traditional Japanese culture. I wanted to tell the next generation about traditional culture. I thought that making a game and letting young people play it would be easier than explaining culture to them. When I first saw the pictures moving, I was really impressed. First, I create the images. Then I run the simulation and they start moving and talking. It's really impressive. Programming is the best way for me to feel a sense of achievement.

🔊 8.1

Host: Hello and welcome to the *Money and Finance* podcast. I'm your host, Ian Brown, and today's topic is **retirement**. In the past, giving up work in their sixties signalled the end of an active, exciting life for people. It was seen as a time for staying at home, doing the gardening and being very careful with money. Twenty years ago, most people planned to leave a large sum of money to their children upon their death and didn't spend a lot on themselves once they started to receive a **pension**.

But times have changed. People nowadays don't usually think of their sixties as old. People who have exercised and eaten a good diet throughout their lives have plenty of energy to enjoy life, no matter what age they retire at. Many of today's older people see retirement as a reward for a lifetime of hard work and, rather than saving their money to give to their children, they're spending it – on luxuries, travel, new cars and meals out, and because they worked hard and saved hard for their retirement, they have plenty of money to spend. As a group, the over-60s in the UK have over 500 billion pounds in **assets**: **property**, money in the bank, investments and so on. Last year, they spent £240 billion on leisure, accounting for more than 60% of all consumer spending. This included £345 million on meals out and £535 million on travel. The average married person between the ages of 65 and 74 spent 26% of their household income on food and entertainment.

Rick and Nadia Jones are typical of this new approach to retirement. I asked them to share their thoughts.

Nadia: Well, in my working life I was a banker and Rick was in business. We both retired at 65, and since that time we've travelled a lot and have had years of fun

ACKNOWLEDGEMENTS

The authors and publishers acknowledge the following sources of copyright material and are grateful for the permissions granted. While every effort has been made, it has not always been possible to identify the sources of all the material used, or to trace all copyright holders. If any omissions are brought to our notice, we will be happy to include the appropriate acknowledgements on reprinting and in the next update to the digital edition, as applicable.

Key: L = Left, R = Right, C = Centre.

Text
Map on p. 63 "Risk of influenza pandemics across the globe," Copyright © Maplecroft, 2012; Text on pp. 154–155, Exercise 2, adapted from "10 Things You Must See in the Louvre" by Daisy de Plume, of THATMuse (Treasure Hunt at the Museum). Reproduced with permission.

Photos
All below images are sourced from Getty Images.

p. 19: mediaphotos/iStock/Getty Images Plus; p. 24: xPACIFICA/ Iconica; p. 30: Quynh Anh Nguyen/Moment Open; p. 33: Inti St Clair/ Blend Images; pp. 36–37: Hero Images; p. 41: GCShutter/E+; p. 50: UpperCut Images; p. 54: Neil Turner/Photographer's Choice; pp. 58–59: Boston Globe; p. 70: Design Pics; p. 72 (lab technician): Fancy/Veer/ Corbis; p. 72 (doctor): JGI/Tom Grill/Blend Images; p. 76 (L): Monkey Business Images Ltd; p. 76 (R): Rubberball/Mike Kemp; pp. 80–81: Keith Douglas/All Canada Photos; p. 87: STR/AFP; p. 91: Alfred Eisenstaedt/ The LIFE Picture Collection; p. 92: Ian Wade Photography/Moment; p. 97 (L): NASA/Getty Images News; p. 97 (C): Hiroya Minakuchi/Minden Pictures; p. 97 (R): Eco/Universal Images Group; pp. 102–103: Martin Child/robertharding; p. 111: Vladitto/iStock; p. 119: DedMityay/iStock/ Getty Images Plus; pp. 124–125: Paul Souders/Photonica World; p. 129: Ian Aitken/AWL Images; p. 136: Spaces Images/Blend Images; p. 138: MicroStockHub/iStock/Getty Images Plus; p. 140: kynny/iStock/Getty Images Plus; pp. 146–147: George Rose/Getty Images News; p. 151: Jeff Spielman/Photographer's Choice; p. 153: Glen_Pearson/iStock Editorial/ Getty Images Plus; p. 158: Massimo Borchi/Atlantide Phototravel/ Photolibrary; pp. 168-169: Chung Sung-Jun/Getty Images New; p. 173: Bloomberg; p. 180: Asanka Brendon Ratnayake/Lonely Planet Images.

The following image is sourced from another library:
pp. 14–15: Nic Cleave Photography/Alamy Stock Photos.

Front cover photography by Daniel Davison/Moment

Video stills
All below stills are sourced from Getty Images.

p. 126 (2): Multi-bits; p. 126 (1, 3, 4): Bloomberg Video – Footage/ Bloomberg; p. 16, p. 170: AFP Footage. p. 60: Sky News/Film Image Partner.

The following stills are sourced from other libraries:
p. 148: AFP; p. 38: ITN; p. 82, p. 104: BBC Worldwide Learning.

Illustration
p. 114: Oxford Designers & Illustration.

Videos
All below clips are sourced from Getty Images and BBC Worldwide Learning.

Sky News/Film Image Partner; AFP Footage; SkyworksFootage/Creatas Video; ITN; nomagnolia/Creatas Video+/Getty Images Plus; Dorling Kindersley; Allstar Picture Library/ Photolibrary Video; Multi-bits/Image Bank Film; topnatthapon/Creatas Video; Multi-bits/Image Bank Film; Bloomberg Video – Footage/Bloomberg; Discovery FootageSource; Reel Entrepreneurs – Footage/Getty Images Editorial Footage; Multi-bits/Image Bank Film; topnatthapon/ Creatas Video; Spoonfilm/Moment Video RF; Kyodo News Video; Eddie Gerald; Video Journalist Africa – Footage; Zhang Peng/Getty Images Editorial Footage; piggyfoto; RPM Media Inc – Roberto & Christina Mitrotti/Image Bank Film; BBC Motion Gallery Editorial/BBC News; BBC Worldwide Learning.

Corpus
Development of this publication has made use of the Cambridge English Corpus (CEC). The CEC is a multi-billion word computer database of contemporary spoken and written English. It includes British English, American English and other varieties of English. It also includes the Cambridge Learner Corpus, developed in collaboration with the University of Cambridge ESOL Examinations. Cambridge University Press has built up the CEC to provide evidence about language use that helps to produce better language teaching materials.

Cambridge Dictionaries
Cambridge dictionaries are the world's most widely used dictionaries for learners of English. The dictionaries are available in print and online at dictionary.cambridge.org. Copyright © Cambridge University Press, reproduced with permission.

Typeset by emc design ltd.

UNLOCK SECOND EDITION ADVISORY PANEL

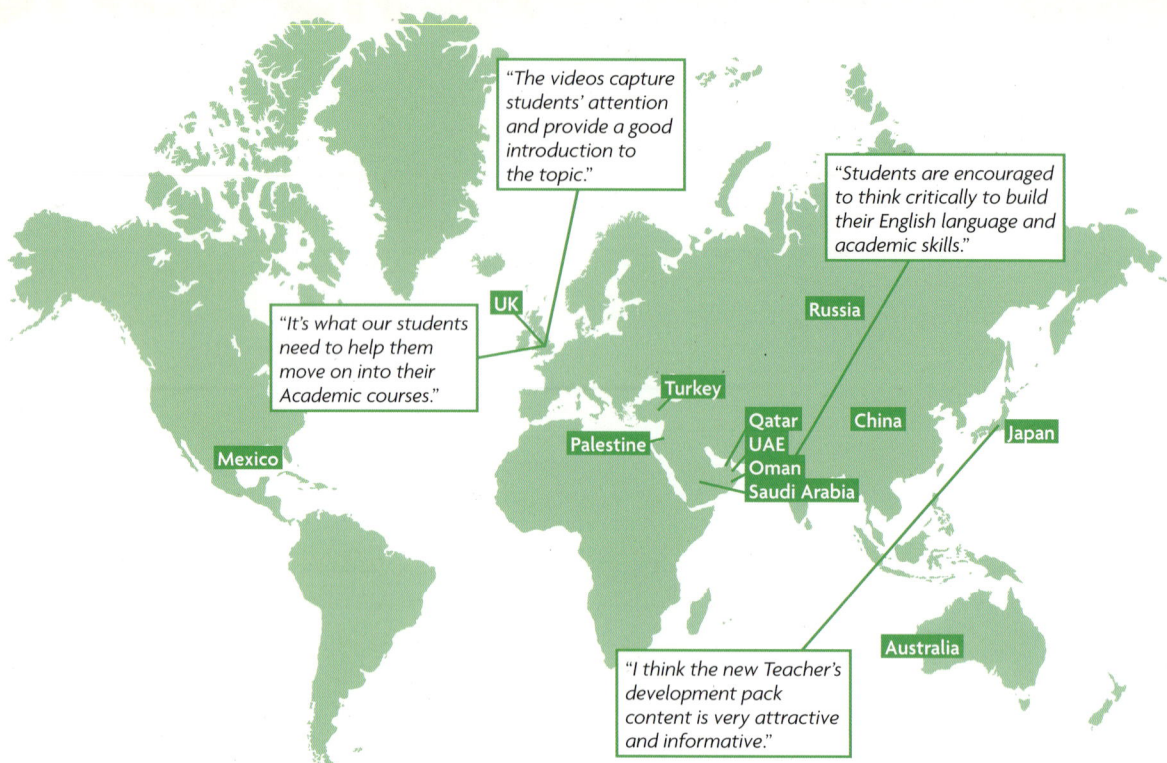

"The videos capture students' attention and provide a good introduction to the topic."

"Students are encouraged to think critically to build their English language and academic skills."

"It's what our students need to help them move on into their Academic courses."

"I think the new Teacher's development pack content is very attractive and informative."

UK

Russia

Turkey

Mexico

Palestine

Qatar
UAE
Oman
Saudi Arabia

China

Japan

Australia

We would like to thank the following ELT professionals all around the world for their support, expertise and input throughout the development of *Unlock* Second Edition:

Adnan Abu Ayyash, Birzeit University, Palestine	Takayuki Hara, Kagoshima University, Japan	Megan Putney, Dhofar University, Oman
Bradley Adrain, University of Queensland, Australia	Esengül Hasdemir, Atilim University, Turkey	Wayne Rimmer, United Kingdom
Sarah Ali, Nottingham Trent International College (NTIC), United Kingdom	Irina Idilova, Moscow Institute of Physics and Technology, Russia	Sana Salam, TED University, Turkey
Ana Maria Astiazaran, Colegio Regis La Salle, Mexico	Meena Inguva, Sultan Qaboos University, Oman	Setenay Şekercioglu, Işık University, Turkey
Asmaa Awad, University of Sharjah, United Arab Emirates	Vasilios Konstantinidis, Prince Sultan University, Kingdom of Saudi Arabia	Robert B. Staehlin, Morioka University, Japan
Jesse Balanyk, Zayed University, United Arab Emirates	Andrew Leichsenring, Tamagawa University, Japan	Yizhi Tang, Xueersi English, TAL Group, China
Lenise Butler, Universidad del Valle de México, Mexico	Alexsandra Minic, Modern College of Business and Science, Oman	Valeria Thomson, Muscat College, Oman
Esin Çağlayan, Izmir University of Economics, Turkey	Daniel Newbury, Fuji University, Japan	Amira Traish, University of Sharjah, United Arab Emirates
Matthew Carey, Qatar University, Qatar	Güliz Özgürel, Yaşar University, Turkey	Poh Leng Wendelkin, INTO City, University of London, United Kingdom
Eileen Dickens, Universidad de las Américas, Mexico	Özlem Perks, Istanbul Ticaret University, Turkey	Yoee Yang, The Affiliated High School of SCNU, China
Mireille Bassam Farah, United Arab Emirates	Claudia Piccoli, Harmon Hall, Mexico	Rola Youhia, University of Adelaide College, Australia
Adriana Ghoul, Arab American University, Palestine	Tom Pritchard, University of Edinburgh, United Kingdom	Long Zhao, Xueersi English, TAL Group, China
Burçin Gönülsen, Işık University, Turkey		

and excitement. A lot of our friends are doing the same. We're still healthy and we love travelling, so why shouldn't we? I had to persuade Rick to agree to the idea at first. It just wasn't like that for our parents. However, we've managed to save enough money to **permit** us to live the life we've always wanted, and I think we've earned it.

Rick: We've been to Australia, New Zealand and South Africa – and Nadia loves the weather in Dubai! We've been there three times.

Host: According to one survey, 20 years ago most of today's older people believed they would work in the garden, read and babysit their grandchildren. However, retired people now want to do more exciting things! Do you agree with this?

Nadia: I do, I think. We worked hard during our careers to **ensure** that our two daughters had a good education. They're both married and working now. I want to be involved in my children's lives, but I do also want adventure! We live close to both our daughters and offer to babysit our grandchildren regularly, but we're not free childminders!

Rick: Exactly. We don't have any **dependents** anymore. Our daughters need to work hard and save their money, just as we've done. Our savings allow us to do what *we* want to do. This is our chance to have some fun, and we don't want to stay at home all day gardening and watching television. Our daughters have agreed to support our choices, and we hope they'll make the same choices for themselves one day.

Nadia: I think our parents' **generation** thought it was really important to save for the next generation, to give money to their children, but our generation doesn't think that way.

Rick: We've talked to our daughters about it. They understand that the money is ours to spend. They also understand that as long as we're in shape and healthy, we might as well enjoy life. Our home is also worth about £500,000. We are not planning on selling it, so they'll get that eventually.

Host: Recent research shows that about two-thirds of older people agree with Rick and Nadia and plan to leave their home to their children, but no money. But what about the next generation? Today's working generation is probably facing a more difficult retirement than their parents. Pensions are getting smaller, many companies are no longer providing pensions at all and the average age of retirement is increasing. According to the United Nations, about 18% of Europeans aged 65 and over are still working, but that number is increasing. By the year 2030, more than 20% of European people aged 65 and over will still have regular jobs. Should these parents be doing more? Rick?

Rick: I think we both feel we've done our bit as parents. We have many happy, healthy years ahead of us and still have other things we want to do with our lives, and now we're doing them. I'd advise everyone else to do the same.

🔊 **8.2**

See script on page 175.

🔊 **8.3**

Mika: Hello. My name is Mika. I'm going to discuss how things are changing for elderly people in Japan. I'll begin by explaining the importance of family in Japan and present some figures that explain how the population is changing. Finally, I'll talk about the way the Japanese government is dealing with the ageing population.

Family in Japan has been very important since the days of my **ancestors**. However, while the extended family is very important in other countries, the focus in Japan is on the bond among children, parents, grandparents, and so on. Of course, this means that in many cases, when elderly people can no longer take care of themselves, they move in with their children.

Japan's population is about 127 million, and it has one of the highest life expectancies in the world. If you look at the data I've provided, you will note that it **indicates** there were about 33 million people in 2014 over the age of 65 in Japan, nearly 26% of the population. By 2050, Japan's population will be about 99 million and 35% of the population will be over 65. The population of children under the age of 14 is expected to fall from about 19 million to about 18 million in 2020 and 12 million by 2050. This can be traced back to a low fertility rate, that is, the number of children being born to a woman during the time she is able to have children. That fertility rate has dropped to just below 1.5 children per woman. Young Japanese people are waiting longer than their parents' generation to get married and, when they do, they're having fewer children. Young people now enjoy a lot of free time in their twenties and thirties, but this also results in the same issues that other countries are facing: more and more elderly people to take care of, with fewer younger people to be **providers**. As the population of Japan is set to decrease by 22% by 2050, this means a loss of about 28 million residents.

The Japanese government has taken steps to deal with the situation. Most Japanese people between the ages of 40 and 65 pay an income tax that goes to help those over 65. The over-65s don't get the money directly, but the government supports them. Even elderly people living at home with family have a care worker who makes sure they have everything they need. Some elderly people go to a day-care centre a few times a week, where they can share meals and **participate** in social activities. Those elderly people who don't live with family generally live in **institutions**, like care homes, with about nine people living in one home. Each has a bedroom, and they share a living room and kitchen. This enables them to have some independence and to feel cared for at the same time.

Ahmet: My name is Ahmet. Thank you, Mika, for your interesting presentation. My topic today is how elderly people are cared for in Turkey. First, I'll give some background on how the elderly are usually cared for. After that, I'll talk about some of the drawbacks and benefits of this system, and I'll finish by explaining the challenges ahead.

Mika explained that many elderly people in Japan live in institutions when their ability to care for themselves declines. Moving old people into care homes allows the younger generation to continue their lives without having to worry about daily care for an ageing parent. However, in Turkey, 80% of households have an older person. Many families see this as the natural solution to dealing with old age. As parents, we **devote** ourselves to our children. In turn, as adults, we devote ourselves to our ageing parents. Most people my age have a grandparent living at home.

The system has drawbacks, both for the families caring for elderly people and for the elderly people themselves. Those responsible for the welfare of an elderly person can feel that they aren't free to do as they like in their own home. The older people being cared for may also not feel completely free and dislike the way things are done by their caregivers. Living closely together in forced circumstances can raise tensions. However, there are many benefits to these arrangements. In many households, older people **contribute** to the family by participating in domestic jobs and helping with childcare. This gives them something to do and a sense of **responsibility**.

Turkey's population is just over 81 million today. If you look at the graph I've provided, you will see that more than 5 million people, or around 6%, are over 65. This is much lower than Japan's 26%. UN projections indicate that by 2050, Turkey's population will reach 92 million and about 18 million people, or 20% of the total, will be over 65. So we can see that in the long-term, the same challenges lie ahead for Turkey as for Japan. However, for now, the solution is for Turks to continue caring for the elderly at home.

 8.4

See script on page 187.